CARRY ON

CARRY ON

A Story of Resilience, Redemption, and
an Unlikely Family

LISA FENN

HARPER WAVE

An Imprint of HarperCollins*Publishers*

Grateful acknowledgment is made for permission to reproduce illustrations on the following pages: Pages 1, 91, and 241: courtesy of Kolman Rosenberg; pages 175 and 289: courtesy of Brownie Harris; page 301: courtesy of the author.

FIRST HARPER WAVE PAPERBACK EDITION PUBLISHED 2017.

The Library of Congress has catalogued the hardcover edition as follows:

Names: Fenn, Lisa, author.
Title: Carry on : a story of resilience, redemption, and an unlikely family / Lisa Fenn.
Description: First edition. | New York, NY : HarperCollins Publishers, [2016]
Identifiers: LCCN 2016012130 (print) | LCCN 2016028025 (ebook) | ISBN 9780062427830 (hardcover) | ISBN 9780062427854 (eBook)
Subjects: LCSH: Crockett, Dartanyon, 1991– | Sutton, Leroy, 1990– | Wrestlers with disabilities—Ohio—Cleveland—Biography. | African Americans with disabilities—Ohio—Cleveland—Biography. | Lincoln-West High School (Cleveland, Ohio) | Fenn, Lisa. | Cleveland (Ohio)--Biography.
Classification: LCC GV1196.C76 F46 2016 (print) | LCC GV1196.C76 (ebook) | DDC 796.812092 [B] — dc23
LC record available at https://lccn.loc.gov/2016012130

ISBN 978-0-06-242784-7 (pbk.)

19 20 21   LSC   10 9

PRAISE FOR
Carry On

Friends of American Writers Award Winner
Christopher Award Winner
Nautilus Award Winner, Silver
NAACP Image Award Finalist

"A poignant memoir by an ex-ESPN producer who befriended two disabled inner-city wrestlers as they struggled to rise."
—*Sports Illustrated*

"*Carry On* is an incredible life-affirming story that would not be believed if it weren't true."
—*Family Circle*

"An engrossing tale that is equal parts despair, hope, and triumph."
—*Ohio Magazine*

"*Carry On* is a surprising book, not only due to the tremendous hearts within these two young men but because the failures and triumphs in their stories don't align with typical narrative rhythms. They arise suddenly, jaggedly, too often shatteringly, as occurs in real life. And as in real life, the moments of understanding, of healing, of unbounded joy will astonish you with the scope of their power."
—Jeff Hobbs, author of the *New York Times* bestseller
The Short and Tragic Life of Robert Peace

"A profoundly moving memoir about two boys who become men in the face of life's toughest challenges: disability, poverty, and torn families. We see the many ways in which one person can carry another, and we are inspired to do the same."

—Tim Howard, author of the *New York Times* bestseller *The Keeper*

"'If you want something you never had, you must be willing to do something you've never done.' This is the philosophy of *Carry On*, an astonishingly beautiful tale about the love we never knew we could experience. And like *The Blind Side* or *Same Kind of Different As Me*, Lisa Fenn's work forces us to reframe our definition of family. By the end, Leroy, Dartanyon, and Lisa had me asking the question that prods us to be better humans: What would you do for a friend?"

—Kevin Salwen, author of *The Power of Half*

"Great sports stories are never about sports. They are always about the trials and triumphs of the human spirit, regardless of the numbers on a scoreboard. No one knows that better than Lisa Fenn, whose heartfelt memoir of faith and the creation of an unlikely family grips you from the first page and pulls at your soul until the end. You need never have watched a second of wrestling, or any sport for that matter, to love this story, and to admire the woman who wrote it."

—Steve Eubanks, *New York Times* bestselling author of *All American*

Each step is like a candle burning in the night. It does not take the darkness away, but it guides us through the darkness. When we look back after many small steps of love, we will discover that we have made a long and beautiful journey.

—HENRI NOUWEN

CARRY ON

Leroy and I never talked about our struggles or our disabilities.
We didn't have to. We just sort of looked at each other like, *You too?*
I thought I was the only one. That's how our friendship started.

—DARTANYON

CHAPTER 1

PRAYING FOR A CHAMPION

If you could reverse the wheels and unbreak the bones, revive the dead and sober up the nights, if you could erase the scars and outrun the ghosts, then perhaps a story could have begun. But instead: The funeral. The accident. The evictions. There is nothing glorious about origins, especially when painfully disguised as endings. To two young men—boys, really—who wandered haunted and hapless, every day felt like a cosmic mistake. Until one fateful fall, on a beat-up high school wrestling mat jammed against some rickety bleachers in a decrepit high school gym, when that hopeless bunch of endings converged to unknowingly begin anew.

THE HEARTLAND SOWS a common dream: that sons will one day become champions. In the world of high school wrestling, there is no more revered path for the molding of those champions than St. Edward High School. Fathers move their families to Ohio, and to the Cleveland area in particular, to give their sons one chance—what they see as the *best* chance—in life: the opportunity to wrestle at St. Ed's, which has built a reputation as both a college prep high school and a wrestling dynasty, holding the state record for most individual state champions (105) and most team championships (30) since 1978.

Every fall, sixty to seventy teens walk onto the St. Ed's wrestling mats to battle for fourteen coveted varsity spots. Few of them are unknown, each grinding out fifty matches a year in youth wrestling feeder programs from the time they are seven years old. They understand the honor at stake; they deem the pressure noble.

The intensity within the St. Edward High School wrestling facility is akin to any Division I college program in the country. The temperature in the room intentionally holds at ninety degrees, dripping with the stench of warriors past. Sights set on identifying the crème de la crème among the talent pool, the head coach circles the room while a dozen technique coaches bark orders, many former collegiate All-Americans in their own rights. The Eagles believe that champions breed champions.

The yearning to uphold the tradition and legacy of the green-and-gold singlet is palpable, and outside of practice, the bar rises ever higher, as many parents drive their sons to additional strength sessions with personal trainers or open mats at wrestling facilities. Athletes opt to ride the stationary bikes during their lunch periods, to cut weight. They feed off one another's contagious enthusiasm and tireless dedication. Through discipline and hard work, they believe, they will be victors, both on the mats and in life.

SEVEN MILES DOWN Lorain Road, a main artery of the city, over crumbling pavement and into boarded-up neighborhoods of stray dogs and lost souls, lies another local high school: Lincoln-West High School, an atrophied limb of Cleveland's decaying city school district. Lincoln's athletes don't funnel out of a system; they straggle in off the streets of this lower-class, predominantly Hispanic neighborhood. Kerry McKinney was substitute teaching at Lincoln-West when he inquired about an open wrestling coach position in 2006.

"Is it JV or varsity?" he asked.

"Uh . . . whatever you want it to be," the athletic director answered.

Kerry McKinney grew up enmeshed in the Ohio wrestling culture and was coached by the legendary John Duplay, an Ohio wrestling Hall of Famer and a pioneer in recruiting African Americans like McKinney to the sport. Twice McKinney advanced to the Ohio State Championships for Warrensville Heights High School. His senior year title match in 1991 is regarded as one of the greatest matches in the history of the state tournament, with McKinney losing in double overtime on the referee's controversial stalling call. Nearly a decade passed before he could walk down the street without someone saying, "Hey, McKinney, you should have won that one!"

McKinney knew what it was like to cut forty pounds in a season. He had spent humid summer days in wool coats and trash bags. He had passed out from dehydration more times than he could count, and shoved twice as many tampons up his nostrils to plug the resulting nosebleeds. He knew what it took to get to the top of Ohio wrestling. And he knew it couldn't be done without shoes. *Why were all these kids barefoot?* he wondered as he walked into Lincoln's first day of practice.

"We only have two pairs of shoes for seven kids," explained assistant coach Torry Robinson, a burly black man who spoke with breathless energy. "It's a waste of time to rotate the shoes during practice. Better to just all practice barefoot. Then we're all equals." Seemed more like insanity than equality to McKinney. Equality was supposed to be about everybody having the same thing, not everybody having nothing.

But it only took one practice to see that the Wolverines were indeed equals, unsurpassed in their respective inabilities. All seven were uniformly horrible. When McKinney told them to line up in their stances, half of them dropped into a three-point football stance, while the others looked around nervously. What should have been as basic as breathing had to be broken down into three deliberate steps: (1) Stand behind your opponent. (2) Bend one knee to the mat. (3) Put one hand on your opponent's belly button and the other hand on his arm.

"No one just shows up as a high-schooler and starts wrestling in Ohio," McKinney said. "And if they do, they gonna get themselves killed!"

Though they lacked experience, these kids came with the nicknames of legends. Weighing in at 145 for the Wolverines was a Latino kid who went by Uno. Then there was Noel, at 160 pounds, who answered to "Christmas" and smelled like a pile of sweat socks because his mother didn't have enough money for all her kids to take baths each day. Christian Keely wrestled at 189; they called him Psycho because of his mile-high Afro and eyes that darted around like pinballs. And Robinson told Shawn "Mama's Boy" Bonilla that if he had half the heart his mother had, he'd be a pretty good wrestler. "We'd get annoyed with him because he was the only kid with wrestling experience, and he could have been good if he had any will," McKinney said. "But then his mom would bring chicken and rice and empanadas to the matches, so everything was cool again."

At 215 pounds, Matt Sifers was known as Blue Ribbon, not for his storied athletic accomplishments but because he moved like he had a case of Pabst Blue Ribbon sloshing around in his fifteen-year-old gut. "He looked like a middle-aged white rapper, all the way down to the money belt buckle," McKinney said. "Nicest and toughest kid I ever met, though. He practiced through injuries, pain, you name it. But he was a terrible wrestler."

The only two Wolverines without nicknames were the two Willies—Willie Diaz and Willie Santiago, the lightest heavyweight in the league. Both desperately wanted fly handles, but nothing materialized. As Latino Opie Taylors of sorts, they were simply too wholesome to tease.

One would have expected Uno to be the team's best wrestler, with a name that translates as Number One. But the kid looked uncoordinated while stretching. "Then we start running, for conditioning, and I see Uno can barely breathe," assistant coach Scott Conklin remembered. "I'm thirty years old, way past my prime, and he can barely keep upright alongside of me."

"What's wrong with you?" Conklin asked. "You're in worse shape than I am!"

"I only have one lung," Uno answered matter-of-factly.

Conklin screeched to a halt. "What do you mean, you only have one lung?" he yelled. "Stop running!" Conklin shared this revelation with McKinney, who echoed Conklin's astonishment: "You only have one *lung*?"

"'Course he only gots one lung," said Christmas. "Why else would we call him Uno?"

Practice ended early that day, in part to avoid asphyxiating Uno and in part to give McKinney a chance to find out what other life-threatening issues he should know about his young wrestlers. On his way out, McKinney tossed his old college wrestling shoes to Christmas. "They're pretty torn up," he said, "but you can have them if they fit."

The next day, Christmas showed up strutting in McKinney's shoes; the holes in the toes were gone. "Stitched 'em all up with some fishing line," Christmas said proudly. "Good as new." McKinney thought of private school wrestling budgets and decided there was something endearing about Christmas cobbling together some hope.

McKinney figured it was best to start with the emergency moves, to get these kids out of the trouble they would surely find themselves in once their matches began. "The first thing I taught them was to escape. I knew they'd be spending a lot of time underneath other people, and it's depressing if you can't escape. We didn't move on to anything else until they could all escape." But teaching even the basics proved difficult, because the kids possessed the technical language of wrestling infants. If he told them to rip the half or reach back or go for the double, they would just stop and stare at him like he had asked them to recite the theory of relativity.

"It's gonna be okay," Robinson would say whenever McKinney pressed his palm to his forehead. "I'm praying." Robinson thought that if God could multiply five loaves and two fish, he might as well see what could be done with seven kids and two pairs of shoes. Truth be told, Robinson didn't have much technical background in the sport either. He had been a horrible high school wrestler and had been ejected from more matches than he actually won. "I'd bite kids, spit on them," remembered Robinson. "One time, I even got in a fight in the locker room and was ejected before the tournament began. I was not the best wrestler, or human being." But Robinson had calmed down since then. He said God had helped him root out the anger and plant joy in its place. Robinson thought wrestling was the ideal sport for instilling structure and character into the lives of young people. He wanted to contribute what he could, so he walked the indoor track above the basketball courts every day before practice and prayed. He prayed for mercy. He prayed for protection. And he prayed for the season to go by fast.

McKinney arrived with renewed expectations and big plans each day, trying to pack in the decade of wrestling these boys had missed, only to leave deflated each night. He began to worry less about the prospect of losing and more about the probability of these kids being slaughtered. One day in early November, just a week before their first meet, they were looking so bad that Robinson told McKinney he was going to go pray *during* practice.

"Sure," McKinney said. "Whatever you can do." So while the boys drilled, Robinson walked the perimeter of the gymnasium, his hands motioning in serious conversation with the heavens. He skipped the pleas for mercy and protection and shot straight for the miracle. "Give us something to work with, someone to build around," Robinson prayed.

And that's when Robinson heard God: *Your ch*

Now Robinson was no Father Teresa. He had made i.,
but he was a spiritual man who ultimately heeded heaven's
even if he took the roundabout path. But this directive required
immediate action, and he had to be sure it was really God. "When
you're 275 pounds of red meat and mashed potatoes, a trip up any
set of stairs had better be for a real good reason," Robinson pointed
out. He stopped under the basketball net and waited to be sure.
The tug came again. *Your champion is upstairs.*

The only thing upstairs was the weight room, and this time Robinson wasted no time hustling up there. He was met at the entrance
by a boy of average height who had muscles bunched like walnuts.
"Kid, you know how to wrestle?" Robinson asked, catching his
breath.

"Uh . . . I don't . . . uh—," the boy answered.

"Don't matter. Come with me."

"I DON'T REALLY want to wrestle," the kid said as they got to the
mat, Robinson still pulling him by the shirt.

"You only gotta stay one day," Robinson said. "If you don't like
it, you don't gotta come back." The kid didn't answer. Robinson
had recruited half of the Lincoln-West team like this. If you walked
upright, or even if you didn't, he'd say, "You should be on the
wrestling team."

"What's your name, kid?" Robinson asked.

"Dartanyon."

"Geezus, you'll fit right in with a crazy name like that," Robinson
said. "You don't even need a nickname."

Like the rest, sophomore Dartanyon Crockett spoke no wrestling
language. Unlike the others, though, he had an uncanny aptitude
for the maneuvers. McKinney explained a drill, and Dartanyon
executed it on his first attempt as though he had done it a thousand

ımes before. "Maybe he *does* need a nickname," Robinson said. "Maybe he's our LeBron."

Born and raised down the interstate in Akron, and drafted directly out of high school into the NBA, LeBron James was Ohio's golden child and this generation's Michael Jordan. The real LeBron stood six-eight. If someone had hit him over the head with a carnival mallet a few times and shrunk him down a foot or so, he indeed could have been mistaken for this man-child now rolling around on the mat. "Dartanyon looked like someone drew him," McKinney said. "Like he had just walked out of a comic book and into our gym." Maybe they wouldn't go winless this season, McKinney thought. With a body like that, Dartanyon could at least scare a few kids into submission.

McKinney skipped over the opening stance lessons with Dartanyon and went straight to throwing. He suspected that a strong kid like this would enjoy tossing other people around, and he guessed correctly, because Dartanyon showed up the next day without anyone dragging him by the collar. With their first meet days away, McKinney showed Dartanyon a headlock and an escape, while Robinson paced and prayed it would make up for his lack of conditioning.

Just before Thanksgiving, McKinney hauled his boys over to the east side of Cleveland for a dual with Collinwood High School, a city school in Lincoln's conference with more experience and an established coaching staff. The Wolverines got their heads handed to them. "From top to bottom, every kid laid an egg," Robinson said. "It was like they were raised on a chicken farm."

The following weekend, they headed an hour east for a tournament in Ashtabula, Ohio. Robinson took note of the rural demographics as they drove into town, and of the halls of white teens as they entered the school. And then he hatched a plan: "Crockett, take off your shirt as we walk into the gym," he said.

Being a boy of few words and even fewer questions, Dartanyon obeyed.

"This big, muscular guy takes his sweats off and looks like a superhero. The other teams were terrified!" McKinney said. "I'm laughing because I know it's not the advantage they think it is." But it was enough. Dartanyon pinned his first two opponents with ease, maintaining the same fixed, expressionless stare from start to finish, as though he could not see anything but the task at hand. He dropped the finals match, settling for second. But in a life engulfed by perpetually losing battles, Dartanyon thought this winning felt pretty good.

MCKINNEY GAVE DARTANYON a lift back that night, as he had been doing once or twice each week. Sometimes Dartanyon wanted to be dropped off at a friend's house, other nights at his dad's work or with a cousin, and once on a street corner. Rarely did McKinney drop him at the same spot twice, and never did the place look like a home. The only constant was the black canvas duffel bag Dartanyon carried with him, large enough to fit a child. Having worked as a detention officer in the juvenile justice system, McKinney knew what that bag meant. "Nobody needs to carry a bag that big unless they are carrying everything they own, to a destination unknown," McKinney said. Dartanyon was transient.

Dartanyon's nomadic existence hardly shocked McKinney. About one-third of Lincoln-West's attendees had no stable place to call home, and nearly the entire student population showed up for the school's free breakfast each morning. He knew he likely had kids on the team who went hungry. The surprising part to him was that all eight of his wrestlers were still turning up for strenuous practices one month in, volunteering to make their lives more difficult. But one look at Dartanyon's duffel bag reminded him that their depleted childhoods prepared these kids for the single most important facet of wrestling: self-preservation. It's unlike other sports: You don't enter the circle with five other guys on a line beside you. No one rebounds your misses and puts them in for you. A wrestler endures alone. Wins alone. Falls alone. Northeast Ohio's powerhouse feeder programs spent years training kids for these battles, but life prepared Lincoln's kids in another way, equipping them with the most important lesson of all: how to get knocked down and get back up. Coach Conklin told the team early on to let him know if they were hungry, and he would get them food. No one spoke up. Life also taught them that pride trumps hunger.

Lincoln's coaches kept the team on a steady diet of JV matches, looking to score a little confidence. The victories came in incremental doses rather than wins per se. If Sifers threw a half nelson from his feet rather than his knees, McKinney counted the bout a success. If Diaz got his opponents on their backs, it was a good day. They almost always ended up losing the match, but those flashes of proper technique, of marginal improvements, were enough to keep them all going.

"They weren't quitters. You have to respect anyone who volunteers to spend their weekends getting beat up," McKinney said. "They weren't much of a team, but they were a family." Dartanyon, especially, lapped up McKinney's direction like a shelter pup. He grew faster on his feet and harder to take down, looking comfortable on the mat in the way natural athletes do when they discover what their bodies are made to do.

Which is why the news caught them all by surprise. Not even Dartanyon is sure how his secret slipped out. Being new to the school, he was hoping to hold on to it for a little longer.

"You're blind?" Robinson exclaimed one day at practice.

Dartanyon took a deep breath and nodded. "Yah, pretty much." Dartanyon suffers from nystagmus and optic neuropathy—

congenital conditions that cause involuntary, roving eye movements and severe nearsightedness that limits his focus to approximately four feet.

"We're cousins," Psycho chimed in. "We have the same eye issues."

"You're related to Psycho?" Robinson asked with a nervous chuckle. "Geezus, now I've heard it all."

"I mean, I can see some things," Dartanyon said. "I just can't see very far, and things are a little blurry."

Robinson huddled up with McKinney and Conklin. How could Dartanyon be blind? He hadn't run into any walls since he showed up. He executed drills better than kids with vision. Sure, the coaches had noticed things here and there, like how Dartanyon held his cell phone a little too close to his face, or how when they talked to him from a foot or two away, his pupils seemed to jog off in different directions. But they'd dismissed it as a wandering eye, behavior no stranger than anyone else's on the team.

"Uno's got some type of lung issue. Sifers is limping around like he's been smoking Camels since the age of two. Christmas is in the corner sewing shoes and can't take a bath. A little jiggle of the eyes hardly stands out as alarming in this group," McKinney said.

"I may be blind, but I can hear everything you're saying," Dartanyon called out as they whispered off to the side.

"Had I known he was blind, I would have dragged some other kid out of the weight room that day," Robinson said later. "Probably better I didn't know."

Dartanyon finished 11–16 that season. Respectable, yet hardly anything to raise an eyebrow at. Still, Robinson's faith told him that God had the right kid, that a champion waited within.

COACH MCKINNEY AND Coach Conklin both moved out of Ohio prior to the 2007–8 season, leaving Coach Robinson at the helm.

Also missing at the start of the season was Dartanyon. He didn't show up for the first practice. Nor the second. Robinson hunted him down in the halls. "Yah, sorry, coach, but I can't wrestle this year," Dartanyon told him.

"Oh, yes, you can," Robinson said. "You got too much talent to waste." He grabbed Dartanyon by the neck and put him in a cradle, but Robinson couldn't hold him. Nor could he blame him when Dartanyon finally offered up his reason. "My dad and me have to move in with my aunt, and she can't afford to feed us both, so I have to work to help out."

Robinson understood, but still he hounded Dartanyon each afternoon that he found him lingering in the halls. "Son, you can go a lot further in life through sports than you can sweeping floors somewhere," he said. "Come wrestle till you find work." Maybe Robinson's needling wore him down. Maybe Dartanyon realized the job prospects for visually impaired teens were dire in a city with the second-highest unemployment rate in the country. Whatever the reason, Dartanyon eventually turned up in the gym.

The team's technical development plateaued with McKinny's departure, but their sense of family strengthened. Early in Robinson's tenure, Lincoln traveled to a city meet where they got their heads handed to them. Robinson went Coach Bobby Knight on them, berating them wildly. "You guys couldn't pin a fish on dry land!" he screamed.

Robinson stormed out of the gym, telling his kids they could all walk home because he wasn't riding with a bus full of losers. Once he was out the door, shame stopped his stride. "I was compelled to go back and tell those kids that I loved them," he remembered. "They were an emotionally broken bunch who needed love more than they needed points and wins." So he hustled back into the gym to find them all sitting like stones right where he'd left them. He told them he was sorry. He asked for their forgiveness. He told them he loved them.

"That was my epiphany," Robinson remembered. "I could have lost every kid right there if I didn't go back." From then on, he looked each of his wrestlers in the eye before they walked on the mat and shouted, "Who loves you?"

"Coach does!" they would answer with proud assurance. With his world mired in perpetual uncertainty, Dartanyon especially grew to trust in this ritual and began to blossom under Robinson's care. He grew a little stronger that year—moving up a weight class from 171 to 189 pounds—and a little fiercer. He was no longer content to toss someone around in a personal display of strength. He was out for the kill, finishing most of his twenty-five wins that season with a punishing headlock. Robinson just looked on and smiled in the impish way you do when you're holding in a secret.

CHAPTER 2

THE NEW KID

The following fall, at the start of the 2008–9 season, Matt Sifers told Robinson that there was a new kid who wanted to wrestle. "I'm not sure what you're going to think of him," Sifers said. "He's . . . well . . . a little different."

Robinson chuckled. "We already got every kind of different on this team. What, is he purple?"

"No, he's not purple," Sifers said. "He's black."

"We already got one of those," Robinson said, pointing to Dartanyon. "What's so different about this one?"

"He doesn't have any legs."

Robinson prided himself as being the king of comebacks, but nothing came out of his gaping mouth this time. He crossed his arms over his chest and thought for a moment. He had long bought into the Wolverines' misfit identity, and he figured if he learned how to coach kids without shoes, he could learn how to coach a kid without legs too. "Tell him to come to practice," he said finally. "We'd love to have him."

Leroy Sutton was a lower-extremity double amputee who'd transferred into Lincoln-West from Akron the previous winter, halfway through his junior year. This being his twelfth school in ten years, Leroy was done trying to make friends. He repelled most people's curiosity with black nail polish, facial piercings, and the heavy metal that blared out of his headphones as he played air drums against the sides of his wheelchair. He successfully creeped out Sifers in the computer class they shared their senior year.

Leroy eventually spoke first, noticing Matt's football jersey one Friday and asking what position he played. "You should come out for the team," Sifers said awkwardly, immediately regretting his insensitivity and reddening.

"Nah, I'm a wrestler," Leroy said.

Sifers wasn't sure how Leroy wrestling could be any more probable than Leroy playing football; he was just glad Leroy had said something that made him feel better instead of worse.

"I wrestle too," Sifers said. "You should come out for the wrestling team this fall." Every day for the next month, Sifers told Leroy that he expected to see him at practice, and the day the mats rolled out, Leroy rolled in.

THE LINCOLN WRESTLING program had expanded to include twelve kids and nine pairs of shoes as that season began, and Justin Hons, a history teacher at Lincoln, came on as Robinson's assistant. Hons, a sinewy young white man, had a background in mixed martial arts but was a little uncertain as to how to convert that into wrestling mechanics. He and Robinson were even less sure what to do with Leroy.

Leroy had wrestled for part of his sophomore and junior year at his previous high school, Akron Firestone, under Coach Mark Avcollie. A grizzled lifer in Ohio wrestling, Avcollie had coached fourteen years at Cleveland's St. Ignatius High School, a chief rival of St. Ed's. In 1988 he led St. Ignatius to their first state wrestling title, keeping the St. Ed's Eagles from a state record eleventh consecutive championship. Avcollie retired from coaching shortly thereafter, but couldn't stay away. Firestone, a public school with a meager wrestling program, eagerly snapped him up, and it wasn't long before his Falcons commanded their own slice of respect throughout the state.

In the fall of 2006 Leroy, then a sophomore at Firestone, tottered into Avcollie's wrestling room on buckling prosthetic legs and crutches. He asked how he might try out for the team. Avcollie, all business, told Leroy the same thing, in the same gravelly voice, that he told every other kid who entered his lair: "Anyone can try out. I don't have to cut anybody. Wrestling is the hardest thing you'll ever do. You'll cut yourself." He usually had sixty kids show up on the first day of practice, and four weeks later he'd be staring down twenty.

Leroy wore a tattered white ribbed tank top that day, revealing his thick shoulders and biceps. "It was obvious he didn't have any legs, but it didn't look like the rest of him had gone to a fat waste," Avcollie remembered. "He had a build on him. If you had only seen him from the waist up, you would have thought he was an athlete."

After only a week of practices, Firestone traveled to St. Ed's for a scrimmage. The coaches told the boys to partner up. Leroy was quickly passed over, as no one knew how to approach a wrestler without legs. He slunk back to the edge of the mats, the odd man out. Just then Andrew Gasber, a two-time Ohio state place winner who would finish his high school career 121–16, walked into the gym like a gladiator into a ring. He was running late. He pointed to Leroy as though he had been searching dark alleys to find him. "I got you," he said. "Let's go."

A wrestling infant versus one of the sport's giants, Leroy hardly made it within arm's reach before Andrew flattened him into the mat, brutalizing him for the next two minutes. Andrew showed no mercy, tossing Leroy around like a German shepherd with a chew toy as coaches winced, mercifully closing their notebooks. When the whistle finally blew, Leroy untangled himself from Andrew's web of limbs and emerged with a wide, satisfied smile. Avcollie knew right then that Leroy Sutton would never quit.

Leroy participated in a handful of junior varsity matches that season. He rarely left with a win, but always with a smile. Leroy's wrestling days at Firestone were limited, though. Academic in-eligibility sidelined him during his sophomore year, and his right femur extruded through the skin to end his junior season early. Following bone revision surgery in 2007, Leroy moved in with his grandmother on the east side of Cleveland and transferred to Lincoln-West.

Most of the kids on the Lincoln team knew Leroy from classes. He'd met Dartanyon the previous spring, when Uno introduced them in the halls. By then, Dartanyon had either acquired a nick-name or given it to himself, depending on whom you ask. "Leroy, meet Muscles," Uno said. "Muscles, this is Leroy Sutton." Leroy cocked his head in a "wassup" sort of way as he looked Dartanyon over. *You ain't the only one with muscles anymore*, he thought, though he said nothing.

In Akron, the story behind Leroy's disability was no secret. Residents young and old could tell you where they were when Leroy Sutton lost his legs. But Cleveland represented new territory, and Leroy wanted to be known for something other than his history. No one dared to ask what happened to him until Dartanyon broke code and spoke unprompted, catching Leroy off guard: "What happened to your legs, man?"

HE DIDN'T KNOW they were gone.

Staring down at the sheets of his bed, the morphine starting to fade, Leroy was still numb, but he knew something was wrong.

"It was when I tried to sit up," Leroy remembered. "I pulled the covers up, and that's when I figured everything out."

December 7, 2001, was a day that started like all others for then eleven-year-old Leroy.

"Redd, getcha butt outta bed!" Leroy's fifteen-year-old brother, Tony, pounded on the wall separating their bedrooms to wake him up. Their mother left at the crack of dawn for a painting job three hours away in Pittsburgh, but even when she was out of a job, the boys still got themselves up for school. Nuzzling children out of slumber and packing lunches with napkin notes was not the kind of mothering Katrina Sutton was about.

The Suttons had moved onto Laird Street a few months prior. Lined with deteriorating Victorian homes, Laird had been built in the early 1900s as a stately dwelling community for the executives of the Goodyear Tire and Rubber Company, whose headquarters were less than a mile away. Once the rubber capital of the world, Akron's population boomed through the 1970s as Goodyear, Goodrich, and Firestone created jobs at insatiable rates. The rubber industry responded to the housing crunch by building homes for their employees.

But like so many other Rust Belt industries, tire companies moved their operations overseas due to multiple labor union strikes in the 1970s and '80s. By 1984, only Goodyear's Formula One racing tire plant remained, and the once-opulent homes of Goodyear Heights were divided into subsidized Section 8 tenant housing. By the time Leroy moved in, the neighborhood was one of the worst areas of Akron, home to drug dealers and the mentally ill, living in destitution. The stench of body odor and uncollected garbage wafted off the hill down onto Market Street, the main thoroughfare, on hot days.

Leroy, a fifth-grader at Hotchkiss Elementary, was too young to understand the bedlam around him. Instead, he awoke excited for his safety patrol shift that morning. Whereas Tony could talk you out of your boots on a snowy day, Leroy was a quiet, sensitive boy. Volunteering on crosswalk duty afforded Leroy a low-pressure outlet in which to make friends, where he could trade hellos with his schoolmates and smiles with the mothers dropping them off. Safety patrol also allowed him to be a few minutes late to his first class, and he felt important sauntering in with an office pass.

That morning, Leroy proudly dressed in the black leather jacket and white New Balance low-tops that Tony had given him the day before. Some of the kids in the neighborhood were saying Leroy was soft, so Tony bought him name-brand clothes to raise his street cred a little. Leroy didn't know where his brother got the money, nor did he know about the slits strategically cut into Tony's own clothes to hide the bags of weed he sold at his high school. Tony was the man of the house, and his mother groomed him to do his part. As a result, he loved Leroy and their four-year-old sister, Keyiera, and resented them in equal parts. He wished he could be a kid himself rather than braiding his sister's hair and minding his brother every day. Tony was Leroy's greatest tormenter and fiercest protector.

That morning Tony and Leroy packed up Keyiera and dropped her with a neighbor, making them a few minutes late. Walking their usual twenty-minute route down and around Market Street would have landed them both tardy, so they headed for a short cut through a neighboring yard and onto the Wheeling and Lake Erie railroad tracks.

Leroy's elementary school was five minutes down the right side of the track; Tony's high school a few minutes farther on the left. The train told time for them each morning. When the boys ran on schedule, the cars shunted by while Leroy was safely in his crossing gear and Tony was climbing the back steps of East High. That morning, the engine rumbled toward them just as the boys emerged from the bushes. They were later than they thought.

"I'm just gonna cross over now, in case it's a real long train," Leroy said.

"All right," Tony replied. "By the time it passes, I be seeing you on the stairs up to your school."

DISPATCH CALLED OUT to Akron Fire Station 2 right at the 7:30 a.m. shift change. The six-person crew—three on the fire engine, two on the med unit, and one swingman—had just finished checking the rigs and replenishing supplies from the previous shift. They had more than forty years of collective emergency response experience among them, enough to expect anything at one of Akron's busiest stations.

Station 2 received an average of twenty med-run calls in a twenty-four-hour period. Its service area included Laird Street—which responders referred to as "Laird Land"—and the adjoining "Willard World," an equally impoverished neighboring street. As is true with most inner-city populations, 911 served as the block's default health care provider. Many runs at Station 2 were for non-emergency calls from residents who used the emergency room as their primary care doctors and the ambulance service as their chauffeur. Responders transported ankle sprains, sore throats, and addicts wanting a free trip to a nearby psychiatric crisis center, hoping to talk their way into a fix when their street drugs ran out. Few of these folks really needed an ambulance, but transporters knew that if they didn't oblige, the resident might scream, throw rocks, and call again an hour later.

The bad days were really bad, though. Babies dead in their cribs and a strung-out mom claiming she'd put her son to bed at 5:00 p.m. "She put him to bed at five p.m. all right. She put him to bed at five p.m. a week ago," paramedic Richard Wendelken remembered. Elderly men and women living surrounded by decades of hoarded newspapers, rotting food, and urine-soaked clothes. Families of ten or more packed together on a bare floor with the television blaring at two o'clock in the morning, the walls teeming with so many cockroaches that they looked like patterned wallpaper.

"When there were children involved, I never left a run without checking the fridge for food, and a lot of times there wasn't much," paramedic Keith Forfia said. Responders were trained to forget their runs, but they could never seem to shake the inescapable hopelessness of Laird.

Station 2 was accustomed to innumerable bogus calls too. Some residents reported kids having been hit by cars, and responders arrived only to find the callers just wanted a ride to the emergency room for a twisted finger and thought flowering up their call would expedite the ambulance. Others made prank calls out of boredom and a warped sense of humor. But those fools were seldom up this early in the morning, which made the first call of the day all the more grave:

CHILD STRUCK BY TRAIN.
SEND MED UNIT TO ELINOR STREET.

"There are calls you dawdle on. There are calls you think, 'I seriously doubt it.' And then there are the ones no one says anything. You just get in the truck and go," Keith said. "This was one of those." Dispatch routinely ordered the med unit out first, and then if a call required help, responders summoned the engine for additional manpower. Lt. Doug Bjerre, a twenty-five-year veteran on the force, knew that if this call were real, the med unit would not be able to handle it alone. He immediately ordered the engine to go along.

Dispatch crossed again.

CHILD STRUCK BY TRAIN.
THIS IS NOT A JOKE.

Paramedic Michelle Dockstader drove the ambulance that morning, only one of a handful of times she remembered taking the turns so aggressively. "Emergencies are relative. Getting somewhere three seconds faster doesn't usually make a difference," she said. "But on that day, there was the unspoken sense that three seconds might matter."

Michelle squeezed the wheel, pressing the gas pedal to the floor with all of her weight. She wondered why dispatch would say it's not a joke. They never talked like that. How would they have confirmed it? Still, even if the call was not a hoax, there was no way this child could be alive. This would surely be a recovery run. They would declare the child dead on-site and wait for the coroner. She turned down Elinor, a short residential street that dead-ended into a cluster of industrial buildings and an exposed train track. As Michelle, Richard, and EMT rookie Danielle Michele pulled onto the gravel with the fire engine right behind, they didn't see anything unusual. There was no sign or sound of a train. "Then once we pulled closer, we looked down and saw a body," Richard remembered. Michelle sprinted toward the tracks, forgetting her bag and her monitor. "I don't know what the Angel of Mercy was going to do with my bare hands, but I started running," she remembered. She came to a halt when the body next to the track ever so slightly lifted his head.

"Oh my God!" Michelle gasped. "He's alive."

"This is my brother, Leroy," Tony cried as he ran toward them. "You gotta help him!" As he and Leroy had walked along their respective sides of the train, Tony looked under each passing car to make sure he could see the glow of Leroy's new white shoes against the gravel. But after the first few cars, they suddenly disappeared. Tony took off running toward the end of the train, but there was seemingly no end to the lumbering cars. When he finally rounded to Leroy's side of the track, his brother lay still on the ground, the train clanking away. Leroy's jeans were ripped in a hundred places, with blood seeping through the slits. Or was that raw flesh? Tony started to vomit in his mouth. "What happened to you?" he screamed.

"I just got sucked under," Leroy said. Both boys masked their panic. Leroy feared his brother being mad at him for ruining his new shoes, and Tony feared his mother coming after him with a baseball bat for getting Leroy killed.

"Let's get you off these tracks," Tony said. He tried to pick Leroy up from under his arms. Leroy shrieked in pain, so Tony set him down just a few feet off the tracks. "I'm going for help. I'll be right back."

Tony raced to a factory twenty feet across the tracks, where a man sat on the loading dock with his morning cigarette and coffee. "My brother just got hit by a train! You gotta help me!" Tony shouted.

"Stop playin', man," the worker said, unfazed, as he took another drag and looked out into the trees.

"Bro, can't you see all this blood on me?" Tony shouted.

The man turned to see Tony's new silver pants splattered with crimson. "Woah, man, I'll call an ambulance!" he said as he dove back into the dock.

THE AMBULANCE ARRIVED after six of the longest minutes of Tony's life. And now the members of the rescue crew stood over Leroy, somewhat unsure. They had never seen a trauma victim so collected. His blood loss was minimal, considering his injuries. He was not in pain, his body numbed into shock. And because he could not sit up, Leroy did not yet know to be afraid. He could not see his lower extremities. "We were all amazed to see how calm he was," Keith said. "He was alert and oriented to person, place, and time."

Leroy stared up at the group, eyes glassy and white, wondering what would happen next. And they stared back, wondering the very same thing. Trauma responders are trained in the A-B-Cs: airway, breathing, circulation. Leroy needed no intervention in those regards. But he did need to be moved, quickly. As is typical in crush injuries, the train's wheels had cauterized Leroy's blood vessels, but they could just as easily open without warning and Leroy could bleed to death. There was no way to know how much time he had. There was also no way of knowing what parts of his legs were attached and what might fall off if they lifted him. "From the waist up, he was a coherent, whole child," Keith said. "But the rest of him was a big jumble of parts and pieces rolled in leaves and dirt, with a shoe dangling backward from what used to be an ankle." His other foot sat fifteen yards down the track. Lifting Leroy posed a risk of further injuring his lower extremities.

"Slide a sheet underneath him, to hold him all together," Lt. Bjerre suggested, unconventionally. They shimmied a sheet under Leroy, scooped him onto a backboard, and ran. Once in the ambulance, Richard made first contact with the Akron Children's Hospital:

> URGENT TRAFFIC. WE HAVE A TRAUMA.
> ELEVEN-YEAR-OLD MALE RUN OVER BY TRAIN.
> CRUSH INJURIES BELOW LEFT KNEE, ABOVE RIGHT KNEE.
> CONSCIOUS. AMPUTATED FOOT.
> WE NEED A TRAUMA TEAM.

Senior firefighter Rick Staeger stayed behind to collect the strewn globs of Leroy's tissue, bone fragments, and his foot. Lt. Bjerre drove the med unit while Keith, Michelle, Richard, and Danielle squeezed in the back with Leroy. There, reality set in. "I'll be the first to say that I *froze*," Michelle remembered. "I was sitting in the back of the rig where his feet should be. He was lying there talking to us, and that's not supposed to happen to a child who gets run over by a train. I wanted to grab his legs and tell him everything was going to be okay. But there was nothing to grab."

Keith started an IV line of fluids and led Leroy through a list of basic questions to keep him alert. What is your name? What is your address? What is your date of birth? "I have a son named Steven who is your age," Keith said. "In a few minutes, I am going to ask you again what his name is." Leroy's answers would assure them blood was reaching his brain. He calmly responded to each question, and as the ambulance pulled into the hospital, Leroy asked one of his own: "Will I be able to run track in the spring?"

Michelle turned away, eyes stinging with salty tears. Danielle gulped down a breath. Richard's lip quivered, and his pen slipped. And Keith thought of his own son, also a fifth-grader. He thought about what he would want someone to say if this was his boy hanging between life and death. He put one hand on Leroy's head, the other across his chest. He said, "Son, as long as your heart and your mind are okay, you will be fine. Your heart and your mind can take you everywhere you want to go. Everything else you can live without."

A sea of doctors and nurses stood waiting for Leroy's stretcher. As she watched his stretcher disappear, Michelle didn't want to forget this run. "Lord, don't let anything happen to this little boy," she whispered. "Don't let him end up a miserable, angry person in a wheelchair who hates the world. Don't let him fall into the system he came from. Help him make something of himself. Show him love in this world."

LEROY ARRIVED AT Akron Children's Hospital less than thirty minutes removed from the accident, well within the Golden Hour trauma teams shoot for to maximize chances of survival. The hospital chaplain took Leroy's hand as they wheeled him into an examining station, asking him where he went to school and what subjects he enjoyed. Dr. John Crow, pediatric surgeon, began unpacking Leroy from the sheet. Though this hospital is located in the heart of Akron, the most horrific injuries tend to come from neighboring Amish communities, where young children wielding aging farming machinery often suffer lost and mutilated limbs. Dr. Crow had yet to see a train accident survivor, though, and as he peeled open the sheet, he immediately knew Leroy fell into the top three traumas he had seen in his nine years of practice. Cinders coated his bloodied lower half, which was butchered into bright red marbled chunks like one would see in a meat market, yet still held loosely together by the ligaments. His jeans were twisted and ground into the wounds. "His injuries were so severe, so grotesque, so dramatic," Dr. Crow recounted. "I will forever remember Leroy coming in as clear as any day I've ever had."

Dr. Crow called up to the operating room to let them know a Trauma III, the highest grade of life-threatening trauma, was on its way. Whether to amputate was never a decision; Leroy's legs could not be saved. The question was whether his life could be spared. No one knew how long Leroy's blood vessels would remain sealed. The team began cleaning out gravel and debriding tissue, harvesting any little bit they might use for future skin grafts, and removing flaps they feared could lead to infection. The skin below Leroy's left knee was salvaged, but the flesh hanging from his right leg proved largely unusable. The more time that passed, the greater the risk of infection, or even worse, sepsis.

That afternoon, Leroy awoke briefly in the intensive care unit with his mother, his grandmother, and his aunt waiting bedside. "I had a dream that I got run over by a train and my legs were gone," Leroy said groggily as he tried to get up.

His mother put her hand on his shoulder and gently pressed him back to the bed. "Baby, that wasn't a dream," she said. Leroy slowly pulled back the covers to find two mounds of bloodied gauze. He looked back at the faces in the room, all eyes puddling with tears. Turning his head away from his family, he noticed that the wall-paper border around the top of his room was a colorful strip of train engines and freight cars. He couldn't look up. He couldn't look down. He closed his eyes and went somewhere else.

Leroy returned to surgery eight times over the next two weeks for repeated tissue cleaning, removing specks of cinder, milking pus, and irrigating his festering, malodorous wounds. The doctors also began stretching muscle tissue and grafting flaps of skin over the ends of his amputated bones. His stumps were wrapped in burn-victim gauze soaked with antibiotic solution, and drainage tubes were used to collect the fluids that oozed from his wounds. Although Leroy developed occasional abscesses and minor infections, surgeons grew increasingly optimistic that he would survive.

While Leroy's body tolerated each procedure well, torment seized his mind every night. "I could not go to sleep, because when I tried to go to sleep, I'd end up hearing the sound of a train and it woke me back up, over and over again," Leroy said. "I just laid awake and asked why. Why?" Leroy had been an athletic child, always among the first picked for neighborhood basketball and football games. He dreamed of becoming an NBA star like Michael Jordan or the Yankee heir to Derek Jeter at shortstop. Now the only dream accessible to him was that of thirteen fifty-ton boxcars sawing through his shins. He could see no further than the long night ahead, the hours primed to torture and haunt him.

The only break he got from the mental anxiety came when surges of excruciating physical pain shot through him without warning. Leroy screamed and howled, gripping the bed rails. Sometimes the pain originated from his open wounds, burning and itching against the gauze. His nurses taught him which button to push for additional doses of morphine, and it calmed his body enough that he could then quietly cry. His ears would pool with cold tears. He did not wipe them away; he hadn't the energy, and the sensation of wet ears was a strangely relieving counter to the burn throughout the rest of his body.

Other times the pain was "phantom," radiating from legs and feet that were no longer there. The nerves that connected his lower body to his brain essentially log-jammed and sent urgent messages in the form of sharp, throbbing pain that something was awry. No cocktail of drugs could combat phantom limb pain.

One night in mid-December, Leroy lay alone in a rare moment when all the different types of pains had eased, allowing him a clear space in which to think. He longed for death's peace more than he wanted to endure the atrocity of his life, and so he reached for the morphine controls, resolved to overdose. He pumped the release button thirteen times, once for each freight car that had crushed his legs and now his spirit. He looked over at his grandmother, who was asleep in the chair, as she had been each night since the accident, and he whispered that he loved her. Then he closed his eyes, content to slip into death.

LEROY DIDN'T SHARE any of that with Dartanyon. Nor did he share his devastation upon learning that the morphine dispenser was equipped with a limiter to prevent overdoses. Instead of skipping across clouds into the arms of God, as he expected, he learned that his stay in hell had been extended. Indefinitely.

"So really, what happened to your legs?" Dartanyon asked again.

"I was hit by a train," Leroy answered simply but firmly, signaling that no further questions would be taken.

The others stood silently. But Dartanyon laughed, heartily. "That's hilarious!" he exclaimed. "I never heard anyone say that before!" Dartanyon couldn't see the awkward twisting of the faces around him; social cues were not his strong suit. Nor could he see Leroy's top lip start to smile as he bit the bottom one down, intrigued by this odd reaction to his misfortune. Leroy was familiar with clumsy expressions of sympathy. He knew the face of pity. But it had been a long time since he'd heard laughter.

LEROY AND DARTANYON didn't cross paths again until the first practice of the 2008–9 season. Though most of the other wrestlers knew Leroy from class, they were unsure how to grapple with him and too nervous to even try. Except Dartanyon, that is.

"Let's do this, Leroy," he called out from the mat. He knew how it felt to be flawed and left out.

Leroy hadn't wrestled in over a year; he quickly grew winded. But what little he could put forth was enough to surprise Dartanyon. "He was a complete powerhouse," Dartanyon said. "I never wrestled anyone as strong as him, being as strong as I am."

Over the coming weeks, it became clear that Leroy's strength was undeniable, yet Robinson and Hons questioned his heart. He seemed leery of everything and everyone. When told to do laps in his wheelchair while the others ran, Leroy weaved through oncoming traffic to disrupt his teammates and coax a few laughs. When Robinson blew the whistle to begin a drill, Leroy would hang back for a minute before starting or purposely alter the exercise. "Leroy always did things on his terms," Robinson said. "The message he was sending was 'I'll do this, but I won't do it your way, because I don't trust you.'"

"None of us knew what Leroy was getting out of this, and any time he got close to opening up to us, he quickly shut back down," Hons said. "Wrestling is a sport of attrition, so if you don't have the goods, you're going to quit. But he didn't quit. He kept coming back. And we couldn't cut a legless kid."

"Sutton, your problem is that you're a turtle," Robinson said one day, laughing, as Leroy lay pancaked under Dartanyon. "Once you're on your back, you're done. You can't roll over!" The kids snickered. Leroy seethed. The way he saw it, the only place Robinson looked like he could roll was down a steep slope with a hard push, which is what Leroy felt like doing to him. Robinson had ballooned to three hundred pounds as that season began.

"I am in shape," he would say when the kids called him Coach Fatboy or Chocolate Thunda. "Round is a shape, so don't y'all discriminate! I used to wrestle at 103, you know."

"Maybe we can give your legs to Leroy and get you back down closer to 103," Dartanyon would shoot back. Leroy liked seeing the jabs hurled in the other direction.

What Leroy didn't know was that Robinson was close to boiling over too. That summer, Robinson had separated from his wife of four years. He plummeted into depression, bankruptcy, and weight gain. He tried to hide his irritability at practice, but his tone was still harsher than usual. And his demonstrations on the mat sometimes seemed personal. "Coach, you changed," Shawn Bonilla said one day. "You ain't the same person you were last year." Robinson still walked the track each day, praying for the Lord to save his kids' lives. But in the next breath, he asked God to take his own. He didn't know how many more days he could go on living with his heart dragging around by his ankles.

Their first match came in late November, a dual against John Marshall High School. Coach Hons thought they were as ready as they could be, but as the big yellow school bus pulled up to load the team, they realized they had neglected one significant element of preparation—how to physically get Leroy on the bus. Five steps connected the door of the gym to the sidewalk, the bus lacked a lift, and the ground was wet. Dartanyon needed just a few seconds to consider both the problem and the solution. "Hop on my back," he said. "I'll carry you." Leroy did as he was told. He raised himself up in the chair, wrapped his arms around Dartanyon's neck, and rode piggyback to the bus.

"What are you two idiots doing?" Robinson asked as they boarded.

"Just helping Leroy get on the bus," Dartanyon answered. "There's no ramp." Dartanyon placed Leroy in a seat and then went back out to break down the wheelchair. When the bus arrived at their destination, Dartanyon carried Leroy off. When Robinson told the team to sit at the top of the bleachers so that they were always looking down on their opponents, Dartanyon put Leroy on his back and carried him up ten wooden rows. Dartanyon didn't think to ask Leroy if he could manage on his own. And Leroy didn't tell Dartanyon that he had been hauling himself onto buses and up and down stairs for the last six years.

The only open weight class on the team for Leroy to fill was heavyweight, and less than fifteen seconds into his first match, he was lifted in the air like a five-pound dumbbell. Half of the gym reacted in laughter, the other half in fright. Leroy was promptly pinned by a kid who had fifty pounds on him. But he was not entirely disheartened by the loss. It had become a familiar place for him. And as Dartanyon carried him onto the bus that night, Leroy noticed something unfamiliar—the consolation of companionship.

The following week, Robinson moved Leroy down to 189 pounds and bumped Dartanyon up to heavyweight. Dartanyon continued mowing people down in robotic fashion. "Even when he weighed forty pounds less than his opponents, kids were still peeing themselves when Dartanyon walked on the mat," Robinson said. "I heard one guy say, 'Oh, Jesus.' Next thing I know I hear him praying in Arabic. I guess he converted. Then I hear a Hail Mary. I'm thinking, 'Hey kid, give up. It's not gonna happen.'"

Leroy intimidated his opponents as well, though in a different way. At times, Robinson heard grumbling from opposing teams who didn't want to wrestle a legless kid; they felt like bullies for taking Leroy down. Then they realized that to lose to him would have been even worse—akin to losing to a girl.

But it was Leroy who lost again and again and again over his next five matches. He belonged in the 171-pound division, where team-mate Joe Pissos fought. Pissos was a decent wrestler who led the team in pranks. Throughout the winter, Pissos shoved handfuls of snow down Leroy's pants while Leroy was riding on Dartanyon's back. But while Pissos got a kick out of torturing Leroy, he couldn't stand to see others do it. "Coach, let Leroy wrestle at 171 instead of me," he told Robinson, serious for the first time all season. "He deserves a fair fight." He figured few battles in Leroy's life had been so.

JOE PISSOS'S WORDS struck a chord with an embattled Robinson. His estranged wife had recently announced that she was pregnant with another man's child. A molten ache churned and scraped in his chest. Robinson was done with psychiatrists, done sitting in groups talking about his feelings. He didn't want to call another prayer chain or take another meeting with his lawyer. Time took intolerably too long to heal all wounds. One night he collected fifty-two prescription Darvocets, poured a fifth of vodka, and invited sorrow's escape. Cupping the tablets in his hand, he thought of his wrestlers. Should he leave them a note? How could he tell them that his life was insufferable, but the blind and the legless should keep going? Shame mounted on top of his anguish. "I'm sorry, Lord," he whispered. "I am out of answers and energy." He swallowed the pills and drifted off.

A crowd closed in on Robinson the next morning. He sat in the center of a stadium, with the throng chanting "Rob-in-son! Rob-in-son!" Their voices amplified, disorienting him until their force shook him from sleep. But there was no stadium, no crowd of allies. He lay in his empty apartment, still alive. One remaining voice spoke: *Your wrestlers need you.* Robinson sensed the voice of God, yet found no comfort in it. "When I came to, I was disappointed because in my heart I was ready to die," he said. "I wanted the pain to go away."

That next week, Leroy recorded his first victory, at 171 pounds, with a pin. The Wolverines swarmed the mat to celebrate— everyone except Robinson. Coach walked out of the gym, leaned against a bank of lockers, and quietly wept. "Leroy was like the kid who practiced every single day but never made the shot. And then he made the shot," Robinson said. "I realized that if he could keep going, if he could win, then so could I."

Leroy unwittingly saved Robinson's life that season. In fact, he invigorated all of the Lincoln wrestlers. They rallied around him, brainstorming how to adapt various techniques for his repertoire. Coach Hons studied videos of other amputee wrestlers like Georgia high school phenom Kyle Maynard and Arizona State University's Anthony Robles. He and Leroy were like two scientists in a lab, altering arm angles and grasps ever so slightly, trying anything to give Leroy a chance. Leroy couldn't fake one way and go the other. He had to come right at his opponents and get just close enough to grab their ankles. From there, he could lock his hands and use his shoulder against their shin for leverage. They adapted low ankle picks, low single legs, and developed a creative variation of a low double leg that showed potential, if even just a sliver. They brought in Dartanyon to test their hypotheses. As if they were playing a game of Twister, he and Leroy experimented with one takedown after another. Those that could be too easily countered in a way that put Leroy on his back were abandoned. Some adjustments worked. Most did not.

"Hate to say it, but you kind of are like a turtle, Leroy," Dartanyon said one day.

"At least he can see better than you," Robinson said. "Turtles are known to have exceptional vision."

"What's wrong with your vision?" Leroy asked.

"You don't know?" Robinson cried. "Son, your ride is blind!"

"Visually impaired," Dartanyon corrected. "I can see some things. Sometimes."

"Won't be long before he's walking the two of you into walls," Robinson said. "You better watch out." Leroy refrained from questions. Dartanyon withheld explanations. He simply continued carrying Leroy into and out of every gym, onto and off of every mat, that season. Each time Dartanyon wrestled, Leroy sat on the edge of the mat. They became each other's competitive constant, and the competition connected them in a way that went beyond the mat. They grew inseparable in the school halls and then outside of school on the weekends. And their respect for one another's physical limitations evolved into self-deprecating humor, with mutual consent.

"Hey Leroy, if you disappeared from your grandmother's house, would you be considered a runaway or a rollaway?" Dartanyon would ask.

"If you were in charge of looking for me, I'd just be gone," Leroy would retort with a deep belly laugh. They became de facto team leaders, with the rest of the Lincoln wrestlers singing backup to their jokes and marveling at their accomplishments. Leroy won nine matches that season, the majority by pinning his opponent. Dartanyon finished 26–3.

In early February 2009, Robinson called Cleveland's newspaper, the *Plain Dealer*, to tell the wrestling beat writer that he had not one, but two disabled kids on the same team. He thought it would be nice to get them a little recognition. He wasn't hoping for much—just a few lines of print and maybe a picture would do.

CHAPTER 3

ROAD TO ESPN

My first mention in a newspaper came in 1984, when I was ten years old. I won a local Junior Olympics 100-yard dash in about seventeen seconds. A volunteer handed me a polyester blue ribbon upon crossing the finish line, and I could not imagine anything more glorious. The local *Sun News* printed the names of the participants in each event. There were probably a hundred names listed in tiny font, but my name had a coveted number 1 in front of it.

Newspapers and sports have long held equally revered places of importance in my family. My grandfather worked nearly his entire career as a journalist for the *Cleveland News* and the *Cleveland Press,* covering Ohio sports and news before transitioning to full-time editing. As children, my cousins and I dug up dust-covered plaques in my grandfather's basement awarding his clever headlines. His regular *Cleveland News* column, "Fenn's Flyers," handicapped the local nightly harness racing with astounding success.

My father began every morning with a cup of coffee and the newspaper, always starting with the sports section. He scoured box scores of professional and local high school teams, looking for buried treasures in the form of triples and stolen bases, particularly admiring of an athlete's speed. And now I was the fastest ten-year-old in that morning's paper. My father circled my name and carried the clipping with him wherever he went.

"You should have seen her. She was lightning fast," he bragged, waving the folded page with a convincing excitement. "No other girl came close. She blew them all away."

Swept up in his excitement, I made a bold decision about my future. "Daddy, I am going to be an Olympic sprinter," I declared.

He laughed. "You can't be an Olympic sprinter," he said. "You're white. You have to be black to be fast enough for the Olympics." My father grew up throughout the 1950s and '60s in a hostile and racially divided Cleveland. He remembers entering Carl F. Shuler Junior High for the ninth grade and being drawn toward a ruckus in the lobby late one afternoon. There, a black teen was violently assaulting a white classmate. It was my father's first encounter with race. He froze. He wanted to defend his white friend, but after assessing the circle of black teens cheering on the culprit, my father retreated instead. "From that point on, I had a fear and a hatred of blacks," my father remembered. "And it was mutual. They feared and hated us too." From there, my father was shaped in circles of friends and family who believed that African Americans were entrenched in poverty due to their poor work ethics, subpar intelligence, and propensity for violent impulsivity. He was taught that separate equaled safe.

"It's not your fault you're white, honey," he reassured me as I clutched my blue track ribbon. "There should be different competitions for those people to keep it fair." My father pointed out that I could still achieve great things. "You'll just need to do them with your mind rather than your body," he said. He drove me to visit all eight Ivy League universities, desiring a grander life for me than the one he felt backed into.

As a teen, my father had longed to study journalism, yet his own father belittled his aspirations. "You can't spell," the editor admonished his son. "You'll never be a writer." My father's dreams were deflated, and he trudged through twenty-five years as a disgruntled greeting card salesman instead. I, on the other hand, spelled proficiently, and when I came home with an A on my third-grade poem entitled "In The Garden"—a haiku of crisp greens and string beans—my grandfather heralded it as Pulitzer Prize material and declared I would be the next writer of the family. Despite the slight, the news liberated my father, for it proved that the journalism gene had been wrapped in his DNA and passed on to me.

But the idea of committing to any type of work unsettled me. For many members of my family, an uninspired sense of permanence seemed to come with choosing a job. My mother served thirty quiet years as a secretary. Her father toiled for fifty years in a factory as a tool and die maker. My father's mother worked second shift as a bank cleric for twenty-five years. They lived in the same modest homes, where they ate the same rotation of meals and stretched their dollars to pay the same basic bills, every week of their adult lives. A job was a means to the mortgage, void of either growth or disdain. Fulfillment came in raising a family—the respectable norm within middle-class Cleveland.

However, the lofty messages I encountered during my college years at Cornell University ran counter to those of my upbringing: Discover your purpose. Settle for nothing. Do what you love, and you'll never work a day in your life. I tried to merge these competing philosophies of success and security, and in doing so, I aimed high. If I too were to remain in one job forever, it needed to be a good one. I applied to the two leading contenders for world dominance: the CIA and ESPN.

I came across the Central Intelligence Agency's job posting in the Sunday newspaper in the spring of 1997. They were recruiting officers in Cleveland to serve on the front lines of human intelligence, forging strong relationships with clandestine sources, and to balance the harvested information with the needs of Washington security and strategy. Candidates needed foreign language proficiency, degrees in politics or science, and extensive foreign travel. I had none of these things, but I had something even more useful propelling me forward: my father's derisive laughter. "Yeah, you could be a CIA officer," he said, choking on his cereal as I read the ad. "You didn't last the week at that seventh-grade summer church camp. I had to come get you because you were crying."

In my defense, the girls in my cabin were really mean and cared only about kissing boys in the woods at night, the fear of which in fact prompted me to fabricate stomach cramps until my counselor called my parents to pick me up. But my skin had thickened since then. During college, I spent a summer serving in a remote region of Siberia. My host family spoke no English, I spoke no Russian, and each night I slept under a tattered mosquito net that left my skin ravaged and swollen by morning. And not once did I ask my dad to fly over and get me, if for no more noble reason than that there were no phones in the village. I deserved to put my camping debacle to rest once and for all. I polished my résumé of irrelevant experiences, slipped into a contrived air of confidence, and made my way to the CIA recruiter that next weekend.

The interview took place in a blank conference room at a budget motel near the airport, with a white man in a dark suit who did not offer his name. I imagined he had chosen this location in case hostile forces caught wind of our meeting and we had to dash aboard a waiting aircraft, sending me into a life on the lam. I anxiously waited for him to probe my love of the dark, experience burrowing underground tunnels, and ability to rappel down caverns on a strand of dental floss.

"Do you feel you work well in teams?" he asked dryly, interrupting my global espionage fantasy. In reality, this position sounded much like the administrative opening at a local radio station that I had interviewed for one week earlier. The intelligence officer spoke of the need to deal with fast-moving situations and exhibit strong intuition. The only difference was the "street sense" requirement, which I did not have but assured him, in a stiff whisper, that I absolutely did. He asked very few questions, instead testing how firmly I could return his unflinching eye contact. He seemed to be gauging my intimidation threshold, waiting to see if I knew what to offer up and what was best kept close to the vest. After twenty minutes, marked by the audible ticking of the plastic clock on the wall, he said he would be in touch.

While waiting for Washington to send me my cape and save-the-world instruction manual, I got busy preparing for my ESPN interview. "Yah, ESPN's going to take you," my dad scoffed again. "Do you even know who was on the mound the last time the Indians won a World Series?"

I did not. I grasped the rules and strategies of the sports I had played, but I did not study them as my father and grandfather did. The names and histories sounded easy enough to learn, though. I scurried to the library and checked out every issue of *Sports Illustrated* and the *Sporting News* on file. For the next three summer months, our back porch looked like the office of a general manager on draft day. Rosters on marked-up poster boards. Team divisions on chalkboards. Depth charts on scrap paper. I had flash cards, baseball cards, notecards. I probably should have written myself a good-luck card as well; anyone who has to study that hard for a sports interview is clearly not a natural fit for the job.

Oddly, my interview at ESPN's headquarters in Bristol, Connecticut, was more uncomfortable than my introduction to the CIA. Al Jaffe, a seasoned and stoic hiring executive, greeted me. And when I say he "greeted" me, I mean he opened the door. No further pleasantries were exchanged. He said he would ask me ten questions, and then he did just that:

"Who is the backup catcher for the Astros?"

"I don't know."

"Name the Bengals offensive line."

"I didn't study the NFL very hard, being that it's the off-season."

"Who won the Vezina trophy this year?"

What's a Vezina trophy?

"Name the starting rotation for the Padres."

"Andy Ashby . . . Sterling Hitchcock . . . umm . . . I know Trevor Hoffman closes."

"Who was the best sixth man in the NBA this year?"

"Tony Kukoč of the Chicago Bulls!"

Al Jaffe said it would be a ten-question quiz, but by my count, he enacted the mercy rule and gave up after eight. His silent disapproval transported me back to college biology, where I memorized the stages of the Krebs cycle until my eyes rolled into the back of my head and still only scraped by with a C on the exam, which was really an F before the curve. Unimpressed with my single correct answer, Al Jaffe said, "Unless you'd like to add anything, we'll give you a call if a position opens up," to which I said, "I do have something to add, because I am certain my phone will never ring."

Was that out loud?

Prior to that moment, I had only dreamed of being bold, of kissing a boy in the moonlit camp woods, or of urging my grandfather to support my father's ambitions. Finally, to my own astonishment, I showed up as the hero in my own life. Al Jaffe remained unruffled. Unlike the CIA officer who had never once broken eyeline, Al Jaffe had yet to glance in the vicinity of my face. His gaze remained locked off to my left, as if David Cone were throwing a no-hitter behind me and he dared not miss a pitch.

I attempted to clarify my position, cautiously at first. "I mean, I could have easily looked up the answers to your questions in a sports almanac and aced your test. But they tell you nothing about my work ethic, my creativity, or my writing abilities. I know I could be a valuable contributor here. All you've done is proven that I am lousy at bar-room sports trivia."

"Is there anything else?" he droned, still looking past me. Finally I turned around. The wall was stark white, and yet I still could not compete with it.

"Yes. There is one more thing," I said, growing in fearlessness, or perhaps foolishness; the line is indeed a fine one. "You have not made eye contact once since I walked in. That's rather rude."

I prepared to leave, awash with an unsettling mix of humiliation (I'd failed the audition) and personal pride (I'd stood up for myself). Except, of course, I knew he wouldn't allow me the last word. I gripped the base of my chair, disoriented, bracing for his retort, the verbal equivalent of a fastball high and tight. Instead, Al Jaffee threw me the most unlikely curve.

"Can you start in two weeks?" he said, finally looking at me.

Huh? For a moment I thought I'd misunderstood. "Excuse me?" I asked.

"You have a bit of, shall we say, spunk," he flatly conceded. "That seems to go far here." He folded his arms across his chest and looked at me, waiting for an answer.

"Yes, I can be here in two weeks," I said.

"Someone from my office will call you with what you need to do from here."

I showed myself out of his office and heard the door shut quickly behind me. I certainly hadn't fooled him. He knew what he was getting. I headed back to my car in a daze, stopping at a stone sign inscribed "ESPN, World Wide Leader in Sports." It was a David versus Goliath moment, causing me to wonder how I, a marginal fan, came to be standing before the gods of sport armed with little more than team flash cards in my satchel.

I RETURNED TO Cleveland and a letter from the CIA, confirming my place in the next round of interviews in Washington, DC, that fall. "Please do not inform anyone of this pursuant path," the letter read. Their secret was safe. No one would have believed I'd duped this many highly intelligent people in one week. I dug my World Dictator flash cards out of my desk to pack alongside my NBA Position Players index cards.

In that same drawer lay a description of my ideal job that I'd compiled shortly after my college graduation eight months prior. Over the summers, I had interned in law, public relations, magazine journalism, and sports communication. The experiences were thoroughly enjoyable, yet none felt like a perfect fit. My father had encouraged me to write down the qualities of my ideal job. After careful thought, my wish list read like this:

No desk
Casual dress
Lack of routine
Irregular hours
Frequent travel
Opportunities to write
Creative, passionate coworkers
Outlets for serving God and caring for people

My father stared at the list for some time. "None of these things point to an actual job," he said. "In fact, your first four requirements are characteristics of people who are perpetually *unemployed*." He seemed distraught that he had paid six figures for an Ivy League education, and all I left with were several early signs of instability. But the succession of ordinary days is the death of me, and I knew I could not wrap myself in a pencil skirt and live happily ever after in a cubicle.

"And this business about serving God is not a real job, so I don't know why that's on the list," my father added. He believed that if there was a God, He had more important things to do than pay attention to us. "He has a universe to run, and the best way we can free Him up to do that is by taking care of ourselves," he would say.

Though we were not a religious family, my parents sent me to a private Lutheran elementary school to avoid the financial and racial tensions within the Cleveland public school system throughout my childhood. As church members, we were granted a tuition break, and so my mother and I sat through just enough Sunday services each year to qualify for the annual discount. When I made my first communion in the fifth grade, I hid the wafer in my pocket because I feared eating it without understanding its significance. I was no more enlightened by my eighth-grade confirmation, which was to be my public declaration of faith. I had prepared for it through after-school catechism courses and that disastrous summer camp. However, neither seemed to hit their intended target. At rehearsal a few days before the confirmation service, I stood at a loss when my teacher said, "Now when you reach the altar, the minister will ask you if you accept Jesus Christ as your Lord and Savior."

That evening, I asked my mother what this decision involved. It sounded more consequential than simply agreeing that God exists.

"Just say yes, if that's what they told you to do," she answered.

"But I can't say yes if I don't understand what I am saying yes to."

"Your father is going," she said nervously. "Just say yes and don't cause any trouble." My father joined us at church for the occasional Christmas or Easter service and special events such as this. He sweated in visible distress in the aisle seat, often ducking out for air and a cigarette. He said that his Catholic school nuns had smacked his backside with wooden rulers for too many years and too many insignificant offenses, and returning to church served as an uncomfortable remembrance for him.

The idea of deceiving a pastor, in a church, in a white dress left me equally troubled. So that night, beside my bed, I kneeled to pray, for the very first time.

"Dear . . . God . . . it's me, Lisa. Tomorrow I have to go to church and tell a lie. I don't want to do it, but if I don't, things will be awkward for you and me both," I explained. "If you will forgive me, I promise that I will find out what the question really means and answer it again."

God did not answer.

I stood before the church that next day with my fingers crossed and professed Jesus as the Lord of my life. My mother nodded with relief. The reverend nodded with approval. My father retreated for air. And I slumped back into my pew, utterly conflicted. A few hours later, during my party to celebrate the charade, I slipped back upstairs to my bedroom and apologized to God again. This time, tingling warmth emanated from my toes and slowly traveled the length of my body, to the tips of my fingers and face. The spiritual realm became real to me that day—not in church or in my lily-white dress, but in my shameful transparency. I did not understand the theology of forgiveness at that moment, but I knew I had received it.

That fall I entered a Lutheran high school and quickly learned what Christians mean when they say they accept Jesus as their Lord and Savior. The formula was simple: acknowledge your sin and yield your will to God for His glory and service. But while the steps appeared straightforward, neither action came naturally to me. I didn't see myself as a sinner. I had never been grounded or uttered a curse word. I was kind to others. I was class salutatorian. I could see no compelling reason to give God holy control of my life when I was wholly proficient at running it myself.

Various teenage afflictions bruised my high school years: my first broken heart, the unraveling of my parents' marriage, a debilitating anemia that hampered me athletically. These disappointments exposed the flimsy nature of my own control, and the fractured relationships left me craving an abiding acceptance—one for which I did not need to strive and strain. I wanted to be guided by someone larger and wiser than me. And as I came to understand the relevance of faith, I found that God was there, waiting.

"Take my will and make it your own," I prayed aloud. The same pulses of warmth I had experienced following my fraudulent confirmation again traveled from the tips of my toes to the top of my head. This time, the message resonated differently. The whisper in my heart said, *You are my beloved.*

My faith deepened in college through my studies of the Bible, and I came to understand that there was nothing that would make God love me more or love me less. This liberating approach to love spurred me around the world in hopes of sharing it with those in need. I cared for orphans in Russia. I delivered Bibles and companionship to remote aboriginal tribes in the Australian outback. The pain of this world drew me in, and faith became more personal than religious, an adventure rather than a duty.

Still, as I clutched my silly crumpled list, I wondered how the heart of God extended to ESPN. I feared I had been so caught up in proving my father wrong or living up to our storied family journalism gene that I had badgered my way past Al Jaffe through my own resolve, and was now drifting away from the kind of service work that had beckoned throughout college. I couldn't imagine the possibility of God having a rooting interest in cable sports television.

ESPN HIRED ME as a production assistant (PA), its entry-level position. In the first month I learned to operate a teleprompter, print scripts for on-camera anchors, and retrieve archived video of legendary sports moments, but my $7-an-hour paycheck rested on one critical responsibility: watching sports on television. Each night between 4:00 and 6:00 p.m., I reported to the screening pit alongside a herd of other PAs. We huddled around the master daily schedule of sporting events taped to the wall, scanning for our name and assigned game. Seasoned PAs received higher-profile games that warranted longer highlights, such as Yankees–Red Sox or Auburn–Alabama. PAs with less experience or skill got events that were not likely to have a highlight on SportsCenter, like

European golf tournaments or Division III college football games. "Score only," we would grumble when forced to watch a humdrum game in its entirety, fully knowing that the only thing that would make the show would be the final score.

We sat before our television monitors with pens in the ready position and kept track of plays by documenting precisely what time, to the second, they happened. If I were assigned to screen a Giants–Diamondbacks game, I wrote down every at-bat, fly ball, home run, stolen base, and pitch count, along with the camera angles of those plays. At the end, I revisited my logs and chose the plays and angles that best told the story of the game in thirty to forty-five seconds. Once approved by highlight supervisors—or hi-supes, as they are hiply known—I carried my stack of beta video tapes of the game to a waiting editor, read off time codes for the plays, and watched the editor splice the highlight together. Next I delivered the tape to the SportsCenter control room, and the description of plays to the anchor. And finally, around one o'clock in the morning, I typed the logs of my game into the library system so that a week or a decade later, if another PA needed to find Barry Bonds striking out against Randy Johnson, she could search the computer for the exact tape and time.

The job required negligible levels of critical thinking. Production assistants were evaluated on speed, organization, and factual accuracy. As a perfectionist, I thrived in this structure. I had no opinion on whether Wally Szczerbiak would make it in the NBA, but I could spell his name correctly and hit his slot in the rundown. While my college friends talked about the stress of their new teaching jobs or the pressures of Wall Street, my workplace possessed a frat-house-meets-Super-Bowl-party sort of vibe, with a crowd of twentysomethings cheering on their favorite teams across forty different screens. The most pressing discourse revolved around whether Ryan Leaf should be drafted ahead of Peyton Manning and whether Miguel Tejada was a better all-around shortstop than

Derek Jeter. The later the nights wore on, the more absurd the predictions grew; during one heated exchange, a PA bet $1,000 that rookie Kobe Bryant would never average 25 points per game. He has yet to pay up.

When my fellow PAs exhausted real-life debates, they moved on to their football and baseball fantasy teams. One oddly zealous PA ran a WNBA fantasy league in which he managed all eight teams and played against himself. I witnessed him alone in an empty conference room late one weekend night conducting the preseason draft—out loud—and wondered if it was time for ESPN to consider setting up a crisis hotline. Production assistants clocked sixty to ninety hours a week, yet for most of them, there was nowhere else they wanted to be. We ordered dozens of pizzas every Saturday and ice cream on Wednesdays. A plastic 7-Eleven Big Gulp labeled "Deep Pool" sat at the hi-supe station. If someone thought the player at the plate would hit a home run in that at-bat, he or she yelled out "Deep Pool!" and tossed a quarter into the cup. (Rates rose to fifty cents for Mark McGwire or Sammy Sosa during their 1998 chase for Roger Maris's home run record.) When correct, the PA won the plunder. Just a month into the job, Jim Thome netted me $16.75 on a bullet down the right field line, more than doubling my hourly wage. I was one of thirteen females in the lot of one hundred PAs, and I was living every man's dream.

The first nine months of the production program served as a training ground. Each month, a group of coordinating producers voted on the production assistants whose nine months were due to expire, either elevating them to full-time employee status or casting them out of Bristol. It was ESPN's method of rotating cheap labor and identifying employee potential before committing long-term. My monthly evaluations were largely positive, yet the system certainly incited nervousness, as I'd frequently seen some of my favorite peers voted out. Somewhere around my third month, I ruminated, anxiously, over how to ask for time off for my second

CIA interview without letting on where I was going. I was still a temporary employee, and management interpreted requests for time off as a lack of dedication. Then one evening, while I was printing scripts for anchors Rich Eisen and Steve Levy, a senior coordinating producer burst out of his office and bounded toward me. At that point, I should have been relatively unknown to the executives. But this one seemed uncomfortably interested in me.

"I got a call this afternoon," he said, distressed. "I don't know who you are or what you're doing, but take off whatever time you need." I nodded solemnly, respecting both this man's agitation and the reach of the CIA. No further dialogue was ever exchanged, and no future schedule requests were ever denied.

Once in Washington, DC, I interviewed with special agents who all began with the same incredulous question: "Why would you ever want to leave ESPN?" To me, working as an undercover international operative sounded far more exciting than logging a Kings–Clippers game at midnight, but when the CIA dismissed me from their consideration after seven months of interviews, polygraphs, and background checks, they seemed to think they were doing me a favor. "You have the best job in the world," one agent, who had always introduced himself with a different name, told me on several occasions. "Why enter a life in hiding when you could be cheering it on out loud?"

I was granted full-time status at the end of my nine months at ESPN, and to my father's delight, I began working on the daily *Baseball Tonight* show. Though I grew up competing in softball, basketball, and track, baseball was our family's year-round love. My father played two years of college ball at Kent State University and told stories of playing alongside teammate Thurman Munson in college. On the day the pro scouts showed up, my father went hitless; Munson went on to be a perennial All-Star and team captain of the New York Yankees. And as my father and I spent summer nights together at Cleveland's Municipal Stadium, cheering on our hometown Indians, I knew he grieved for his lost opportunity.

Between 1998 and 2003 I lived baseball for ESPN, and my father lived it vicariously through me. "At least one of us made it to the majors," he would say. Each February I reported to spring training with pitchers and catchers to produce team preview features for either Florida's Citrus League or Arizona's Cactus League. I worked alongside Peter Gammons and Tim Kurkjian, assessing teams' lineups, pitching staffs, and off-season changes. During the season I traveled to a different major league stadium nearly every week to produce two- to three-minute stories for our nightly shows. If I were covering the success of the Oakland Athletics pitching rotation, I flew to wherever the team played that week and interviewed their starting staff and their coaches, identifying reasons for their surge. I wrapped up after batting practice but stayed for that night's game just in case a no-hitter broke out and ESPN needed us for news coverage. During those summers, filled with bat cracks and the aroma of roasted peanuts, I realized that the CIA had advised me correctly. Summers in ballparks far surpassed summers in Saudi Arabia.

Each October I hit the road again for four weeks of baseball playoffs, culminating in the World Series. I worked up to 120 hours a week, producing game previews and postgame reports and following my assigned series from city to city. In 2001 I stood beside the Yankees dugout when Tino Martinez and Scott Brosius hit game-tying ninth-inning home runs in Games 4 and 5 of the World Series, and I was doused in champagne two days later when the Arizona Diamondbacks won Game 7 on Luis Gonzalez's ninth-inning RBI broken-bat liner up the middle off Mariano Rivera, the greatest closer of all time.

People often asked me if I found it difficult to be a woman navigating professional sports locker rooms. To me, it seemed easier than being a man. In most clubhouses there was no shortage of balding white male reporters working for a gaggle of television, radio, print, and Internet outlets. These men had to work harder to differentiate themselves from one another than the subset of women in the locker rooms. A CIA officer once told me that one of the reasons the agency was interested in me was that I was un-assuming: because of my petite stature and pale skin, he could have either used me as a trustworthy adult or disguised me as a child and sent me off to school with the teenage family members of potential informants. I thought he was joking. "The CIA doesn't joke," he said. Either way, he believed people would have an easy time saying yes to me because physically, I looked like someone who wouldn't do them wrong. This turned out to be a quality that also allowed me to move about major league locker rooms with ease. No athlete ever ignored my questions, and most answered them politely.

During those years I began to gravitate toward features that highlighted interesting tidbits of players' personal lives. I spent a weekend with Gary Sheffield and his wife DeLeon, a professional gospel singer. I toured Sammy Sosa's designer shoe collection. I featured Ryan Klesko surfing on his days off, and Scott Brosius homeschooling his brood. In 2000 I followed Deion Sanders around the minor leagues. A two-sport phenom for fourteen years, Neon Deion was the only man to play in both a Super Bowl and a World Series. During the 1989 season he clubbed a home run for the Atlanta Braves in the afternoon and then scored a touchdown that night for the Atlanta Falcons. The only thing as electrifying as his athletic ability was his charisma. I caught up with Deion in the twilight of his baseball career, when he was grinding out a comeback with the AAA Louisville River Bats baseball team. After one afternoon game in Kentucky, the team boarded a bus to Richmond, Virginia, but Deion climbed into his own tricked-out coach, complete with a bed and a wet bar. My camera crew and I joined him for an eight-hour trip down memory lane, during which he relived what seemed like every one of his twenty-two career NFL touchdowns and their corresponding end-zone dances.

We arrived at the Richmond Super 8 Motel just after one o'clock in the morning, ahead of the rest of the team. A young man walking through the lobby looked quizzically at Deion, struggling to be certain before he approached. "Are you Deion Sanders?" the man asked. "I am a huge fan!"

"Man, you crazy!" Deion exclaimed. "Tell me, *what* would Deion Sanders be doing in a place like *this*?"

The man froze in terrible embarrassment. "Wow, you're right," he said. "I wasn't sure . . . you kinda looked like him . . . but yeah, you're right." The man backpedaled. "Sorry, sir. Have a good night." Sanders, who was known as Prime Time, couldn't have the word getting out that he stayed in two-star motels.

I spent a memorable weekend with pitcher Barry Zito watching his father compose classical music for the Buffalo Symphony Orchestra. His ability to create beauty out of nothing both intoxicated and intimidated me. Though a classical pianist myself, I could not even imagine where to begin with such a task.

"Ahh, but you could," the elder Zito told me. "If you conceive and then believe, you will achieve." These were the same words he imparted to his young son as they tossed a ball in the backyard. Barry meditated himself all the way to the Cy Young Award in 2002.

When I learned that St. Louis Cardinal pitcher Steve Kline had never washed his cap out of superstition—and that the team equipment manager packed it in a container separate from the rest of the team's hats—I traced Kline's roots to a pig farm in western Pennsylvania. The townspeople were dumbfounded that we considered this newsworthy. "Steve smelled like dung his whole life," they said matter-of-factly. "The hat hasn't changed anything."

After the 2002 baseball season, ESPN created a unit dedicated to developing long-form, more emotional feature stories on amateur athletes with meaningful accomplishments. I was asked to join a handful of other producers in spearheading this initiative. My first assignment was on a high school basketball player in Winston-Salem, North Carolina, named Chris Paul. Little known at the time, Chris grew up in a close-knit Bible-believing family where his grandfather, Nathaniel Jones, ran a local service station. Nathaniel was the rock of the family and never missed one of Chris's games, until the day he would miss them all. Five teenagers bludgeoned Nathaniel to death in broad daylight in his own driveway, after his empty wallet. Though few expected Chris to attend his next basketball game, just days later, he decided to play as a tribute to his grandfather. And despite his previous game high of 43 points, Chris told his aunt that he was going to score one point for every year of his grandfather's life. All sixty-one of them. Chris went out playing like he was the only boy in that gym. Staying within the flow of the game—and without his parents knowing what he had planned—Chris scored 24 points in the second quarter alone.

"The whole game I was just thinking about my granddad, watching me from heaven. He's watching this game," Chris said. "This was one of those times that I just felt like there's no way, I don't care what kind of defense you play, who you put in front of me, there's no way you're gonna stop me from getting to that goal. And as the course of the game went on, I said, 'I can do this.'"

With less than two minutes to go in the fourth quarter, Chris had scored 59 points. Then he drove to the hoop, took a hard foul, and the shot dropped. He had his 61 points. Chris fell to the floor, cheered on by every soul in the gym as they honored the one who wasn't. "I just felt like I coulda died and went to heaven right there," he said. "It felt like my purpose for being here was fulfilled."

Chris's total left him just six points away from the state record for most points in a game. But as he stood at the foul line, the record didn't matter. Sixty-one did. Chris walked to the free throw line, received the ball, and intentionally shot an air ball right out of bounds. As he took himself out of the game and collapsed in the arms of his waiting coach, his total stood at 61.

ESPN reporter Chris Connelly and I interviewed Chris Paul and his family less than a week after this remarkable event. They were lovely people, and when our crew wrapped for the day, I hung back, drawn to this family's ability to handle tragedy with such dignity. They shared pictures of Chris's childhood and stories of their beloved Nathaniel, who was known for handing out spare dollar bills and station pumping jobs to those in need.

"He was one of those people who tried to change the world one little life at a time," Chris's mother said. Before I left, we prayed together for healthy grieving and justice in court, and we promised to keep in touch.

I returned home exhilarated by my tender connection with the Paul family. My years covering baseball, though thrilling, had been void of such depth. Shortly after we aired Chris's story in December 2002, the Paul family phoned to tell me that thanks in part to the media coverage generated by my story, the judge had granted their wish to prosecute the killers as adults. "We cherished my father's life, and they took something very special away from us," Chris's mother said. "Thank you for giving us something special to remember him by."

A few months later, I won my first Emmy Award as producer of Chris's story. My first call from the ceremony's lobby was to Chris himself, who sounded just as excited as me. Together we felt we had achieved something special for Nathaniel. Chris went on to star at Wake Forest University, become the fourth pick in the 2005 NBA draft, and win Olympic gold. Yet whenever I saw him around, I would say, "Hey there, little Chris Paul," to which he would say, "Hope you're still praying for me, Miss Lisa."

Then there was feisty Katie Morris, whom I met through ESPN's partnership with the Make-a-Wish Foundation. Each summer ESPN selected five critically ill children with sports-related wishes and blew the doors off of their requests. Katie was a ten-year-old brain cancer fighter who wished to treat the fifteen boys on her former Little League team to a Seattle Mariners game. Her best friend on the team, Bryce, had moved out of state just before Katie's diagnosis, and I told Katie that Bryce could not attend. Then, while staging a pregame team photo in the center field of Safeco Field, the public address announcer came over the speakers and said, "Katie, we understand this is not a complete team photo and is missing one of your teammates and your very good friend. We direct your attention to the area in center field. Turn around and welcome back your friend and teammate, Bryce Aberg!"

Ten-year-old fresh-faced Bryce came sprinting out of that center-field wall like he had run all the way from Tennessee to find his Katie, and the two precious kids wept in one another's arms with their team and the Mariner Moose mascot gathered around. It was a love as fierce and pure as I have ever witnessed.

Katie died ten months later. Her family asked me to participate in her eulogy. "You gave Katie her last happy day," her mother said. "We want you to help everyone remember her that way." I flew to Oregon without hesitation, filled with love for Katie and the understanding that it would have been disingenuous to celebrate with her family one year and let them cry alone the next.

In 2005 I produced a story on Travis Roy, a hockey legend for all of the wrong reasons. Travis grew up on the ice of Yarmouth, Maine, with a stick always in his hand and a loving father always coaching by his side. In 1995, Travis was a highly touted high school hockey recruit. He committed to defending national champs Boston University under legendary coach Jack Parker. The arena was electric for the first home game and the raising of the team's championship banner from the previous season. Travis did not start on the first line but was waved on early in the first period, alongside future Stanley Cup winner Chris Drury, his centerman. Drury took the face-off, sending the puck into the offensive zone. Travis gave chase but arrived a split second after his opponent. Travis leaned in to bodycheck, eager to send a message in his first appearance on the ice. He thought he'd angled himself just right, as he had nearly every day for the last fifteen years of his life. But instead, he deflected off the 185-pound defenseman. Momentum sent him headfirst into the boards.

Get up! Get back in the game! Travis thought to himself as he lay facedown on the ice. With the trainers hovering over him, Travis asked for his father to be summoned from the stands. Travis had fallen a thousand times before. But this one felt different.

"Come on, Trav, get up!" his father, Lee, said as he made his way to his son.

"Dad, I am in big trouble. I can't feel anything. I can't move anything," Travis said. "But Dad . . . I made it." Travis thought that this fall might be his last. And if it were indeed to be his final time on ice, he wanted his father beside him to share this dream of Division I college hockey. It was a dream that spanned just eleven seconds.

The fall burst Travis's fourth and fifth cervical vertebrate, rendering him quadriplegic. He instantly went from a strapping NHL prospect to requiring round-the-clock care. Slowly Travis rebuilt his life. He finished school with the help of aides. He began a foundation to purchase adaptive equipment for other victims of paralysis. But he never regained movement. ESPN reporter Tom Rinaldi and I were charged with looking back on Travis's accident and where he was ten years later.

"Travis, when you dream about playing hockey, what do you see?" Tom asked to start the interview. Travis had answered hundreds of routine questions over the years, but Tom Rinaldi interviews are infamously disarming. Travis began to cry.

"No one's ever asked me that before," Travis started slowly, as though he was about to share a secret. "Occasionally I have those dreams, and they are amazing. They are real. Too real. I can feel that ice. I can play that puck with such ease and put it where I want. I wish those dreams came more often."

I had never met a quadriplegic before, and I came into our interview with Travis apprehensively. After Tom's first question, guilt replaced nerves. I felt as though we were rubbing fresh salt in old wounds. I was unsure what to do, until Travis told me: "Lisa, can you please wipe away my tears?"

Tom asked ninety more minutes of questions under hot, invasive lights. Some were factual, others intended to till hardened ground: "How have you reconciled hope against disappointment?" "When you cry, what are you crying for?" Travis revealed that when he weeps at night, tears puddle in his ears, and he is unable to wipe them dry. He shared his loneliness and how he felt like an oddity, known on the streets as "that hockey player who was in the accident."

I stayed another week to film with Travis. I captured his daily care routine, his strolls around Boston, a meeting with his charitable foundation, and a trip to a Boston University hockey game. I asked him how his accident had affected his faith, either positively or negatively. He said religion left a sour taste in his mouth because in the months following his accident, Christians from around the world had mailed him Bibles and books by other disabled individuals of faith. "They were all very concerned with where I was going after this life but not terribly interested in sitting with me through the hard times of this one," he said.

I told Travis that I knew I was late on the scene, but if he was still taking applications for friends, I would like to be considered. So once the cameras stopped filming, I made the two-hour trip to Boston for lunches and movies together when our schedules allowed, and the developing friendship nourished both of our souls.

Though engaged to be married myself, I said, "Travis, you are every girl's dream come true. All you can do is sit and listen!" He laughed and told me to start lining up prospects. "Not many people can see past Travis the circumstance to see Travis the person," he said.

These were just three of a hundred features I produced over ten years, and just three of a hundred where I learned that feature reporting was not a job. It was a privilege. I grew comfortable with the intimacy of this work and the influence of my behind-the-scenes role. The camera forced subjects into buried emotional spaces, where they risked the vulnerability needed to share the dreams and fears that accompanied them on their extraordinary journeys. And once the camera stopped rolling and my reporter jetted out, the subjects looked for continued connection with me. Certainly they understood that their participation was ultimately intended for the world, on a broadcast months away. But in the hours and days following their interviews, their wanting eyes were on me, awaiting useful responses to their pain and courage. Their hearts expanded as they realized the healing power of putting words to emotions, of illuminating dark memories. I drew strength from these exceptional individuals, as each shaped my understanding of how we are called to live. With whom could I sit and wipe away tears? In what way could I be someone's happiest day? How could I impact the world, one life at a time?

Shortly after meeting Travis, while sorting a stash of boxes in my flooded basement, I once again came across my old crumpled description of the perfect job. I smiled, realizing that God had woven all of my odd requirements together into an unlikely calling: knitting together stories of the heart within the drama of sports. And it was in that theater that I discovered two leading characters who entered my life . . . and never left.

CHAPTER 4

THE CALL

The phone rang early on that blustery February morning in 2009. Through the haze of sleep, I made out my father's number on the caller ID. My parents divorced shortly after I began working at ESPN, and my father frequently called in the late afternoons for cooking instructions and laundry tips. Those calls were endearing. But these early-morning ones only meant one thing.

"Listen, I'm sorry to wake you," my dad said, "but there's something in the *Plain Dealer* you might be interested in."

Since I had moved away, my father and grandfather started their mornings together, reading the sports section over fried eggs and crusty Italian bread with butter patted an inch thick. If soaring cholesterol from that breakfast didn't ultimately do them in, high blood pressure related to Cleveland's cursed sports teams likely would. For years my father and grandfather had pitched me story ideas on why the Indians couldn't field a competitive team, how the Browns couldn't play worse blindfolded, and did I ever notice how great teams in other cities were made up of players who started in Cleveland under owners too cheap to keep them? Even with the Cavs at the top of the league in 2009, their discussions revolved largely around how the front office would screw this one up too. They served as my own personal Statler and Waldorf, the two curmudgeonly Muppets in the balcony who are happiest when complaining.

"There's two handicapped wrestlers from Lincoln-West High School on the front page of the sports section," my father continued. "You remember Lincoln, it's like ten minutes from here—real bad area off West Twenty-Fifth. Anyway, looks like it might be in your wheelhouse, so see if you can punch it up." My dad had been using computers for nearly a decade, but still said things like "Punch it up" and "Do a double click—one, two—and you're good to go."

With a slow yawn, I pulled my laptop up from under my bed and went to the newspaper's website. There they were: a legless teenage boy perched on the back of another kid, walking through a high school gym. Both were black, with defined, muscular upper bodies. "Willing and Able," read the headline. I scanned the accompanying article, picking out that the boy on top, Leroy Sutton, had lost his legs in a childhood train accident, and the teammate carrying him, Dartanyon Crockett, was legally blind. Still, as interesting as those details were, I could not divert my eyes from the photograph for more than a few seconds.

"I can go scout them out for you," my father offered. "They're wrestling at Midpark High School this afternoon. Just up the road."

They were seniors, so at that afternoon's Greater Cleveland sectional meet they would possibly wrestle the final matches of their high school careers. "I think I might like to see them myself," I said. "I'll call you back in a few hours."

This photo did what photos are designed to do: reveal. And in this case, the image revealed the need for further revelation. Leroy Sutton and Dartanyon Crockett. However did life join these individuals together? Why did Leroy's knowing grin cause me to smile back so warmly, without even realizing I was doing it? Where were they going? How much were they carrying? What could we learn? And what in the world kind of name is *Dartanyon Crockett*?

I dressed quickly and packed an overnight bag in the slim chance that Victor Vitarelli, coordinating producer of the ESPN features unit, let me hop a plane to find these boys. I arrived at my desk just after 8:30 a.m., about two hours earlier than any other morning.

Fridays are typically busy days for the features department, preparing for a slew of weekend edits. Victor was already convening with fellow coordinating producer Valerie Gordon and manager Tom McCollum on scripts. I poked my head into the office.

"Hello, Lisa," Victor said. "How are you this morning?" No matter who you were or why you'd come, Victor was always genuinely pleased to see you.

"Sorry to interrupt," I said. "But there's a story in the Cleveland newspaper today about two disabled high school wrestlers." Tom pulled it up on his computer as I dove into the backstory.

"The blind one carries the one with no legs around between their matches," I explained. "Today is their sectional meet, so if we're going to do this story, we have to shoot it today in case they don't advance to districts."

Victor leaned over for a better look. "In . . . ter . . . est . . . ing," he said, which is Victor's way of saying "not . . . so . . . fast." At that time, ESPN was producing a surplus of feature stories on athletes with disabilities. A young runner with cystic fibrosis gasping for the finish line as his school cheered him on. A teen with Down syndrome finding his father's acceptance through golf. An autistic high school basketball player who managed equipment before emerging from the shadows as a shooting savant. These kids possessed a unique brand of courage that made it easy to inspire viewers. But recently our features had grown similar and saccharine, and we were quietly mandated to pitch fewer stories on people with disabilities.

So my timing was not the greatest. Nor was my research.

"Are they good athletes?" Tom asked.

"Probably not the best," I said. "It's city league wrestling, and one has no legs."

"Are they articulate?" asked Valerie.

"I have not spoken to them," I said.

"Are they friends?" Victor asked.

"They must be. You don't carry acquaintances around on your back. And their school is in a rough part of Cleveland, so I'm sure they're poor in addition to disabled," I said, as though poverty counted as bonus points.

"Lisa, what exactly is the story?" Victor asked, turning back to the script in his hands. "Being blind, and maybe poor, and getting hit by a train seven years ago, while all very tragic, is not exactly current news."

"I know I'm lacking specifics here," I admitted. "If I had to boil it down to a tagline, I would say it's about the one who can't walk being carried by the one who can't see."

Begging for story approval was not my usual mode of operation. Victor expected his producers to do their homework, to preinterview subjects, to forecast shooting budgets. And then we engaged in an educated discussion with him. I had done none of that. But instead of pointing me back to my desk, Victor uncharacteristically rolled the dice.

"Give me your honest gut feeling," he said.

I nodded cautiously, leaned in, and lowered my voice. "Victor, think about it: *the one who cannot walk being carried by the one who cannot see*," I repeated slowly.

He looked at the picture again, slowly scrunching his mouth from side to side three times before stopping on a sideways smirk and granting the permission that would permanently alter the course of three lives: "Have a nice trip to Cleveland."

THAT MORNING STARTED like every other for Dartanyon—flat back to the hard oak floor. He'd been staying with his teammate, Matt Sifers, on the lower west side that year, along with Matt's little sister and their mom, Laura. Theirs was a simple place, just two bedrooms, a kitchen, and a small area to the left of it with a cracked leather reclining chair. After Dartanyon and his dad, Arthur, lost their place the previous fall, Arthur slept on that chair for a few weeks. Dartanyon didn't mind, though; at least he knew where his dad was each night.

Arthur's sister on the east side eventually agreed to take him in, but the sense was that she never cared much for Dartanyon; the last time he stayed with her, she'd accused him of eating too much food. So Laura said Dartanyon could stay for a while, and she'd make sure he got to school and back with Matt. Though no one treated him as a burden, Dartanyon knew Laura struggled to make rent each month too, so he minded his manners and remembered to be grateful for his patched-up air mattress, which leaked most of its breath by morning.

Dartanyon rolled to his side, his back creaking in rhythm with the floorboards. He could feel winter in his bones, but still found it easier to get up on that morning than others. Today was the city sectional wrestling tournament—the first qualifying meet on the road to the state championships—and Dartanyon's confidence was high. One week earlier, he'd won the Senate Conference championship and earned league MVP. His dad had come to that meet as well, sober, making for three milestones in a day.

Dartanyon quietly slipped out of the house and reached the bus stop just as the 7:00 a.m. westbound arrived. A few folks on the bus looked Dartanyon over as he got on, as though trying to place where they had seen him before. As the bus continued on, Dartanyon thought two men pointed at him and whispered to one another, but he couldn't quite tell. Then an older black gentleman sitting opposite slowly glanced up from his newspaper, over his bifocals, down again to his paper, and then shot his head back up, chuckling at Dartanyon. The man pushed his fistful of newspaper onto Dartanyon's chest. "Look at you man, you a hero!" he declared. And with that, the man hopped off the bus.

Dartanyon pulled the page up close to his face. A color picture of him and Leroy sat smack in the middle of the sports section.

He remembered the reporter at their conference championship last weekend, asking them questions about how they wrestled with their disabilities. But he certainly didn't get the sense that the guy liked them enough to do a whole story on them. Dartanyon thought maybe there would be a few lines in the high school roundup notes, but he didn't know when, or that there would be such a large photo. Poverty had taught him that he didn't have the right to answers, and so he had gotten out of the habit of asking questions.

Dartanyon walked off that bus a few inches taller. He thought about showing the article around the halls at school but instead placed it carefully on the top shelf of his locker. Following their last eviction, Dartanyon's dad put their few remaining belongings into a storage unit, but when he stopped making payments two months later, the owner confiscated Dartanyon's athletic trophies and plaques and sold them off for scrap. Dartanyon vowed to protect his joy from that point on.

Before first period, Coach Hons hung the article on his classroom blackboard with a magnet, feeling somewhat puzzled as he did. Certainly it was unique to have two disabled wrestlers on the same team—but front-page-worthy? Must have been a slow day in Cleveland sports, he thought. This was an incredible acknowledgment for his team, though. As each one of his wrestlers circled in to see the article, they beamed proudly in front of that blackboard. People in these neighborhoods make their names in the crime blotter, so when the Wolverine wrestlers saw two of their own representing good news, they felt they'd achieved something honorable together.

"Congratulations on your boys, Hons!" Fellow teachers saluted Justin throughout the morning, and Dartanyon strutted those halls like he was The Man. This was strong momentum to take into sectionals, Coach Hons thought.

"*Pssst.* Mr. Hons . . . ," the school secretary said, poking her head around his classroom door. "*Pssst.* A woman from ESPN is on the phone. She wants to talk to you."

"We're just about to start class," he said. "Can I call her back?"

"Um, well . . . I'm not a huge sports fan, but this sounds kind of important," she replied. "I think she's on her way to Cleveland."

MY FATHER PICKED me up at the airport later that afternoon, pleased his phone call resulted in a visit from his daughter. "I don't know if you saw it," he said, shaking his head as we drove out of the airport, "but the Cavs didn't do anything at the trade deadline last night. Shaq stays in Phoenix. When will these general managers ever learn?" A minute later, he puffed his chest like a proud parent as he described the *Plain Dealer*'s recent ranking of LeBron's best games so far that season.

"You know," he continued eagerly, "if this thing with the wrestlers doesn't work out, maybe you could do something with that—a LeBron highlights thing, you know. Now *that* could make a good story for you."

"Thanks, Dad—I'll keep it in mind."

Midpark High School, site of the Greater Cleveland sectional meet, was a short drive from the airport, past the billowing smoke stacks of the Ford and Chevy motor plants and just over the city line into the blue-collar suburb of Brook Park.

"Does this happen often?" my father asked as we pulled in to the parking lot.

"What do you mean?"

"You know, where they let you just get on a plane like this?"

I shook my head. "Never," I replied.

"Jeez, well, they may never let you do this again either, because I don't think these two are going to be ESPN-worthy wrestlers," he said, a tinge of worry in his voice. "I mean, if they were, they'd be wrestling over at St. Ed's."

My videographer, Rick Hines, and his audio tech, Jon Wermuth, were waiting for me outside the gymnasium, and as we entered, there they were, walking straight at us: Leroy Sutton, riding on the back of Dartanyon Crockett. Rick hoisted his camera onto his shoulder, not wanting to miss a possible TV moment. A sudden knot in my chest prompted misgivings.

"Please don't film yet," I said. "Just hang back for a bit." That morning's frenzy of fielding my father's call, gaining Victor's approval, and racing to the airport had me intensely focused on pursuing this story. I had forgotten that walking toward me now was not a *story*, but rather two young kids just trying to get around and blend in. And here I appeared in ambush without even the respect of an introduction. I didn't feel like a respectable journalist. I felt like paparazzi.

A thundering voice from off to the side jolted me straight. "You the ESPN lady?"

I turned to see a hefty man rumbling toward me, hustling in a sort of slow motion. "Oh, um, yes. Hi. My name is Lisa," I stammered. "You must be Coach—"

"Robinson, but that don't matter," he said as he reached me. He meant business. "All that matters is one thing and one thing only: You been sent here today by God, you know."

I extended my hand and smiled nervously. "Oh, thank you, it's so nice to meet you. I—"

"You hear me?" He leaned in, his face inches from mine. "Every day I walk our track, praying for my boys. This year, I prayed hard for Sutton and Crockett. Because they good kids. Real good kids. But once they graduate, there ain't nothin' for them out there." He paused to take a breath and a sly smile crept out, blowing his stern cover. "And then ESPN walks in the door? That ain't no coincidence, little lady. You've been sent here for a reason."

I left the house each morning looking for glimpses of what God was doing in the world and the chance to be a part of it. But learning that someone else expected me to be the answer to a prayer applied a pressure I was not ready to assume.

"Listen, I'll introduce myself to the boys and then get out of the way during filming," I said. "I know a lot rides on this tournament, so I don't want my presence to make Leroy and Dartanyon uncomfortable. I can talk to you all later."

"Okay," Robinson replied. "Just remember what I told you." Robinson waved his index finger above his head as he turned to join his team on the warm-up mats across the gym. Most teams were decked out in brightly colored nylon tracksuits, sending the message that they had their act together. In contrast, the Lincoln-West kids, several of whom were barefoot, wore cheap navy-blue T-shirts that read "Matthew 18:20" on the front in white block letters; on the back, in both English and Spanish, they read:

WOLVERINES PRAYER:
WE PRAY NOT FOR EASIER LIVES BUT TO BE STRONGER MEN

Robinson said he experienced God's presence most profoundly when he was with his team. "For where two or three gather in my name, there am I with them," the scripture from Matthew reads. He spent every practice praying for those kids, and so in his mind, they were congregating in the Lord's name. Robinson didn't bother explaining the message to his boys, and none of them asked. They were just happy to look legit and to have a coach who loved them enough to put shirts on their backs.

The buzzer signaled the end of warm-ups. *"Please rise for the singing of our national anthem."* Dartanyon bent down to the ground. Leroy rose on his left knee, wrapping his arms around Dartanyon's neck as Dartanyon hoisted him. Dartanyon stumbled three steps left and one to the right before securing his balance.

Leroy pointed toward the flag so Dartanyon could align himself accordingly. He supported Leroy's knee with his left hand; he kept his right hand on Leroy's wrists, which were over Dartanyon's heart. The surrounding wrestlers stood alongside as though this was perfectly natural.

Following the anthem, Dartanyon scaled the bleachers, Leroy still on his back. Wrestling at 171 pounds, Leroy was not a light load. Dartanyon took the stairs in one fluid motion, harnessing momentum. Once they settled near the top, I headed up and slid beside Dartanyon. I explained that I was a producer for ESPN, had seen their picture in the paper that morning, and was interested in filming their matches. They said nothing. Dartanyon's wandering eyes made it difficult for me to tell if he could see me, but I was certain from Leroy's icy glare toward the mats that he chose not to.

"So . . . do I have your permission to film you today?" I asked, more directly this time.

"Sure!" Dartanyon exclaimed. "Anything for ESPN!"

"Great, and then we can talk more later. I'll just want to learn a little more about your lives, who you are, how you became friends. Those sorts of things."

Leroy slipped his earbuds back in. The letters P-A-I-N were written in pen across the four fingers of his left hand; he tapped them frenetically against his thigh. He was not interested in letting people get to know him, and he certainly wasn't going to make an exception for me.

Dartanyon, on the other hand, was enthusiastic. "What do you want to know?"

"Well, how has your season been?" I asked. "Do you have any favorite wins from this year?"

Dartanyon pondered for a moment, as though it was a question that had never occurred to him. "No, I don't remember any of my wins," he said finally. "I only remember the losses."

DARTANYON'S FIRST LOSS had smelled uncomfortably like roses at every turn. There was the deep crimson rose on his father's dashboard when he picked Dartanyon up early from school to tell him the news. Then the small white bud his sister pinned on his shirt before they all headed to the church. And now the ground where he stood was literally covered in petals of red and pearl, their fragrance thickening the air in his throat as he leaned over the open grave. When you come across a rose petal, you know how it takes a few strokes in between your fingers and your thumb before you can tell whether it's real or artificial? Well, that's similar to how Dartanyon felt, leaning over this open grave with a handful of velvety petals. He knew that was his mother in the casket, but was she really not coming back?

Dartanyon was with his second-grade class the week before when Mrs. McKenna told him to pack up his things, that his father had come to get him. Dartanyon panicked, scrolling through his day, trying to figure out what he could have done wrong to warrant his father showing up to school. But Dartanyon was the one wronged this time. "Your mother is dead," his dad told him when they reached the car. "She had a stroke and died this morning." Arthur thought there was no other way to say it to a child than point-blank, to make sure he understood. Dartanyon didn't think a little sympathy would have muddied the message any.

"Do you want to go see her?" Arthur asked. Dartanyon nodded. His five older siblings were already at the morgue, crying and holding one another up. Dartanyon ran to his mother's side and slipped his hands into hers. "Come on, Mama, please get up," he whispered as he leaned in closer. "Let's go home." He knew his mother was sick, but he never had any reason to believe she wouldn't get better. Mothers just don't up and leave their seven children. Especially not Juanita Crockett. She held her family and half the neighborhood together. She could patch her own drywall, change a tire, and serve up Thanksgiving dinner for thirty people in the same afternoon, all while chasing around her house full of kids. Juanita was seventeen years old when she had her first child with Darnell Crockett. Irquois, as he was known, was both her first love and—as a light-skinned black man—her crown jewel. Back in that day, if a dark-skinned black woman like Juanita could get herself a lighter black man who could turn even a few heads on the block, she reeled him in as fast as she could. Juanita got one and could never let go.

The problem was that she had hooked herself some trouble rather than a big fish. As the story goes, Irquois took a hit to the head while working at the Ford motor factory when he was twenty-one years old and was never quite right after that. Most felt he could have gone back to work, but the disability income from social security covered his liquor just fine. Juanita worked long days as a stylist at Mirror Mirror Salon and then came home to Irquois and his no-good drinking cronies. As far as anyone could tell, he never used a dime of his monthly checks to buy groceries, never paid a bill, never diapered a baby. But Juanita didn't complain. No matter what condition Irquois was in, she was just glad he was still there when she came home from work each day.

However, it wasn't long before Irquois was lured away by the neighborhood mistress: crack. He would disappear for stretches of time, but he always seemed to remember his vows toward the end of the month when he ran low on cash and rocks. Juanita would take him back, part hoping she could change him and part fearing he'd beat her if she didn't.

Juanita took up with a few other men along the way until she could figure out how to clean Irquois up and keep him home for good. And because of that, she was never quite sure about the paternity of some of her seven children. Some were lighter in complexion, some darker. Either way, she quietly listed Darnell Crockett as the father on all of their birth certificates. To further connect them, she named each child according to Irquois's initials, D.C.:

Dionna, Darnell Jr., Darlene, Dominique, Davielle, Dartanyon, and Danielle. She said she did so to ensure all of her kids grew unified as a family, and there was probably some truth to that. But her desire to hold on to Irquois was equally true.

Juanita carried all of her babies home like the gold at a rainbow's end. She tucked them into their beds each night, and by morning, a pack of three or four of them would be sleeping beside her, right up under her like a litter of puppies. And that's the way she liked things. She was comfortable with chaos, with kids running wild, the banister hanging by its hinge and crusted ketchup on the couch. It was the type of bedlam that gave holy purpose to her struggles.

Juanita thought Dartanyon would be her last child. She hemorrhaged badly during his delivery, and her obstetrician said that additional pregnancies could threaten her life. Perhaps that's why she always looked at him with an extra twinkle in her eye, held him a little dearer. She'd nestle her new boy into her cheek and say, "Isn't he just the cutest baby you've ever seen?"

It didn't take long before Juanita was certain of one more thing too: Irquois wasn't the father.

"This one's Arty Harris's," she told a friend. "Looks just like Arty, with his square head and thick body." Juanita named him Dartanyon, maybe after the unlikely hero of the Three Musketeers, or maybe not. No one is sure, because no one was beside her to ask as she wrote "Dartanyon Davon Crockett" on his birth certificate, just in case she and Irquois worked things out one day.

Juanita and Arthur had met at the Laundromat less than a year earlier and had been living together off and on. Though they were on the outs when Dartanyon was born, Juanita took him back soon after. She appreciated that Arthur always pitched in with the cooking and the cleaning up and minding her kids while she worked. He had five kids of his own scattered across town, but Dartanyon was the first one he cared for from early infancy. As

Arthur fumbled with diapers and rocked away the nights, he held his son in his palm and thought, *Awful big name for a little baby. You're going to have to grow into something strong with a name like that.* With his fingertip, he connected the freckles on Dartanyon's cheek. There were seven of them, resembling the Big Dipper, and as Arthur gazed at this boy, he felt like he held the whole world in his hands.

Unfortunately, Arthur had trouble holding on to good things. He'd be cool for a minute, then mess up with the drinking and the drugs. Juanita developed headaches after giving birth to Dartanyon, and Arthur's lying and arguing made her temples throb even worse. By Dartanyon's third birthday, she'd kicked Arthur out for good. He still picked up Dartanyon on weekends, along with Davielle and Dominique. Just three years separated the three brothers, who shared varying degrees of visual impairment. Juanita called them her stair steps, and if you were taking one, you better be taking them all.

To be closer to her children, Juanita did hair at home. Micro braids, kinky twists, sew-ins, weaves. Her following was faithful, and she could fill most Saturdays with twelve hours of heads lined up across the living room. Juanita started the braiding assembly line, and then passed them off to her oldest daughter, Dionna, to finish while she started the next one. If she hustled, she could pull in $1,500, even with all those boys sitting up under her. But Juanita could be financially fit on a Saturday and be trading hair for food stamps by Monday, because there are two kinds of broke in this world: the kind that comes from not being able to earn money, and the kind that comes from not being able to keep money. Juanita was the latter. She gave freely to her struggling sisters, and then there were the boyfriends whose habits depleted her as she tried to help them too. "Juanita, why you picking the same bad men over and over again?" her friends would fuss. Juanita loved the Lord, but churchgoing men never were her type. The kind of man she liked wasn't the kind that stayed around when he finished spending her money.

As a result, she was always grappling with something that needed solving—finding the next place to stay or falling behind on the bills. Yet even when they were eating syrup sandwiches for dinner, her kids felt as though they were living like kings. The Crocketts may not have had much, but their house was a home. In that sense, they had everything. "People told us we was lucky because we kept our own place," Dominique said. "That's what people kept telling me about our mother. She never moved back with her mama when times were hard. She kept her own spots until the day she died." Her children were fiercely loyal, and after long summer days of braiding, she would pile her brood into the minivan and head to the drive-in movies, splurging on caramel corn and cotton candy while they sat on the roof, waiting for Jim Carrey or Denzel Washington to do their things.

But Juanita wanted to do better by them. Sometimes they'd be driving, and she would stop off at Lake Erie on East Fifty-Fifth. "You stay in the car," she'd tell the kids. "I'll be right back." She grabbed her Bible and headed to her rock overlooking the water. Her children watched in reverent solidarity as their mama prayed and pleaded from her rock to the One who was her Rock. By the time she got back to the car, a song had returned to her lips.

"Let not your heart be troubled, His tender Word I hear," Juanita would sing to them. "And resting on His goodness, I lose my doubts and fears."

"Why you always singing, Mama?" they would ask her.

"So no one can kill my joy," she would reply.

Still, no dosage of Jesus could ward off those headaches that seemed to worsen each week. By the time Dartanyon started school, Juanita was up to a dozen Tylenol a day. She didn't think about checking her blood pressure or hypertension. She figured six kids pound on your head like that. She never complained, just kept a cup of black tea near at all times.

In August 1999, Juanita gave birth to her seventh child, Danielle Crockett, even though she had legally divorced Irquois by then. Juanita brought her new bundle home, but this time her bliss was subdued by the now crippling headaches. One week later, she finally sought help. It was too late. Juanita had developed a blood clot after labor that traveled up to her brain and caused a stroke. A craniotomy saved her life but not her mobility, leaving her left side paralyzed. She entered a nursing home for rehabilitation, needing help for basic care.

Lying in bed, she sang gospel as loud as her feeble voice allowed, for though her body betrayed her, her faith would not. "I think she knew she was going to die," Arthur said, "because two weeks before she passed, she told me, 'I tried to walk the walk and talk the talk, Arty. Not saying I did it perfect, but I tried. Now you do the same.'" Her last words to Arthur were "Take care of my son."

Dartanyon never had any reason to believe his mama wouldn't recover. She told him and the others to get themselves to school and mind their business and she would be back soon. But now here they were, sending her home with her favorite hymn, "His Eye Is on the Sparrow."

> When songs give place to sighing, when hope within me dies,
> I draw the closer to Him, from care he sets me free;
> His eye is on the sparrow, and I know He watches me;
> His eye is on the sparrow, and I know He watches me.
>
> —CIVILLA D. MARTIN, 1905

The minister spoke at the song's conclusion, but the only thing Dartanyon could hear with any clarity were golf balls pinging off tees at the public course a few hundred feet away. He wondered why the whole world didn't stop when his mother did.

As Juanita's casket lowered into the ground, Dominique collapsed beside it. "Nooo, Mama, she can't go!" he cried. "Take me instead!" He could neither go with her, nor did he know how to go on without her.

Dartanyon and Davielle knelt on each side of their brother, their cheeks glistening with tears as the crowd wailed around them. The boys sat bewildered until Dartanyon picked up a handful of rose petals and dropped them softly over the casket, watching in resignation as they fluttered down like butterflies. The smell of those petals just made him sad anyway, so he thought maybe his mama could take them with her, to decorate her new place in heaven. Davielle followed suit, and without a word, Dominique too. There were hundreds of petals strewn about the ground, but Juanita's boys found a holy purpose in their struggle, and in doing what they did best: they sat up under their mama, pushing every last petal into the ground until she was blanketed in their love for eternity. And there wasn't a soul there that day who ever forgot the way the Crockett boys slowed their tears to honor the woman who kept a roof over their heads and a fire in their hearts.

THEY SAY YOU die twice. One time when you stop breathing, and a second time, a bit later on, when you are forgotten. Juanita Crockett was still very much alive, for the first thing Dartanyon wanted me to know about him was that his mother was both gone and still here with him now.

"Her watching me is my motivation for everything I do," Dartanyon said. "I'm hoping when I see her someday, she'll be proud of me." He looked away, his thoughts trailing off into solemn remembrance.

Leroy tapped Dartanyon on the shoulder, signaling his match was up soon. Dartanyon moved down a step, allowing Leroy to climb on for their trip down the bleachers. Spectators stole glances as they passed, unsure if it was appropriate to watch. Dartanyon took Leroy to an alcove on the far side of the gym where they stretched and engaged in some sort of Eastern breathing ritual, extending their arms parallel to the floor and then over their heads, breathing deeply with their eyes tight. They didn't strike me as the yoga types.

"I've never seen them do that before," Coach Hons said. "That might be new for the camera."

Dartanyon delivered Leroy to his mat, where Robinson waited to pump him up with a hard smack across the cheek. Leroy flew onto the mat with a primal roar, frantically shaking out his hands, as though they'd fallen asleep. This dramatic entrance signaled to the gym that now it was okay to look. Leroy had pinned Jacob Simpson, his Midpark High opponent, earlier this season. But this time Jacob was more prepared to wrestle an amputee, and within ten seconds, Leroy was on his back. He rolled out, but Jacob quickly registered a second takedown, wringing the air out of Leroy's throat with his forearm.

"Roll him, Leroy, you got this!" Dartanyon yelled from the side of the mat as Leroy grunted and gasped. He refused to succumb, battling off his back better than many kids with legs. Finally Leroy escaped, but he was denied the point. By definition, an escape ends in a standing position, and it is impossible to land on your feet when you have none.

Jacob quickly attacked again, folding his legs around Leroy's torso, controlling his hips and shoulders. At the two-minute mark, he flattened Leroy out for good. Leroy slid back to Dartanyon, who patted him on the head as if to say he'd get 'em next time. Leroy smiled, seemingly unaffected by the loss. As he made his way back to the bleachers, wrestlers from other schools streamed over to shake his hand. Winning came in this acceptance.

Dartanyon was up soon after, and he walked to his mat with his navy-blue singlet straps down by his waist, just as Robinson taught him to do. His muscles bulged and shined like those of an action figure.

"Do you know anything about Dartanyon?" I asked one of the tournament organizers. "Does he have a chance to make it out of sectionals?"

"I have never seen him wrestle, but I'm sure he'll get through easily," he said.

"Why is that?" I asked.

"All these white kids see a black kid who looks like *that* come out on the mat, and it's all they can do not to pee their unitard," he said with a laugh.

But Dartanyon's first opponent wasn't white. He was one of the handful of black kids in the gym, as well as Dartanyon's Senate Conference rival. Dartanyon had defeated Irayel Williams the previous week for the city championship, as well as in every match for the last two years. Dartanyon was confident; Irayel was hungry.

"Make him cry," Leroy said to Dartanyon, who squatted down beside him.

"I'm gonna break his spirit," Dartanyon declared. "Just gonna break his spirit." Dartanyon rose, slapping his shoulders and releasing a guttural growl, like a lion announcing to the forest that he's about to slaughter.

Known as Rock, Irayel was a natural athlete. His arms and legs were strong, though not as sculpted as Dartanyon's. He knew he would have to pass through Dartanyon to get out of sectionals. He also knew Dartanyon was graduating, making this his last chance for retribution. And Rock was ready. His coach, James Greenwood, wrestled at Navy and was the best technical coach in the gym. Greenwood preached wrestling not as a way of life but as the *only* way. Like Robinson, Greenwood strived to shape boys into warriors, but he did it with discipline and drills instead of prayers and T-shirts. He'd held Rock in the gym till eight o'clock every night that week, watching tape on Dartanyon and mapping out strategy.

The vendetta on Rock's shoulders pushed him low into his stance. Both wrestlers pounced at the whistle like dancing cougars. Rock attacked first, taking Dartanyon down for two quick points. He wasted no time scoring a second takedown, giving him a 4–0 lead and leaving Dartanyon with his headgear down over his eyes. Lincoln-West was known for having the worst headgear in the city, Robinson said. Having been passed down for so many years, it looked as sturdy as a set of earmuffs strung together with rubber bands. Robinson ripped off Dartanyon's headgear and motioned to Leroy, who tossed his set to Dartanyon. Leroy was the only Lincoln wrestler with his own, thanks to his grandmother putting up the forty dollars for him.

As Robinson strapped it on, Dartanyon breathed heavily and stood a little less sure, wondering why he couldn't shake Rock off like he had so many times before. Back on the mat, Rock worked like a military strategist, making subtle moves to gain small yet critical advantages. Occupy space and don't give it up, Coach Greenwood had taught him. He scored again to make it 6–0. This time Dartanyon did not get up. Rock drove Dartanyon's head into the mat for emphasis, to let him know who was in charge now. Dartanyon returned to center but quickly flopped back down, grabbing his right knee. He hobbled over to Robinson, who lifted him by the shoulders like an angry bear and pressed his forehead to Dartanyon's. "Son, you never show your opponent where you're hurt!" Leroy sat on the corner of the mat with his pant legs spread wide on the floor, covering limbs that weren't there, hollering for a hope that was ebbing away. Robinson hastily shoved Dartanyon back out onto the mat.

Dartanyon let out another roar and surprised us all by lifting Rock into the air. Any other day, Dartanyon would have flipped him up and over to finish that move; instead, he landed facedown on the mat with Rock spread over his back: 10–0. He was out of gas. Rock yanked the injured leg. I covered my eyes and watched the rest from between my fingers.

Dartanyon hobbled back to center, kneeling into position. He looked for a reversal, tried a switch, but couldn't hit a thing. The ref noticed his busted lip and mercifully whistled for time. Coach Hons hurried Dartanyon over to the trash can, where he heaved and spewed blood. Leroy had never witnessed his friend self-destruct like this.

Dartanyon limped back in for one last try, but we all knew he was finished, including Rock, who wasted no time picking him up by his right leg and laying him flat. Victorious by 15 points. But neither appeared happy. Dartanyon had suffered the disgrace, and Rock was denied the satisfaction of the pin.

Dartanyon stumbled toward Robinson and fell at his feet. Robinson picked him up by the back of his neck and walked him backward off the mat. Dartanyon winced in agony. He collapsed to the ground as they reached the wall, one hand over his eyes, the other over his knee. Leroy scooted over while Robinson tried to calm his boy.

We continued filming, and the audio tech extended that fuzzy microphone that looks like a hedgehog on a long pole to pick up their conversation. I hoped Dartanyon's vision was poor enough that he could not see us. Leroy scowled at me for heaping on the disgrace, and with my eyes, I pleaded with him to understand that this saddling up to real-time heartache was the part of producing that I disliked as well. But Leroy was not interested in what I liked or disliked. He followed Dartanyon and Robinson to the trainer's room and slammed the door.

COACH ROBINSON EMERGED from the trainer's room a few minutes later. "His ego's pretty beat up, but his leg is fine," he said.

"Really? It looked like he could hardly walk," I said.

"You get manhandled by a sophomore you've beaten before, and you need some kind of excuse," Robinson said. "I'm not saying the boy's not hurt some, but the only reason you put on a show like that is so people think your knee gave out instead of your heart."

"And I'm sure he was a little nervous with the cameras," Coach Hons added earnestly. "It's not like you're the local Channel 8 News. You're ESPN, and he's just a kid who's going to see his worst loss ever on SportsCenter tonight."

"Oh gosh, oh, no, no no . . . he's not," I stammered. "This won't be on SportsCenter."

"You ain't running the highlights tonight?" Robinson asked.

"No, I'm sorry, I guess I didn't explain myself well," I said. "I am a features producer. I tell longer stories that take weeks and months to put together." Their assumptions were understandable. When working with amateur athletes, especially kids, I typically fly in a day early to get to know people before subjecting them to cameras. We sit together, casually, as I explain the filming process, the schedule, the equipment. We talk about what they are comfortable shooting and what might be off-limits. But I hadn't had time to prepare Leroy or Dartanyon for my arrival.

"Listen, let me talk to him and ease his mind," I said. "I feel awful that he felt that pressure."

Dartanyon limped from the training room with an ice pack wrapped around his knee. Leroy scooted behind him, focusing on keeping his fingers out from under oncoming shoes. They settled into the bleachers a few rows below my father. I made the slow trek up their way, unsure of how to make things right. As Leroy noticed me coming, he preemptively put in his ear buds.

"How are you feeling?" I asked Dartanyon.

"I'm okay," he said. "Split my lip and this old knee injury from lifting weights flared up again. Just gottta fight through it." The first day of the tournament had finished. The other Lincoln wrestlers collected their things and headed toward the door. Leroy stayed.

I assured Dartanyon that no one would ever see the footage of his match. He shrugged like it wouldn't matter to him, but his expression relaxed nonetheless.

"You know, your mother's still proud of you, Dartanyon. If she were here, I think she would tell you that one loss doesn't change that."

Dartanyon lowered his head. He needed her. I placed my hand on his shoulder and felt tears in my eyes. "You know what else, Dartanyon? I'll bet your mother is going to gather all of heaven together to cheer you on tomorrow."

He looked up and squeezed out a smile. "Yeah, maybe. I was the mama's boy of our family," he said, nodding. "You gonna be here tomorrow?"

"I would like to, if that's okay with you guys," I answered.

"Fine with me," he said as he slowly stood up. "We gotta get on the bus now. See you tomorrow." Dartanyon retrieved Leroy's wheelchair from under the bleachers. He walked out free of a limp, and I smiled, knowing Robinson had diagnosed correctly.

My father had been watching the scene from a few rows up in the stands, biting the insides of his cheeks. "You can't be getting close to kids like that," he said to me. I was tempted to ask him, Kids like *what*? But I already knew. He meant black kids. "You just never know what these people are thinking," he added. I wanted to tell him that times had changed. I wanted to tell him that I had black friends, that I regularly interviewed black athletes. I wanted to tell him, *Actually, Dad, you'd be surprised what you can know about a person if you just ask.* Instead, I took a handful of his popcorn and stuffed it in my mouth before those fighting words came out. I was not ready to engage in this battle—not just yet.

THE NEXT MORNING, Dartanyon walked off the bus with Leroy on his back and the spring back in his step. I was struck even more by how much Dartanyon resembled a store-bought action figure. His head was planted squarely on his shoulders, rather than on a neck. He had six well-cut abdominal muscles protruding from his gray Lycra shirt, and his short sleeves were forced up under his shoulders by his ballooning biceps.

Leroy wore a white Lincoln-West T-shirt with his nickname on the back: Cripple. I reckoned he wanted to say it before anyone else could, to tell you that he knew what you were thinking and where you were looking. If he couldn't ward off the world's labeling system, he would embrace it and use it to make someone who stared at him feel just as uncomfortable as they were making him.

"Huddle up!" Coach Robinson called out once inside the gym. "You are all great wrestlers. There is no one and nothing that can stop you!" These were bold statements to make to kids who shared headgear and threadbare shoes and hadn't pulled out a single win the day before. But the kids hung on his every word. They needed to believe it.

Leroy lost quickly that morning by pin, ending his wrestling career. Still, he burst into smile, and his opponent hugged him twice before they left the mat. Even with two matches in progress on other mats, the entire crowd applauded Leroy, thereby validating what I'd experienced when I first saw him in the newspaper: when Leroy smiles, it is impossible to look anywhere else.

"Two words, Crockett! Two words," Robinson shouted as Dartanyon walked out for his first match of the day, eyes to the sky. He never returned to his mother's grave in the years following her funeral, and his family spoke little of her death. But sometimes, when Dartanyon did something of which he was proud, or when he watched other moms pick up his friends from school, his brother Davielle would quietly remind him: "She's watching." Those two words anchored Dartanyon through every storm.

Dartanyon had defeated Chase Bell from Cleveland Heights earlier in the season. Chase lacked both Dartanyon's strength and Rock's technical proficiency. Here again, Dartanyon pinned him in less than a minute.

"Two words," Robinson whispered to himself, as Dartanyon kissed his fist and pointed to the sky. "Only two words that matter to that boy, so we gonna ride those today." As Dartanyon strutted into the quarterfinals, his whole body seemed to be asking, *Who's next?*

"Crockett, I want you to make this next match so brutal that you send whoever you fight after him to his knees too," Robinson said. "You hear what I'm saying? I want this kid's mother running out of the stands yelling, 'Ooh, stop doing that to my baby.'"

Dartanyon nodded obediently as they walked to the mat. "Be brutal, son," Robinson reminded, then looked down at Leroy on his other side. "What are you doing down there?" Leroy paused, smiled slyly, and broke into a little dance that made Robinson chuckle. "Don't bite any ankles down there, Sutton."

Dartanyon's quarterfinal match pitted him against Carl Slaton of Valley Forge High School. Redheaded with freckled skin, Carl was the type of thick, squishy kid the tournament director had alluded to the day before. Right from the whistle, Dartanyon darted around like a mouse playing games with a house cat. Once behind Carl, Dartanyon wedged his right hand under Carl's arm and his left hand under his left thigh, flipping him upside down. Carl landed on his back with a thud.

"My God . . . ," Robinson whispered to Hons while Carl saw stars. "Is he crying? Is he *crying*?"

Dartanyon returned to his corner while the referee checked Carl over. "Listen, son, break him right now," Robinson implored. "The kid you wrestle next is watching. Break this kid and you win the next match too."

Carl chose to go on, cautiously. Less than a minute later, Dartanyon wrapped his arms around Carl's torso and lifted him off the ground like he'd just pulled an old oak tree out of the earth, roots and all. With Carl's legs dangling, Dartanyon walked him four seconds to his right, heaved him over, and fell on top for the easy pin.

Dartanyon hopped back to center to be declared the winner, but Carl stayed down, grimacing and grasping his shoulder.

"Leave him broken," Robinson said. "Let's go. And don't put your clothes back on till you get up to the top of the bleachers. Keep your singlet straps down." Dartanyon followed orders, walking with his chest bare, and from behind, his back looked like two seismic plates divided down the middle by a fault line an inch deep. And then Robinson got his first wish—to incite the opponent's mother. Carl's mom stormed out of the stands. And she was looking for *me*. "Are you in charge of that ESPN camera?" she demanded to know.

I smiled warmly, extending my hand. "Yes, my name is Lisa. How can I help you?"

"You can give me those tapes right now, because you didn't have permission to film my son!" she said angrily.

This predicament was new to me: most people jumped to be on ESPN. I constructed a quick defense. "This is a public sporting event, and I do have the permission of the tournament organizer to film."

"My son's a minor. You can't film him without my consent!" she yelled. "Your kid *hurt* him!"

I boiled at her accusation, and it was in that moment that Dartanyon became my kid. I wanted to tell her that my kid was as gentle as a dove, and that if her kid would lay off the Doritos, he might stand a chance next time. I didn't know if either were true, and fortunately neither left my mouth, because I noticed Carl peeking at us from about ten feet behind her, standing on that thin line between humility and humiliation. I chose the kinder road instead.

"How is he doing?" I asked.

"His shoulder is all messed up from your kid acting like an animal out there!" she yelled again.

"Ma'am, Dartanyon wrestled cleanly. The ref never penalized him for unsportsmanlike conduct," I said. "Calling him an animal is out of line."

"What's your name? You'll be hearing from my lawyer!" she screamed.

"Please do have him get in touch," I said. "I would be happy to speak with him." I pulled a business card from my bag, knowing she sorely lacked a case. ESPN made its name on lesser athletes falling at the mercy of the naturally gifted. This practice was not litigated; it was celebrated. There was no use arguing the issue any further, but as I turned away, I saw Dartanyon standing within earshot, looking touched that someone might fight for him.

DARTANYON'S SEMIFINAL OPPONENT came out like a full-court press. Peter Heggs of Shaw High School entered fresh off of a third-round loss. Both he and Dartanyon needed the win to stay in qualifying contention. Peter appeared solid and carried himself in a no-nonsense sort of way, and from the first whistle he went about his business. He capitalized on Dartanyon's slightest mistakes, quietly ticking up the score. By the start of the third period, Peter was up 8–3. Robinson sat in the corner alternating between "Two words!" and "Come on, Crockett!" but neither pearl of coaching expertise was enough to help Dartanyon close the gap. He lost, 10–4.

Dartanyon fell to the ground, mourning the loss of a sport that gave him a reason to get out of bed each day. "Crockett, what are you doing?" Robinson said. "Get up and pull yourself together. You lost, but you gave it everything you had. This is a life lesson. You quit here, you quit in life."

Dartanyon took no comfort in lessons. Life had taught him all he cared to know about losing. Dartanyon looked like he'd rather crawl under the scorer's table than be seen in the consolation match later that afternoon. The top four in each weight class advanced to the district meet, and this bout was for fifth place, or first guy staying home. Just yesterday, the man on the bus had told Dartanyon he was a hero; one day later, he was in the loser's bracket.

"Crockett, end on a high note," Robinson said. "Don't die here. God's got other plans for you today."

Dartanyon's heart was not in that match, but his body was all he needed. He scored an early takedown, then a reversal. Leroy sat somberly at his post, knowing there was nothing to be won here.

"Two words, son," Robinson called out, and as I watched Juanita's boy fight for dignity, I suddenly sensed her voice in my own mind, prodding me: *Take care of my son.*

I stopped, stock-still, my head tilted as if waiting for more. Though I could see the crowd cheering around me, this whisper was all I could hear, reverberating between my head and my heart.

"What?" I whispered aloud, leaning forward, drawn into the conversation. Her voice came to me again, like high tide washing through my body. *Take care of my son.* The plea could not have been clearer if she was seated beside me, and it was wrapped in an entrancing sense of peace. The rest of the match moved in slow motion, and Dartanyon got the pin just after the four-minute mark, raising his fist, as he always did, to acknowledge the woman who had left his world and entered mine. I felt like I was watching a film in which I had just been cast.

Here we were almost adults, and we still couldn't
put thoughts together with any ease, and when we could, we didn't
have the courage to tell them to anyone. It made people assume
we didn't feel anything, or that we didn't care. But we cared a lot.
It was trust that we were missing.

—LEROY

CHAPTER 5

PLAYING FOR TRUST

L et's see whatcha got!" Victor said as I walked into the office on Monday morning. He rubbed his hands together, eager to see what his gamble had netted. I nervously rewound the first tape, feeling fifteen years old again, about to show my dad what I'd bought at the mall with his credit card and hoping he approved. The tape stopped on Dartanyon picking up Leroy for the national anthem.

"Whoa," Victor said. And then captive silence as I scrolled through the boys' trips up and down the bleachers, Leroy's vigor on the mat, Dartanyon tossing the redheaded kid around like a rag doll, and their warming laughter as they headed to the bus. I skipped over Dartanyon's losses and the woeful trash can episode.

"Are we sure the one with legs is blind?" Victor asked. "Because he seems to hunt down his opponents pretty easily."

"His coach said everything is shadowy."

"When do you shoot again?"

"I'm still not sure what it is that I'm shooting. Their wrestling seasons are over, although I'm not sure this is a story about wrestling anyway. I think it's a friendship story, but I didn't get to know them well enough to say so with certainty."

"Can I see that anthem shot again?" Victor asked, with a hint of disbelief. The script of sports emphasizes competitive bonds and the meaning of a teammate. Dartanyon carrying Leroy legitimized that bond in a tangible way. Their connection was immediately seen and understood. And Victor's reaction confirmed my suspicion that this was one of the most striking images I had ever seen pass through a frame of video.

"I was thinking I might go back for a few days, to learn more about their lives and figure out what I need to make this work," I said. "I can stay with my parents. It wouldn't cost us anything but the flight." I conveniently omitted the part about how one half of the story refused to speak to me.

"That's . . . just . . . wow," he said, replaying the anthem clip over and over again. "Yah, get to know them. There's something there."

I had also left out the bit about hearing voices in the bleachers, even though that was the part of the weekend that had unmoored me. I believed that God desires to speak to us in different ways and through various means: dreams and visions, strangers and friends, nature and events, reason and silence. And though I had never heard audible voices, I had discerned God communicating in the form of unexpected thoughts that suddenly apprehended my own, causing me to either change direction or notice something I would not have been drawn toward otherwise. These nudges were like taps on the shoulder that whispered, "Pay attention over here." I had grown attuned to this soft, small voice beneath the whirlwind of ordinary life, pointing me to look past the surface to the connectedness of our lives. Still, this directive was startlingly specific. It had not occurred to me that Juanita's son needed taking care of, and yet the plea could not have been clearer.

"Maybe we're supposed to adopt him," I said to my husband, Navid, upon arriving home from Cleveland.

"Sure, let's take in a seventeen-year-old blind kid for the spring, get him off to college in the fall, and then retire early," Navid said wryly. "Those years between infancy and adulthood can be parenting nightmares anyway."

Navid was in the final four months of his family medicine residency at Middlesex Hospital in central Connecticut. From an early age, my husband had believed he had two callings in life, both strongly influenced by his own upbringing: doctoring and fathering. When I met him in 2003, Navid was pressing through medical school and came from a family that could have started its own health care system, boasting a pediatrician, a dentist, a pathologist, an immunologist, an occupational therapist, a public health specialist, and a pharmaceutical salesman.

Navid's mother, Shirin Mahooti, practiced pediatrics for forty-eight years and was still running a solo office at the age of sixty-eight. Born in Iran, Shirin did her schooling in England. Upon returning to Iran after medical school, she married Navid's father, a petroleum engineer for the National Iranian Oil Company, and together they applied for green cards to the United States. Seven years later, their requests were granted. The family immigrated in the summer of 1976.

The Mahootis settled in Woodbury, Connecticut, near the only hospital that offered Shirin a chance to repeat her residency. Then, in 1979, political hell broke loose in the shape of the Iranian Revolution, and the rebels seized sixty American diplomats in Tehran. The Iran hostage crisis dominated the headlines, as helpless, blindfolded Americans were paraded through the streets and the images were aired across American news outlets. The hostages were held for 444 days. Potent surges of anti-Iranian sentiment swept through the United States. The value of the Iranian rial plummeted against the US dollar, and the family's net worth, which they had maintained in the Bank of Iran, was decimated. The Mahootis were forced to start over in every way.

Shirin slaved through hundred-hour workweeks in a residency program that embraced neither Middle Easterners nor women. Navid's father, a Fulbright scholar, worked factory jobs to make ends meet. Teachers targeted the Mahooti children with public humiliation and wore anti-Iranian armbands in support of the hostages. The family led an insular life, with no one to depend on but one another. And as they did, they found that togetherness was all the sustenance they needed.

The family unit was therefore sacred to Navid, and he longed for a gaggle of kids of his own, to replicate the closeness that had emerged from the trenches of his childhood. Though I too desired children, birthing them was not a priority. I was ten years old when my mother relented and bought me my first Cabbage Patch Kid, the must-have doll of my childhood era. She was a perky redhead named Hedda Kate. Hedda came with her own birth certificate, and my mom said that when I clutched that piece of paper, I cried real tears, rejoicing that this orphan doll finally had a home. Hedda Kate was soon followed by Lindy Ana and Emma Courtney. Each addition further stirred my interest in adoption. Serving in inner-city shelters throughout my teen years and in Eastern European orphanages during college cemented my conviction that with such a surplus of children in need of parents, the world didn't need me to make more.

Navid and I talked about these issues on our first few dates. I found that, as certain as I was that I would one day adopt, he was equally certain that he would not. "I don't know if I will be able to love an adopted child as fully as a biological child," he confessed. "It's not a risk I want to take, for either me or the child." His concerns were honest and thoughtful, and I prayed for Navid's desires to one day merge with mine.

Four years into our marriage, we conceived. And then we miscarried. One miscarriage led to another, which led to a total of four. Each occurred early in their terms, eight weeks or fewer, with the last miscarriage falling on Christmas Eve of 2008. The havoc that the miscarriages wreaked on my body paled in comparison with how they ravaged Navid's heart. Why would he be denied this cherished gift of fatherhood, a role he would hold so fiercely and so tenderly?

One week before meeting Leroy and Dartanyon, I drove with Navid through Woodbury, toward the bucolic ball field where he had pitched Little League. He pulled over, missing his own father, who had passed away a year before, and on a snow-capped mound, our wishes converged. "I just want to be a dad, however it's meant to happen," Navid said.

I wrapped my arms tightly around my husband and his dream. "We can continue trying," I responded, "but perhaps we can start looking into adoption as well."

"Yes," he agreed. "Maybe there is someone out there who needs us just as much as we need them."

MY FATHER WAS adamant that I not go to Lincoln-West High School alone on my first Monday morning back in Cleveland. I had returned on a five-day scouting expedition of sorts, to gain a clearer picture of Leroy and Dartanyon's lives and personalities. I needed to decide if they possessed a story that would make for powerful television, and if so, begin laying the groundwork for future shoots. "Let me drive you over there," my father said. "I'll bring the newspaper and wait for you in the car."

"I'll be fine," I replied.

"It is not safe for little girls like you to be over there by yourself," he contended. At scarcely five-one, I am indeed slight, but I knew my father was speaking to me as someone even smaller: his five-year-old pigtailed, freckle-faced girl, whom he had nobly protected from crude urban life. Technically, I was a city kid too—raised in Cleveland eight miles and half a world away from Leroy and Dartanyon's high school. In 1978 I entered kindergarten two blocks from my west Cleveland home. My father liked to reminisce about how he walked me to my first day of school. He said I squeezed his hand nervously, and that when we reached the classroom, I refused to release my grip from his. "It was the first time I had to let you go for your own good," he said. "And even though I had to let you go a hundred times more throughout your life, it never got easier."

My public school career lasted one month. That year, Ohio appellate court judge Frank Battisti upheld a previous ruling to desegregate the Cleveland public schools and drafted a sixteen-point plan to ensure that black students and white students would receive equal educations. Of greatest concern to citizens on my side of town was that the predominantly African American schools on the east side of the city and the white schools on the west side of the city would have to exchange enough students to achieve racial balance. This plan, commonly known as busing, was met with great resistance among white residents. Judge Battisti received death threats, and the Cleveland public school teachers went on strike in the fall of my kindergarten year. Like most parents in our neighborhood, and in cities enacting similar desegregation plans, my father grew concerned. His protective instincts could not allow his blue-eyed, blond-haired daughter to ride a public school bus to the hood each day once the strike ended, yet he knew that his income as a greeting card salesman could neither fund a private education nor afford a suburban mortgage.

My father, a shrewd card player, scrambled to up his weekend poker participation. My mother soon returned to the workforce. Together they took on odd jobs. Their extra earnings enabled me to attend the private Lutheran elementary school five miles over the city line, where I went years without seeing a black person. My mother chauffeured me to after-school piano and ballet lessons alongside the other suburban children. A few times during high school, I volunteered at an inner-city soup kitchen as part of a service assignment. I also accompanied my aunt, an attorney, downtown to Cuyahoga County Juvenile Court to watch her prosecute parents accused of neglecting or abusing their children. My sole exposures to black people during my formative years involved worst-case scenarios, as I was either handing them a Styrofoam plate of slop or seeing them prosecuted for unspeakable crimes. I was ignorant of the paths that had delivered them to those points. And though I was grateful for the risks my parents took to shield me from life's rougher edges, I was now curious to see what was on the other side.

"You don't need to worry," I assured my father. His right hand began to twitch, reflexively, down next to his thigh, as it did when an uncomfortable situation closed in on him.

"You just don't understand how this world works, Lisa," he said, turning back to scrub dishes in the sink. We stood gridlocked for an uncomfortably long time before my father handed me his car keys.

I drove toward Lincoln-West down potholed roads that grew quickly dreary as I passed storefronts such as Dollar Loans, Payday Furniture Rental, and Cash Smart Check Cashing. Cleveland's push for desegregation had inadvertently impacted the city's economy, for as white families fled to the west side of town and to suburbs, local businesses went with them. The result was that the remaining children were bused from a predominantly black school on the east side of town to a now predominantly black school on the west side of town. Racial balance became impossible to achieve. And rather than investing in updated textbooks, upgraded facilities, or better technology, more than half a billion dollars had been poured into transporting students, often an hour away from their homes. Cleveland wearily ended its desegregation efforts in 1996, with the court crediting school officials for doing their best to carry out a flawed experiment that united few and left the city's education system in shambles.

Outside Lincoln's main entrance, half a dozen kids congregated and smoked cigarettes. Their nicotine clouds drifted up the brick wall toward metallic letters spelling "Lincoln-West High School." The *L* had loosened and hung carelessly at an angle. Inside the door, I joined a shuffling line of black and Hispanic teens, herded by a uniformed police officer. "Bags open so we can see what's inside!" he shouted. The boy in front of me, wearing no coat on this blustery morning, was turned away. "You were expelled last week, but since you didn't show up, they couldn't tell you," the officer informed him.

I passed through the metal detector—the ominous gate into Leroy and Dartanyon's daily world—and into my first immersive encounter with American poverty. My inner alarms sounded. I hated that my father's beliefs seemed woven into my fabric. I was, in fact, afraid.

I had planned to meet Dartanyon outside the school office, although when I called him the day before to confirm, his phone number was no longer in service. The school had not responded to my request to shadow Dartanyon through his classes. As I waited uneasily, watching students trudge past me in sleepy indifference, I suddenly wished I had chosen a more casual ensemble. I was dressed in gray polyester slacks, a powder-blue button-down blouse, and spool-heeled boots. It would be difficult to meld with urban teen culture while inadvertently masquerading as a preppy flight attendant.

Dartanyon emerged from a pack. "Good morning, Lisa," he said, from about fifteen feet away.

"Hi, wow, how did you know it was me?" I asked. "I mean, it's just, I thought you couldn't see so well."

"I just remembered that's how your shadow stands. And you had a pony tail at sectionals too." His mind had seemingly photographed my outline and committed it to memory. "You ready?"

Dartanyon was one of just three students in his first-period computer skills class. Impressed, I commented to the teacher on this wonderfully small class size. My naïveté amused her.

"We started the year with twenty-three," she said. "This is all that's left." One of the last three standing; his mother would be proud, I thought. Students worked independently, and Dartanyon positioned himself mere inches from the outdated computer monitor, his eyes ricocheting through the lesson.

"The font is small for you, no?" I asked, peeking over his shoulder. "Can you see it?"

"Yah, I just get close to it. And I can figure out a lot of words by the shape of them. Like the word *the*—the tops of the first two letters are taller, and then it goes flat for the *e*. Or like the word *and* is short, with two flat parts and a sticky-uppy thing at the end."

My attempts at conversation with Dartanyon were forced as I followed him through the rest of his day.

"How is your knee feeling?" I asked.

"Fine, thank you."

"How do you like Lincoln-West?"

"It's good. It's a school."

"Are you going to miss wrestling?"

"Yes, ma'am, I will."

"Do you do any other sports?"

"Powerlifting starts this week."

His answers to my questions, though brief, were respectful, and he insisted that I pass through each door ahead of him, as a gentleman would. When his mother was dying, she'd told her boys to treat girls like queens, and Dartanyon never disrespected his mother. His chivalry stood out as almost peculiar in a day marked by irreverent students. In English class, a group of girls formed a circle with their chairs to page through back issues of *Shape* magazine while their instructor tried to facilitate a discussion. Security broke up a fight after fourth period. Teachers collected books after each class, as they couldn't be sure that either the book or the student would return. And all the while Dartanyon moved through the pandemonium with poise.

Thirty-three languages were spoken throughout the Lincoln-West student population, representing fifty countries. Despite the challenges of teaching a student body so diverse, and in spite of its 40 percent graduation rate, Lincoln-West was considered the country club of the Cleveland public school district. Although skirmishes broke out in the parking lot from time to time—typically forewarned when a midday fire alarm was pulled—violence was largely absent from the hallways and classrooms. Teachers battled perpetual mischief but were safe from the more dangerous episodes that plagued other Cleveland public schools.

Lincoln-West also housed the city's program for the visually impaired. When Dartanyon entered Lincoln-West as a tenth-grader, he took all of his classes in the same cramped room alongside twenty-four other visually impaired students. The rest of the school knew them by their glass dome magnifiers and the large-print books they carried through the halls.

"Large-print books weren't just bigger words," explained Dartanyon. "The whole book was huge, like a giant magazine. They didn't even fit in a backpack. You don't know the torture."

"To hear Dartanyon tell it, he could see everything," said Val Barkley, Lincoln's lead teacher for the visually impaired. "But in reality, he needed at least twenty-point font, and he needed to sit in the front of the room to have any chance at following along."

By his junior year, Dartanyon was sick of being lumped with the "blind kids." He began resisting aides and adaptive devices. He swore up and down that he could see the chalkboard, that he had no limitations. Barkley sensed the program's approach grating on Dartanyon and approved his transition into mainstream classes during his junior year, along with an assistant to guide his note taking. But Dartanyon ducked the assistant as well, hiding in the back of the room or coming in late to avoid being seen with her. He remembered his mama's words: *You don't need special help. You can do anything anyone else can do.*

The spirit of Juanita's counsel was pure; the practicality of it caused Dartanyon's grades to plummet. Only sports forced him to accept the help he needed, as he could only fake it for so long before his eligibility caught up with him. He and Leroy became regulars at Coach Hons's after-school tutoring club, where they sat side by side. Dartanyon would get up to sharpen Leroy's pencils; Leroy ensured that Dartanyon could understand directions in small print. Yet each time I allowed myself to revel in their gentleness, they reverted to a teenage humor with a twist that only they could share.

"Did you guys do your homework?" asked Coach Hons.

"Dartanyon tried," said Leroy, "but he couldn't see it."

"So Leroy ran over and read it to me last night," Dartanyon said. He played it so smoothly that it felt like an old joke, yet their classmates laughed heartily, signaling that this was new, improv material. Afterward, the pair barreled down the halls together, their echoing laughter the brightest light in those dreary halls. Still, I could not coax a smile from Leroy in my direction. He suspected that I had come to probe his heart, and that was a place he had locked up eight years before.

I ASKED COACH Robinson to accompany me to Leroy's house later that night, hoping he could help me break the ice. Leroy lived with his grandmother on the east side of Cleveland, a predominantly African American community that had been hit hard by the city's economic decline. Robinson led me off the highway, through blocks of boarded-up homes. Many of the stop signs had been painted blue by the Crips. Farther along, Leroy's neighborhood was Bloods territory, so its stop signs remained red. Perhaps the street's most eye-catching sign had been hung by Leroy's grandmother in her front porch window:

THIS HOUSE IS GUARDED BY SHOTGUN
THREE NIGHTS PER WEEK.
YOU GUESS WHICH THREE.

"Don't worry, this neighborhood isn't as bad as the one off the highway," Robinson assured me. "No one gets shot around here unless they need to be." He hadn't called ahead to say we were coming, yet Patricia Sutton greeted us warmly. "Big Ma, this is Lisa from ESPN," he said. "We're here to see Leroy."

"All right, then," she replied. "He just downstairs doin' whatever and stuff. Go on through the kitchen there." Big Ma was preoccupied, watching *Wheel of Fortune* on a wide-screen television; artificial plants, ceramic elephants, and decorative crosses filled in the remaining space. The air hung heavy, saturated with cooking oil.

In the musty cinder-block basement, Leroy was hunkered down on a stained carpet with his Xbox controller in hand. He was uninterested in our arrival. "Hey, kid, Lisa's here," Robinson said.

"Hey," Leroy grunted, without looking away from the television. Robinson cleared a pile of crumpled T-shirts and dishes crusted with old food from a floral crushed-velvet sofa behind Leroy, motioning for me to take a seat. Dampness permeated my pants.

Coach Robinson and I made small talk about the wrestling season and what it's like to work at ESPN. I didn't lob any questions to Leroy. I had not touched a video game since Q*bert debuted on my Atari 5200 twenty-five years earlier, and any conversation I faked would have simply exposed me. My hope was that if he simply observed his coach's acceptance of me, Leroy would find permission to do the same. After an hour, I asked Leroy if it would be okay to stop by again the next night. He grunted in a way that communicated neither a yes nor a no.

"He'll come around," Robinson said on our way out. "He just doesn't trust you yet. Probably thinks you're a turkey lady."

"A what?" I asked.

"You know, a turkey lady," he repeated. "One of them white people who only come into the hood to drop off Thanksgiving dinner. That's their good deed for the year, and then they go back to their side of town."

I ARRIVED THE next night on my own to find Leroy squared up to his console, still refusing to greet me. This time I opted for the floor to show him that he could not scare me away, that I was not here on a service project. If he wanted me to leave, he would have to say so. Until he did, I would play along. After an hour of silence, I thanked Leroy for having me and said I would see him tomorrow.

Upstairs I found Big Ma calling out letters to Vanna White. Curiously, in two visits, she had yet to ask my purpose. So during a commercial, I took the liberty of telling her. I told her that I found her grandson to be an admirable wrestler. I told her that I wanted to learn more about him and his family. And I told her that I was interested in featuring him on television. "All right then, sounds good," she said, nodding approvingly. "Now here come round two. These boards are tough today."

After Big Ma beat out the contestant from Oklahoma in the bonus round, I asked her if she had any photos of Leroy as a child that I might see. She dug a stack out of a china cabinet drawer in the dining room. "Ooohhh! These here are good. These are from my retirement party. Forty years I worked for the board of education. I worked and saved up and got me this house. Mmmm, I love my house."

"You worked as a security guard?" I asked, noticing her blue uniform and shiny gold badge in one of the photos.

"No, I was a security *officer*," she corrected. "Guards are for buildings. Officers are for people. I looked after *people*." She shuffled through photos from the retirement celebration, reminiscing about the party, the cake, and the nice things people wrote in cards. This period of Big Ma's life served as a source of great pride.

"Mrs. Sutton, do you think there might be photos of Leroy in there?" I asked.

"I probably got some somewhere," she said. "I gotta dig around. You comin' back tomorrow?"

"Yes. I'll be back."

BIG MA STOOD waiting with a handful of Leroy's baby pictures the next night. Unlike my childhood milestones, which are lovingly held in albums resistant to ultraviolet rays, Leroy's had not been preserved with any degree of care—torn corners, creased edges, melded together by hot summers and clumped food. She told me how Leroy was born as chubby as a baby walrus and that his nickname was Redd due to his ruddy coloring at birth. "He got a cousin a few years younger we call Smurf cuz he blue when he came out." She chuckled, sliding her glasses back up with her index finger.

I came to a photo of Leroy in a hospital bed, hooked up to a pale blue ventilator tube. "Tell me about his accident," I said.

"Oh, that was bad. Real bad. But I was there every day by his bed, praying," Big Ma said. "I never left, every day, all day. I was so tired, but I stayed with him even when his mama went home." Propped up on the large hospital bed, little Leroy looked like a doll, eyes wide and scared.

"How would you describe Leroy's state of mind in those first few weeks?"

"Oh, he was fine, cuz I just prayed and prayed," she said. "I left work that morning when the call came, and I said 'I don't know when I'm comin' back because my grandson been hit by a train.'"

"Did he have counseling in the hospital or when he left?"

"Oh, no, he didn't need that. He did real good, cuz he knew I was with him. The nurses said 'Pat, you go home and get some sleep,' but I said, 'No, no, I'm stayin' right here.' Never left, not even when I got hungry." Pat clearly loved her grandson, but at times it seemed she leaned toward framing his suffering as a tale of her own virtue.

"But losing one's legs is traumatic at any age. It must have been confusing for an eleven-year-old boy," I pressed. "What types of things did he say to you as you sat together all of those days in the hospital?"

"He didn't say nothing. He knew he was gonna be just fine 'cuz I was right there," she said.

Big Ma had done as she was trained to do—guard people. She posted at her grandson's bedside day and night. She wielded her battalion of prayer and besieged the angels to walk with him through his valley of the shadow of death. She trusted God to make everything better, and she had convinced herself that He did. He had to, for she knew no other way. She herself was unequipped to give Leroy the tools he needed most—words to unlock the pain anchoring him to the basement beneath her.

"Oh, I got this here to show you too." Big Ma headed to the entryway closet and pulled out a black leather jacket with slices down its sleeves. "This is the jacket Redd had on when he was hit by the train. I don't know why he won't wear it no more. I cleaned it up real good."

I thanked Big Ma for her time and headed downstairs, now understanding that waiting out Leroy would not get him to open up to me. His ability to express himself remained locked up in chasms and closets that he could not open. He had never been given the language or the permission to be anything other than "just fine." I found him in his usual spot, controller in hand, slaying dragons and conquering demons in worlds he could control, perhaps a symbolic sort of therapy for him.

Leroy wasn't playing a game with me, though. Unbeknownst to me, the media had pursued him before. And he had learned that precious little comes of that.

Akron Beacon Journal reporter Jim Carney arrived to an empty newsroom on the morning of December 7, 2001. A twenty-four-year veteran on the staff, he looked the part. He was sparse in the scalp, silver in the beard, and quick on a tip. Most days he went straight out on assignment, but that Tuesday was the sixtieth anniversary of Pearl Harbor, and Jim was assigned to write a commemorative piece. As he settled in, activity on the police blotter piqued his attention.

CHILD STRUCK BY TRAIN.
ELINOR STREET, OFF OF MARKET.

Jim's oldest son, Will, worked as a railroad engineer in St. Louis and had volunteered on these same local lines as a teenager. Because of Will's passion, trains had long been a centerpiece in the Carney family. Jim was familiar with the city's routes. He had seen photographs of engines that had plowed into abandoned cars stuck on the tracks. Jim shuddered, thinking of how a two-hundred-ton screaming locomotive had surely just obliterated a child.

CHILD RESPONDENT AND
EN ROUTE TO AKRON
CHILDREN'S HOSPITAL.

This child was still alive? Jim slipped his coat back on and dashed to the tracks. By the time he arrived, the emergency crews had departed. The train had lumbered on, its conductor unaware that he had run over a young boy. Other than a few smears of blood, nothing noteworthy could be seen. Jim gathered what limited details existed from the hospital public relations staff and wrote up five hundred words about the hazards of walking along open tracks for the next morning's edition.

At a hospital press conference one week later, Jim spoke with Leroy's mother about the possibility of meeting Leroy and following his recovery for the paper. Katrina said that would be all right, and just like that, Jim and photographer Ed Suba became regular fixtures in Leroy's hospital room during his two-month in-patient stay. They observed Leroy's care and rehabilitative routines. Ed documented Leroy's bandage changes, wound cleanings, and dunks into the whirlpool for "soapy bubbly baths." Leroy shaped suds into cottony eyebrows and beards to make everyone laugh by pretending he was a bubble-horned sea creature. Both Jim and Ed were surprised by how well the boy seemed to be handling the trauma.

"As a father, I felt terrible for Leroy, for what he had been through," Jim said. "But what really got me from the very beginning was his contagious smile. He was just a sweet-faced kid with this humongous tragedy that changed everything for him, yet he didn't seem to be bummed. He joked around. He didn't display any anger. I was really interested in telling his story as he went through the healing and therapy because he seemed to be taking it so well. It seemed like we could all learn from him."

But it was Leroy who needed guidance, particularly after hospital visiting hours, when the train returned. Neither Jim nor Ed was privy to the night terrors that engulfed Leroy in a looping film strip of screeching steel and creaking boxcars, their graffiti flashing in startling detail. The heat from the wheels smelled like burned toast when they sliced through his legs that day, and the same nauseating aroma filled Leroy's nose at night. These flashbacks triggered piercing phantom limb pain, which left Leroy wondering if he was losing his sanity.

The torment typically subsided by morning, and Leroy greeted his care team and visitors with the smile that was beginning to garner him praise. The floor psychologist knew better, though; each time she visited, she charted the same thing in terms of the clinical stages of grief—denial, depression, anger, and acceptance. Leroy was in denial. In his opinion, denial was the only thing keeping him sane—the only antidote to those nights that kept coming for him.

Untrained in trauma recovery, Jim and Ed continued to marvel at Leroy's daytime disposition. His affect confused others at the hospital as well. Clinicians enrolled him in a pediatric trauma study testing whether Inderal, a beta blocker that controls blood pressure and heart rate, could also relieve initial symptoms of post-traumatic stress disorder. Psychologists randomized Leroy into the control group where he did not receive the trial drug. Yet they found Leroy responded to his stress better than many children who had received the trial medication. One psychologist hypothesized that Leroy's stress was instead alleviated by the tenderness of his nursing staff, considered an "unmeasured intervention" by researchers.

"His care team gave him loving attention. They caressed him with healing physical touch. They wallpapered his room with get-well cards from the community. They spoke encouraging words. And we started to think that perhaps these were not expressions Leroy was accustomed to in his family relationships. He responded to his care team in ways that were more positive and more pronounced than children who come from attentive families," Dr. Norman Christopher, director of pediatric emergency medicine, explained. "Leroy skewed our data, but that was a good thing in his case."

The nursing staff nicknamed him King Leroy for the way his smile lured them into his service. He lapped up their positive energy and enjoyed being the center of warmth and attention—a role far different from his usual place as the shy middle child in a family where his mother's preferred communication style was yelling. In his hospital room, Leroy enjoyed video games and a television, amenities he did not have at home. Growing up, the Suttons were so poor that Leroy and Tony imagined watching programs together at night.

"What kind of show you watching?" Leroy would say from the bottom bunk.

"A dog show," Tony would answer. "But I'm getting real tired of these stuck-up poodles. Switching over to some cartoons." They clicked their imaginary remote controls and launched into animated voices for their adventuresome story lines.

Jim and Ed followed Leroy home from the hospital in February 2002, where they were immediately faced with the unkind realities of Leroy's new normal. Though the residents of the Akron area raised about $9,000 for Leroy's accommodations, the front porch still lacked a ramp. Tony and Katrina scrambled to hoist Leroy up five steps to the stoop while the wheelchair remained parked in the muddied snow.

"When we went into the house, I was kinda like 'Whoa,'" Ed remembered. "The place was dilapidated, no furniture, trash on the floor everywhere. If there was anything that was going to set Leroy back, that would cause him to be depressed, it was this. He's home, but he's home to this. To have to deal with this on a daily basis as a normal kid would be hard enough, but to be there after what happened to him, well, I just went 'whew.'"

But Leroy had not learned about the haves and the have-nots yet; to him, this was his home, and it felt good to be back. His mother, brother, and sister camped out beside him on the living room floor, and that's where they stayed for the next two months. Katrina used the donations to buy things that would keep the kids entertained—gaming systems, Pokémon cards, board games, action figures. For a while it felt like a perennial family pajama party, wrapped in a renewed appreciation for one another. When Leroy needed to go to the bathroom or to bed, Katrina slung him onto her back and carried him up the stairs. She spoke gently to Leroy and stroked his head. Tony no longer zipped Leroy into a sleeping bag and flung him down the stairs. Little Keyiera curled up on Leroy's lap when he was in his wheelchair and snuggled beside him when he lay in bed. She begged to help change his bandages, angling the gauze into the gaps in Leroy's tissue to clean them out just right. Big Ma brought heaps of chicken and greens down from Cleveland on the weekends. Ed snapped pictures. Everyone laughed. And little King Leroy continued to feel like royalty.

Jim and Ed followed Leroy through all of his milestones that spring—physical therapy, doctor's appointments, and in April 2002, his return to school. The Akron school district re-assigned Leroy to Case Elementary, a school with a single-floor layout across town from Leroy's neighborhood elementary school. Administrators excitedly began enhancing their disability accommodations with great care once they learned of Leroy's enrollment.

"When I found out he was coming here, I told my mom, 'This is the boy we've been praying for,'" said Tracy Cason, one of Leroy's fifth-grade teachers at Case. "He was on the prayer list at most everyone's church."

The staff measured desks and doorways to ensure Leroy's wheel-chair would fit. They lowered the shelves in his locker and nailed together wooden ramps. Helpers were assigned to carry Leroy's books and open doors. When Leroy finally arrived, the students who had followed his recovery in the news welcomed him as a sort of superhero who had stared down the mighty locomotive.

"The reporter from the Akron paper was here and the photo-grapher with a camera lens that was about fourteen feet long," remembered Mary Anne Maxwell, another of Leroy's teachers. "Leroy had a lot of eyes on him."

"I wondered how being unlucky enough to be hit by a train warranted such fanfare," Leroy remembered. "Then I looked at the date on the wall. It was April 1, 2002. April Fool's Day. My life felt like a big joke." The irony was reinforced by his classmates' stares—innocent ogles that left him feeling like a deflated punch line. So Leroy reached back for the trick he learned in the hospital: he smiled.

"It is hard to fit in with that entourage. But Leroy had that million-dollar Ronald McDonald smile, and it really helped the rest of the kids to relax," Mary Anne remembered.

Two weeks after his return to mainstream life, Leroy underwent additional surgery to increase the range of motion in his left knee. Ed and Jim attended Leroy's weekly physical therapy appointments, where Leroy floundered on his new prosthetic legs. "Are you practicing at home?" Jody Kreitzburg, Leroy's physical therapist, would ask. "You have to be up and walking on these every day." Neither Leroy nor Katrina answered. Jody's bubbly youthfulness clashed with Katrina's austerity. When Leroy faltered, Katrina blamed Jody for letting her son fall forward; Jody believed Katrina was holding him back.

"Leroy didn't want to wear his legs," Katrina said years later, "and I wasn't gonna make him."

At the time, Ed scratched his head, realizing he hadn't photographed Leroy practicing with the legs at home, and how, as the weeks wore on, he hadn't noticed much of Katrina either. Though she had seemed attentive initially, the permanence of her son's condition and the reality of the effort required to manage his care had begun to take a toll on her.

"One photo I took seemed to say it all—Katrina alone in a corner, her forehead pressed into her palm and the weight of the world upon her shoulders," Ed remembered. "She came in to this as a young, struggling mother, and now you throw in multiple weekly doctor appointments, more surgeries, and more expenses. There was always a problem to solve. I got the sense that if she could have avoided it all, she would have."

Katrina didn't nuzzle up to Leroy on the floor anymore. Nor did she carry him up to bed; she said his dead weight threw her shoulder out. By necessity, Leroy grew more independent. He scooted around on his hands, pulled himself up the stairs by the railing, and stood on his left stump to use the sink. By May, Leroy was a no-show at twenty-seven out of forty-six physical therapy appointments—sessions he didn't know he had. Jody documented dozens of voice mails left for Katrina before logging her final note in Leroy's chart: "After no response from patient's family over the last three months, patient is to be discontinued from physical therapy at this time."

This was fine by Katrina; haggling with the transportation service for all those appointments got to be a hassle, she said. Out of a job and out of donations, Katrina was scraping her family through each day on food stamps and Leroy's monthly disability check. She fretted over past-due rent, broken-down cars, and her aching shoulder—all within earshot of Leroy. Tony stopped playing video games beside Leroy; being with his little brother for too long triggered his own flashbacks and induced guilt for letting Leroy out of his sight that day. "I started to think it was my fault that everyone was in such a bad mood," Leroy said.

His smile no longer worked at home, but he kept beaming for the public. Ed continued visiting; there wasn't much to photograph, but he still came just in case. One woman who saw Leroy in the national news flew clear from Texas to visit him. The emergency responders who pulled Leroy from the tracks were honored with a Star of Life award for their prompt, lifesaving action. At the banquet, Leroy was interviewed alongside the response team, who squeezed him tightly and celebrated his recovery. Even the Akron Children's Hospital Miracle Network named Leroy one of their eight "Miracle Kids" for that year's telethon. Television producer Laurie Moline interviewed the family for the hospital's campaign.

"When I pulled up in front of his house at ten or eleven o'clock in the morning, there were twelve or thirteen guys sitting on the porch drinking beer and talking loudly," Laurie remembered. "When I went in, looking for a place to shoot Leroy's interview, it looked like an abandoned house. There was one ripped black couch in the middle of the room. Open trash bags everywhere."

Laurie took Leroy, Tony, and then Katrina out on a side patch of grass and immediately noticed the difference between the resilience levels of the Suttons and other families she interviewed for these awards. "They weren't forthcoming or comfortable sharing their feelings," Laurie remembered. "None of them said much more than a yes or a no." The Suttons lacked the words to describe the noose of helplessness, failure, and guilt they each felt tightening around their necks.

Leroy's hospital care team tried scheduling the family for counseling after the accident. The note from their initial May 2002 visit read: "Patient states that he was 'run over by a train while on my way over to school.' Patient drops his head and refuses to answer any more questions related to this incident."

Katrina never took her sons back. "We could counsel ourselves at home just as well," she said.

Hospital psychologists knew therapy was imperative; young trauma victims learn how to process their ordeals through the messages communicated to them by trusted adults. They rely on those around them to equip them with the correct language to navigate their feelings and accurately interpret facts. Leroy was receiving conflicting messages. Members of the media and event coordinators praised his courage and treated him as an inspirational wonder boy; but at home, Leroy felt beguiled more than beloved. The dissonant tug-of-war between his public trauma narrative and his private truth left him anxiously wondering: Was he a victor or a villain?

In one candid moment, Katrina admitted to Jim that coordinating Leroy's follow-up care wore her down and prevented her from working consistently. "I need help," he quoted her as saying in the paper. "I need assistance from somewhere."

Jim and Ed genuinely cared about Leroy and felt bad for Katrina's stress. But trained to maintain journalistic distance, they did not take steps to try to alleviate the family's hardships. Leroy's story was one of the biggest they had ever worked on, and they focused intently on *what* was happening, earnestly documenting Leroy's daily activities, appointments, and events. Yet they overlooked the critical *why* questions: Why was this family languishing in poverty in the wake of public support? Why was Leroy still scooting around on his hands instead of walking on prosthetic legs? Why wasn't this young trauma victim receiving psychological counseling?

In their defense, Katrina typically confounded their under-standing of what was happening beneath the surface, tossing out explanations that always seemed just plausible enough to satisfy their suspicions. She was just about to get a car, just about to get that new place, just about to get herself a job. Then everything would be better, she would say. If you didn't probe into her cyclical patterns of unemployment, transience, and drug use, your tendency would be to suppress your misgivings and sympathize with her.

"Something felt amiss when I filmed at Leroy's house that day," remembered Laurie, "but it never occurred to me that a parent would not or could not do everything possible to support a child. It wasn't even in my realm of possibility that a mom would not take a kid in Leroy's position to physical therapy or counseling."

Like his mother, Leroy grew skilled at telling people what they wanted to hear, avoiding deeper questions. He guaranteed Jim that he wanted to walk. Just need to get these pressure sores healed up, just need to get through one more surgery. Then everything would be better, he would say. Leroy repeated a collection of upbeat clichés, such as "The past is past. The future is now." And then there was his smile, that bedazzling grin, reassuring people that he was indeed the world's most resilient child.

Leroy cut the ribbon at the Akron Holiday Tree Festival in November 2002. Wheeling in and out of more than two hundred sparkling Christmas trees, he declared that he was thankful for how the loss of his legs had positively transformed his life. This implausible perspective closed out the *Akron Beacon Journal*'s one-year anniversary article on Leroy's accident. The six-page spread, entitled "Comeback Kid," depicted Leroy's recovery and his new life as a double amputee, incorporating eighteen of Ed's three thousand photographs taken throughout the year. *Beacon Journal* editor Jan Leach penned a preface that encouraged readers to "look beyond Leroy Sutton's pain and scars and see the face of courage."

"We wanted to share his triumphant spirit," Leach wrote. On those pages, Leroy publicly declared that his life was better now than before the accident. Readers closed this chapter festive and content that Leroy had successfully overcome this most horrific experience. Ed won the Ohio Understanding Award for his work. The *Beacon Journal* nominated the coverage for a Pulitzer Prize.

And that is where the story of Leroy Sutton's first trauma ended, and his second one began.

THE NIGHTLY WINNING lottery numbers were announced just after *Wheel of Fortune*, and Big Ma watched with her yellowed, taped-up copy of *The Original Lucky Three Wise Men Dream Book* on the coffee table. This eighty-page booklet purported to decode numerology and predict lottery combinations based on one's "vibrations of life," such as zodiac signs, seasons, and dreams.

Big Ma placed great importance on dreams. She said the Hebrews and Egyptians were warned of future peril in biblical visions. So any time Big Ma saw a celebration, a death, or an old friend in her sleep, she'd play the corresponding Pick 3 at the Quick & Easy convenience store at the top of her street. And anytime Leroy dreamed about the train, the two of them hoped that 15-45-63 was going to win them both some better living.

Though they never spoke directly of his accident, or the incidents that ultimately delivered him to her, Leroy appreciated the consistency of Big Ma's company. He sat beside her each night for dinner and then some television. She tried to get him to sleep in the upstairs bedroom next to hers, but Leroy insisted on the basement. "He calls it his dungeon," she said. The dungeon's only visitor was Dartanyon.

"You gonna be talking to him too?" Big Ma asked me.

"Yes, I have spent some time with Dartanyon already," I answered. "How well do you know him?"

"I love that child like I birthed him myself! He come around here with his silly jokes, but he's always polite. He don't curse, and there's no sag in his pants." She said Dartanyon often spent the weekend playing video games with Leroy and making up songs on an old guitar. "They have a good time watching movies, talking about girls and whatever and stuff." One time, after Big Ma's heart medication caused her hair to fall out in clumps, Dartanyon shaved her head. "He did a real nice job," she said. "If it happens again, I won't let anyone shave it but him. Got myself a blind barber."

Big Ma would fry up chicken and pork chops for the boys. She watched Dartanyon clean his plate before moving on to her stash of chips, ice cream, and juice. She was on a tight budget, but she knew Dartanyon didn't have a mother to keep him full, so she didn't mind. Dartanyon often slept on the couch in the basement, or sometimes on the floor beside Leroy's bed. On Monday mornings, Leroy's driver would let Dartanyon hitch a ride to school on the wheelchair bus.

"Dartanyon hugs me when he leaves, so I know he appreciates coming," Big Ma said. "He and Leroy are like brothers."

"How did Leroy come to live with you?" I asked.

Big Ma shook her head and lowered her voice. "His mother wasn't happy with me, I'll tell you that."

RIGHT AROUND THE time of the Akron Holiday Tree Festival in November 2002, Katrina picked up again, heading to Hudson, Ohio, an affluent community twenty minutes north of Akron. It marked Leroy's tenth move in his twelve years, and each one had come without warning. "Get your stuff!" Katrina would yell. "We headed somewhere better."

Hudson was the first place that actually looked like somewhere better. The hills that rolled through this whimsical town were dotted with wraparound porches and backyard gazebos, people rode bikes as a form of exercise rather than transportation, and the town square featured yoga, farmer's markets, poetry readings, and wine tastings. What stood out most to Leroy about Hudson was its color. His previous neighborhoods were washed out in a sooty gray. Hudson was *green*, burgeoning with lush grass, flowering shrubbery, and wise old elm trees. Leroy reveled in the surrounding nature, spotting deer and rabbits and even a coyote. Life grew in every nook of this small town, and the Suttons dared to wonder if perhaps they could regain their vibrancy here too.

At first, things were working out nicely for the family. Katrina received a coveted Section 8 housing voucher in Hudson; her subsidized monthly rent totaled $27. Their dwelling resembled more of a shanty than a house, aging off the road behind a larger, newer home. But for them, the place's most desirable feature was its distance from the clattering trains that thundered through their old Akron neighborhoods and battered their souls like storms.

"I chose Hudson because we didn't have to hear the trains, the ambulances, the fire trucks. We didn't have to be in the hood anymore," Katrina said. "In Akron, every time we'd hear a siren or a train whistle, it would take us right back to the accident."

Katrina began a job in home health care. Tony, now age fifteen, joined Hudson High School's basketball team. And Leroy's new middle school warmly welcomed the inspiring young man they had all read about in the newspapers. But Hudson's starry country nights could only satiate Katrina and Tony for so long before they were lured back to what they knew best—hustling. Tony soon realized that rich white suburbanites liked their street drugs just as much as city folk. "The people in Hudson were just smarter about it," he said. "They partied hard but still went to work and school the next day."

By the spring of 2003, Tony was making weekly runs up to Cleveland to pick up marijuana supplies. "My uncle had a super deal where we could get weed from California for $250 a pound," Tony remembered. "Because kids in Hudson had so much money, I could flip that for $1,600. That's a sick come-up."

Tony shared his spoils with Katrina so she could pay the electricity and food bills—or at least that's what he thought she was doing with the money, until the electric company sent shutoff notices.

"Here she was flipping my money and Leroy's disability checks with other dealers on the side," Tony remembered. "She always did it with grimy dudes, though, who would take off with her money. She always trusted the wrong people."

Tony started paying some of the bills himself, leading to heated arguments with his mother. Katrina slipped into avoidance, sometimes disappearing for days at a time. With Tony splitting time between Hudson and Cleveland, twelve-year-old Leroy was often left alone to care for five-year-old Keyiera. He braided her hair, fixed her breakfast, and if Keyiera's school bus came late, he missed his own in order to see his sister off. School records show Leroy absent for fourteen days in the spring of 2003. And though he fell substantially behind in Hudson's rigorous curriculum, his teachers gave him unending second chances.

"He definitely had his own set of rules and learned to use them to his advantage early on," said Shawn Gaskins, Leroy's science teacher. "He was a smart kid, but he used his smile to get by rather than his brain. He became the class clown, which was strange. We expected someone in Leroy's position to be the opposite."

The "class clown" title gave Leroy an identity other than that of the "kid with no legs," and his classmates' laughter compensated for the attention he lacked at home. But during the summer months, isolated from his audience of peers, Leroy grew sullen. His mother was often unreachable. Tony was out dealing all day. The get-well cards and fund-raisers had long ceased. His story no longer drew media attention. And Leroy discovered something worse than being an amputee—being forgotten.

Leroy wondered why everyone had left him, and each time he looked down at his lower half, he settled on the same conclusion: he deserved abandonment. His first trauma had torn off his legs; this one tore out his heart. Desperate for acceptance, Leroy started bagging weed for his brother that summer. Desperate to dull his heartache, he began smoking it.

"We had the biggest parties ever, like several times a week," Tony said. "So many girls, cases of liquor, pot, raves. And Leroy was the drunkest dude there."

Leroy tried it all—mushrooms, ecstasy, and every last strand and strength of weed. Pineapple Express, Starburst, Banana Kush, and perhaps most fittingly, Trainwreck. He sold his own prescription pain pills, since being drunk and baked numbed his phantom limb pain better than oxycodone anyway. Even when the summer debauchery wound down, Leroy continued using heavily. As he entered the seventh grade, he estimates that he attended school hungover and high 75 percent of the time.

Hudson High school was ranked in the top 4 percent of schools in the country in 2003, with an astounding 98 percent college placement rate; the other 2 percent entered the military forces. Hudson specialized in high achievers. No one slipped through the cracks in this system, and so when Leroy finished his fall quarter with two Ds and two Fs, with comments like "Leroy unable to finish test because he fell asleep" on the tops of his papers, red flags shot up. Furthermore, the school district had paid for an onsite physical therapist to get Leroy walking, but Leroy rarely showed up to his sessions, and when he did, it was without his prosthetic legs. Administrators grew impatient with Katrina's failure to return calls and attend meetings. In a community of involved parents, this type of noncompliance was incomprehensible. When Hudson's administration finally cornered Katrina in late October, they informed her that if Leroy did not bring his prosthetics to school, they would pursue neglect charges against her.

Leroy arrived on time the next day with tears instead of legs. "I'm supposed to get all of my stuff," he said to Mr. Gaskins. "We're moving this morning." This time he had no smile to mask his disappointment.

"Where are you moving?" Mr. Gaskins asked. He peered out the window at the waiting van.

"My mom didn't say. Just said it was somewhere better." Leroy lowered his head and wheeled out the door.

"His mother literally plucked him out of a first-rate school, out of an environment that was committed to helping him," Mr. Gaskins remembered. "He had this look on his face like he knew he had lost a great opportunity. He was very upset. I'll never forget it as long as I live."

The Suttons returned to Akron, where Leroy continued smoking marijuana and drinking while attending Litchfield Middle School. His work was undeserving, but teachers handed him just enough Ds to pass him along. Tony built up his weed clientele again, while Katrina flipped Leroy's disability checks with neighborhood dealers. Tony grew hot that his mother wouldn't invest her money with him yet always wanted a cut of his profits. Leroy hid in his room, trying to block out all of the yelling. One day, Katrina hit Tony in the face with a milk crate during an altercation. He stormed out, saying he was never coming back.

"You're giving up on me too?" Leroy called out from the porch. "I thought you were my hero, but you're just as cowardly as everyone else!"

"You never give me no props for saving your life anyway!" Tony screamed back. "Everyone acts like you the hero, like you saved yourself. All you did was get hit by a train! I'm done, man." Tony threw his hands in the air and kept walking. Nine years would pass before Leroy saw his brother again.

Katrina shuffled Leroy and Keyiera around Akron four more times between 2004 and 2007, always headed "somewhere better." They crashed on couches and floors, and as they dragged their black trash bags of worn-out stuff from one run-down place to another, Leroy's only constant was the belief that this vagabond lifestyle was his fault. And no matter how many times they moved, he couldn't escape the reminders of his accident. Physical problems plagued him, and the environmental and emotional stressors in his life added to his sense of defeat. His wheelchair had irreparably broken down, and he forced himself onto prosthetics that he remained unfit to use. He missed weeks of school due to the resulting skin ulcers and infections between his upper thigh and groin area. The Akron Children's Hospital emergency department records noted pain, swelling, and tissue breakdown four times between 2004 and 2006. In February 2007, Leroy underwent a stump revision surgery to shave his right femur, which was protruding out of his deteriorating skin.

"A lot of times that revision is avoidable with good therapy and good follow-up at home," said Dr. Crow, Leroy's pediatric surgeon. "But my impression was that home was not optimal for him."

Leroy would smile and assure his doctor that everything was good, and he did the same with Jim and Ed when they pursued a follow-up story in 2005. Their article highlighted how Leroy "learned to deal with the unimaginable, kept smiling, and held on to his faith," and Leroy did not object. He knew his truth was not fit for print. The truth was that in lieu of physical therapy, he smoked a blunt each morning to combat the pain of his prosthetic legs gouging through his skin. The truth was that when the buzz wore off around third period, it was impossible to make it down the school hallway without pain shooting through his lower back. That pain then triggered a stress response that aggravated his phantom limb pain, and Leroy stabbed himself with pens and etched words like PAIN and NO LOVE and DEATH into his forearms with safety pins to divert his focus from the pangs. The truth was that he lit the hair on his arms on fire, bit holes through his skin, and sliced his wrists with six-inch blades. The truth was that he wore long sleeves to school to cover these bloodied pleas for help, but at home he left his wounds exposed, inviting his mother to notice his pain. She did.

"She came at me swinging with whatever she had in her hands," Leroy remembered. "I got hit with extension cords, brooms, wooden spoons, switches, you name it." But Katrina's attempts to discipline Leroy missed the mark. She confiscated Leroy's knife collection but never cut to the underlying issues. If his mother couldn't handle his truth, Leroy knew he could never entrust it to anyone else either.

His final cry for help came in the fall of 2007 at Firestone High School, where Leroy sprayed aerosol deodorant into the choir practice room and ignited it with a lighter. No damage resulted, but Firestone expelled him for attempted arson. Leroy barreled home to tell his mother, certain she would storm the school in his defense.

"I guess you gonna have to find something else to do before you end up doing nothing with your life," Katrina told him flatly. The truth was that feeling like nothing was something Leroy was already used to.

Big Ma caught wind of her grandson's expulsion through one of Firestone's security officers. The two had worked together up in Cleveland back in the day. As soon as Big Ma got the call, she drove down to collect her grandson.

"I want you to finish school," she told him. "You can do that if you come stay with me." Katrina yelled at Big Ma for undermining her; Big Ma bellowed back about Katrina blowing through money. From an adjacent room, Uncle Vonn hollered for Redd not to be taking the video games if he be leavin'. Leroy was done with the yelling, done with people fighting for everything but him. Akron's wonder boy tossed some clothes in a plastic bag and followed Big Ma unceremoniously out of town.

THE LOSSES NEVER leave. The hurt never ceases. But life persists.

My presence returned Leroy to places and times he had worked desperately to forget. The whir of the camera, the scribbles in notepads, the clichéd sound bites. Once he moved into Big Ma's house, Leroy gave up the alcohol and the weed. He put down the safety pins and the lighters. He was ready to forgo the public charade as well. He had learned that letting people tell stories about him would not ease his plight. He did not want to be the focus of my job. He did not want to be my protagonist. He wanted to suffer the punishment of his folly alone, and he had spent a year in coveted anonymity before I, the media, found him once again.

But Leroy did not tell me any of that, because no parent, no therapist, no teacher, no journalist, had taught him the language of suffering. Instead he had stacked up stones to keep himself safe, each stone a truth he had gleaned from his experiences: I am unlovable. I am unworthy. I am invisible. He used these stones to build a wall of protection—a wall that also served as his prison.

And although Leroy acted as though he wanted to be left alone, he had not yet said no to filming with me. As I sat on the floor in Leroy's dungeon, I thought of how the great poet Maya Angelou famously said that there is no greater agony than bearing an untold story inside of you. I thought of Leroy's hospital photos and the tattered black leather relic in the closet. I stopped caring about doing a story and started caring about the broken boy before me. I thought back on Robinson's audacious first words to me and wondered if perhaps I could be part of the solution to this boy's pain, rather than an additional cause. With that, I broke the silence.

"Leroy, I want to thank you for allowing me to hang out with you these last few nights," I started gently. "I can tell these visits have not been comfortable for you, so I will not be back tomorrow." Leroy paused his game but continued staring at the television.

"Deep inside of you, I think you have a lot to say," I said. I told him how I admired his caution in choosing with whom to share it, that he was wise to shield his heart. "If you decide to talk to me, know that it's your story to tell. I am just here to help you do it in the most meaningful way possible," I explained. "And if you don't want to be on TV, but you do want a friend, I am even more interested in that."

Leroy resumed his game. I trudged up the stairs and sank into the couch with Pat Sajak and Pat Sutton for one last round of *Wheel of Fortune*, wishing I could buy Big Ma an *e* for empathy. I wanted to tell her that no child—no human being—gets hit by a train and emerges unscathed. But I took a deep breath instead, reminding myself that Big Ma likely knew as much, otherwise she wouldn't have earned the name Big Ma. She just didn't know what to do about it. So she showed her love by doing what she knew best—standing guard.

As Vanna White doled out prizes, Leroy rounded the corner. "Hey. I got a new game today," he said to me sternly, looking right at me for the first time. "You wanna see it?"

I nodded slowly, understanding the deeper significance of his invitation. As Socrates wrote, sometimes you put walls up not to keep people out, but to see who cares enough to break them down. I had proven enough to get in. I didn't know just how much I was in for.

CHAPTER 6

DESTINED FOR GREATNESS

Every coach at Lincoln-West can recall the moment he realized Dartanyon Crockett just might be the real deal. For Kyro Taylor, the Wolverine football coach, the moment came at the start of the 2006 school year, when a new student sauntered past his open door and out of view. A few seconds later, the same kid arched backward, poking his head through the door. "Uh, what sport do you coach?" he asked.

Taylor quickly sized up the boy's athletic build. "Son, whatever you want to play, I'll coach it," he answered. Taylor had the chiseled charm of Deion Sanders, the heart of Mother Teresa, and a coaching record of lopsided losses. He salivated, thinking about handing the ball to this truck of a boy and running him up the middle all day long. Taylor invited him to practice that afternoon, but the kid seemed uncertain, shifting in his stance.

"You ever play football?" Taylor asked.

"No," he answered.

"What's your name?"

"Dartanyon." Though his answers were short, Taylor noticed that the moments between them were prolonged by the unusual hitch in Dartanyon's stare.

"Well, Dartanyon, we'd love to have you," he said. "The bus heads over to the practice field at three."

Dartanyon lined up for the bus that afternoon, and when they reached the field, Taylor tossed him a football from about fifteen yards away. "Glad you came, man," he said. The pass deflected squarely off Dartanyon's face mask and onto the ground.

"Don't worry about it," Taylor called out. "Here's another one." He lofted a perfect spiral toward Dartanyon's numbers. This one bounced off his shoulder pads and through his arms, as though Dartanyon had never seen it coming. Yes, he'd make him a running back, Taylor thought.

As the team gathered to stretch, Dartanyon quietly revealed his secret. "I am legally blind," he told Taylor, "but I can still play football."

"You ever play before?" Taylor asked.

"No," Dartanyon answered.

Taylor puzzled over this predicament, if only for a moment, before walking Dartanyon over to the linemen. The Wolverines had been winless the previous season; sight or no sight, Taylor couldn't afford to leave a strapping body like Dartanyon's on the sideline. Instead, he'd turn him into a nose tackle—the defensive lineman directly across from the center. Never mind that nose tackles are usually the largest players on defense, clogging the middle of the line to stifle the offensive running game and to allow the other defensive players to make plays. Dartanyon was at least three inches shorter and seventy-five pounds lighter than the other lineman in his conference, but Taylor figured that at nose tackle, Dartanyon would know exactly where the ball was at the start of a down and could listen for the snap. And what the boy lacked in girth, Taylor hoped he'd make up for in agility and quickness.

Taylor's instincts proved correct. Dartanyon easily darted around behemoth opposing centers and wreaked havoc in their backfield. He started every game that season, and the Wolverines miraculously pulled out four wins. And when they were far enough down in their losses, Taylor had his quarterback hand off the ball to Dartanyon, who rumbled and tumbled down the field for a bit of fun.

"Looking back, I am amazed he played football," Taylor said. "He played for two years, and each year, I was more in awe of the talents he had. How do you play football when you can hardly see? At that point, I didn't know he was hardly eating either."

After Dartanyon's first football season, Taylor invited him to train with the school's powerlifting team, which many Lincoln football players used as their off-season lifting program. Dartanyon quickly fell in love with the sport, finding weights to be a great equalizer. One hundred pounds weighs one hundred pounds for the visually impaired and the sighted alike. Dartanyon didn't have to be the "blind lifter." He could simply be the strongest, with no asterisk.

The sport of powerlifting is comprised of three events: squat, bench press, and deadlift. Athletes are allotted three attempts in each category, strategically increasing their weights based on who is ahead of them. Individual winners are awarded in each event, as well as an overall winner for the combined highest totals for all three categories. Dartanyon, like most kids who are new to the sport, initially thought powerlifting involved throwing around as much weight as he possibly could. He was unfamiliar with nuanced techniques and competition strategies, as well as the mental aspects of powerlifting. More important than strength is patience, because progress is incremental. Taylor told him that good lifters see increases of five pounds or maybe ten pounds in a three- to four-week span. Dartanyon, however, was an anomaly, known to jump fifty pounds in a week.

"Dartanyon was definitely unique when it came to the word *progression*," Taylor remembered. "He seemed to accomplish what he wanted, when he wanted it."

Mark Julius, Lincoln's track coach, was the second coach after Robinson to drag Dartanyon out of the weight room. "Look, Muscles, as strong and explosive as you are, you should be sprinting," Julius told him. Though Dartanyon was already wrestling and powerlifting, he joined the indoor track team for his in-between moments. And while three-sport athletes are not uncommon in high school, no sane person takes on three sports in the same season.

"Had I told him he should be running marathons, he probably would have said okay to that too," Julius said.

Dartanyon was instantly Julius's top sprinter—at times too fast for his own relay teams. As he awaited the handoff, Dartanyon would burst forward on his "go" command. And yet often, his oncoming teammate could not catch him in time to pass the baton before Dartanyon reached the end of the exchange zone. If Julius started Dartanyon off the blocks, he would overrun his hand-off to the second leg. He was disqualified from as many relays as he finished. But Julius never troubled himself over winning and losing. His philosophy was that if his kids were running laps, they weren't running the streets.

Dartanyon's crash course in high school sports concluded at the Senate Conference powerlifting championships in the late spring of 2007, where he deadlifted five hundred pounds—a 66 percent increase from the three hundred pounds he'd lifted at the state competition just a few weeks earlier.

Coaches marveled, asking Taylor how this kid was lifting so much as a sophomore. Taylor shrugged and forced a smile. He knew that when you're already carrying around the weight of the world, piling on a few more pounds hardly makes a difference.

DARTANYON LOST NOT only his mother at that funeral but all of his brothers and sisters as well. As the burial luncheon wound down, a group of reluctant fathers circled around Juanita's children and—as if at an awkward middle school dance—tried to figure out who should go with whom. Dionna, then twenty-five years old, had a one-bedroom apartment and a baby girl of her own, so she took her two teenage siblings, Darlene and Darnell, to crowd in with her. Dominique, age ten, was pretty sure that Irquois Crockett was his biological father because his mama always threatened to hand him over when he misbehaved, and so the boy, in an act of surrender, walked over to Irquois. Then Irquois and a man named Curtis, who Juanita had gone with on and off, both declared the rights to Davielle. Davielle looked on, wondering why either of them had waited nine years to take notice of him. As their squabbling escalated, Davielle looked at Curtis, then looked at his brother, standing sunken next to Irquois, and settled it himself.

"I'll just go with him," Davielle said, pointing at Dominique. "There's really no winning either way, so we might as well stick together." Irquois hotfooted the boys to the car and sped away. Curtis walked out clutching new baby Danielle instead. No one disputed Arthur taking Dartanyon. Despite Arthur's issues, he was considered the most reliable father of the bunch by virtue of having shown up every other weekend to see his boy. Still, minding a child every day was a challenge Arthur had already failed.

In 1978, when Arthur's oldest son, Lil Arty, was six months old, the child's mother left him in Arthur's care and never returned. Arthur carried the boy up to the church, where his grandfather was the pastor at the time. "I asked him to pray over Lil Arty because I knew he was going to have a hard life," Arthur said.

At the time, Arthur worked as a dairy manager at the Pick-N-Pay grocery store during the day while his own mother watched Lil Arty. But Mr. Life of the Party suited him better than Mr. Mom. His love for fast living and fast women led him to father two more children around town. The ensuing stress caused him to escape deeper into nightlife. Arthur routinely missed work, and what little remained in his paychecks went to feeding his three children.

"I was an iffy employee at best," he remembered. "Finally I grew sick and tired of being sick and tired." In 1984 Arthur, then thirty-two years old, saw a commercial for the US Navy and enlisted.

He packed up six-year-old Lil Arty and drove west, where the San Diego sea air felt like it could wash his slate clean. Left to his own, he had never been one to tend to fine details, but in the navy, with multiple levels of oversight, he was forced into the kind of success that results from seeing a task through. And his commanders treated him with a respect he'd never found stocking milk jugs and battling baby mamas.

Arthur might have made a career out of the navy had he not been introduced to methamphetamine, also known as crystal meth. He quickly became hooked, and it wasn't long before he went from second in command of his line to meth addict. The navy sent Arthur to rehab for three months. Though he emerged clean and determined to regain the respect of the uniform, he could not cope with graveyard shifts and the pressures of parenting. Arthur began drinking heavily, trading one vice for another. Lil Arty, ten years old by then, bore the brunt of his father's rage. "I started whupping him hard like my father used to whup me," Arthur said. "I couldn't control my anger." Arthur drove his son to the police station and requested they put the boy into foster care. Lil Arty wailed and hung onto his father's leg, pleading with him not to leave, but Arthur saw no other choice. "I don't want to hurt you any more," he told his son. "You will be safer this way."

Arthur was honorably discharged from the navy one year later, in 1990. He left Lil Arty in foster care and hopped a Greyhound bus back to Cleveland, wondering how many times a man had to start over before he could finish right.

Not much had changed in Cleveland, although after a few months back home, Arthur did make two life-altering discoveries at the corner Laundromat: Juanita Crockett looked awfully fine folding clothes, and outside in the parking lot, crack cocaine sold for a lot less than crystal meth. All Arthur had to show for the years that followed was a disabling drug addiction and a blind son.

Now, as Arthur drove off from Juanita's funeral with eight-year-old Dartanyon sitting heartsick beside him, he dug his nails deep into the vinyl steering wheel and prayed a different sort of prayer than the one he prayed for Lil Arty.

"This time, I prayed 'Lord, don't let me screw this one up,'" Arthur remembered. "Help me do the best I can." Fraught with regret over his previous parenting failures, Arthur knew raising Dartanyon on his own was going to require a holy intervention, for they were both in need of some saving.

Arthur and Dartanyon settled into the top half of a two-family home on Kinsman Avenue, situated in an area of Cleveland's east side known as Mount Pleasant. Arthur had spent a period of his own youth in this neighborhood, at a time when Kinsman was lined with regal homes and manicured yards. But by the 1990s, Mount Pleasant had devolved into a crime-ridden urban wasteland. Crack was readily available on just about every corner, and as Arthur faced Dartanyon's earnest brown eyes each day, he leaned on that one feeble prayer: *Don't let me mess this one up.*

Arthur handled his business for their first year on Kinsman, walking the straight line of a full-time parent. He earned decent money as a server at the Beachmont Country Club and paid the rent. Dartanyon waited alone in the apartment after school, playing video games and watching cartoons until his father returned around ten o'clock with a meal for him. Together they watched Bruce Lee and Jackie Chan movies. Arthur taught him to play Connect Four and chess. He enjoyed his son's inquisitive nature and grew to understand Dartanyon's challenges. Previously, Arthur had heard Juanita use the term *visually impaired* in passing, and he had detected a twitch in Dartanyon's eyes, but beyond that he had given it little thought. Now that they were together every day, he noticed Dartanyon walking into walls as he turned corners and sitting up close to the television.

"Sometimes I wanted to grab him and help him, but I didn't, because the world is not like that," Arthur remembered. "When I saw him fumbling around or trying to find something I see right there, I had to sit there and wait. Might seem like a cruel lesson to some people, but he had to learn that the world don't help you. I never let him feel sorry for himself."

But eventually Arthur began to pity his own single-parent plight. As the late movie nights caught up with Dartanyon, his middle school teachers sent homework plans to address his poor grades and contacted Arthur for parent meetings. Only functionally literate himself, Arthur buckled under the pressure. Though he had quit seeking out crack, it never quit looking for him.

"It hit me that I got this little kid now. What am I supposed to do with this little kid?" Arthur said. "So I go do the coward thing and relapse again. Sometimes I would be cool. Most of the time I wasn't."

Dartanyon noticed changes in his father, like how he stopped coming home every night, giving Dartanyon no advance warning as to when he'd be going to bed hungry. When Arthur did return, it was usually with a can of Colt 45 in his hand. Eventually he told Dartanyon that he'd lost his job. He said that he and his boss didn't agree on some things, but he was really sorry and would find another job soon. Dartanyon sympathized with his father, because he loved him. He was too young to recognize the patterns of an addict.

One day Arthur told Dartanyon to get his things together; they were moving into the downstairs first-floor apartment with Arthur's brother, Marcus, so he could help them out with rent. Marcus made Dartanyon skittish. He was an alcoholic in a backward sort of way. When he staggered around drunk, he danced and sang and told Dartanyon jokes. But when Marcus sobered up, he grew inexplicably mean, and once they were living to-gether, Dartanyon became a preferred target. If Dartanyon used a spoon, Marcus threw it away in disgust. One morning Dartanyon woke up ill and tried to call his sister for help; Marcus ripped the phone out of the wall, berating him for using a service for which he was not paying. Another time, Marcus swung at Dartanyon for "looking at him with those funny eyes." Arthur blocked the punch but promptly excused it.

"Marcus did not like Dartanyon," Arthur admitted. "I think he thought Dar put a gap between me and him getting high together."

Dartanyon wished he had that sort of influence, but he hardly grasped what was happening himself. All he knew for certain was that he missed how his mother's hands smelled like shea butter when she held him after a day of braiding hair. He missed her famous soul spaghetti and the way she'd bring home a birthday cake from the grocery store even when no one was having a birthday. "Some days you gotta make your own fun," she would say. He missed clean clothes and talking smack with his brothers. And as he crawled into the bed he shared with Arthur each night, twelve-year-old Dartanyon whispered his own scared prayer: *Mommy, please come back.*

Most kids in Dartanyon's class were from single-parent homes, but that parent was never the father. None of his friends understood the pain of losing a mother. Dartanyon cried in the bathroom when it came time to make Mother's Day crafts, and he tackled classmates for making "Yo Mama" jokes.

"Even though it wasn't personal, it made me feel like I was the only kid without a mom," Dartanyon remembered. "Kids already teased me for my eyes, and this was just another thing that made me feel different from everyone else." The school counselor tried to get Dartanyon to open up and also tried to involve Arthur. But Dartanyon remained tight-lipped, and tracking down Arthur was like trying to catch a wave between your hands.

"When I got home from school, my dad was either at a job or drinking somewhere with Marcus," Dartanyon said. "I'd go to the corner store to get food on credit or go to sleep without eating." He learned to stretch kitchen staples to new lengths. Potato chip sandwiches with hot sauce. Fried bologna with mayonnaise. And steam-ironed grilled cheese when the gas bill was past due. "As long as the electricity was still on, I could put the sandwich in a paper bag, run the clothes iron over it, and melt the cheese," he said. "Tasted pretty good."

And so it was always a treat when Arthur said they could get take-out from Captain Mike's Shrimp Boat restaurant at the top of the street. Shrimp Boat served up authentic New Orleans shrimp, gumbo, scampi, and lobsters, although Dartanyon's order never changed—a jumbo catfish sandwich for his dad and a sausage po' boy topped with coleslaw for himself.

Father and son would split up to fetch dinner—Arthur went down to the corner store to get his beer while Dartanyon picked up the food. One of those outings, when Dartanyon was thirteen years old, would take his life in a new direction. He started back with the sandwiches around ten o'clock on a brisk fall night. Halfway home, he heard a voice come up from behind, on his left. "Hey, you got a lighter?"

As Dartanyon turned to answer, a second man blindsided him from the right, bashing him with a blunt object—one blow to the side of Dartanyon's skull, followed by another to the jaw. Dartanyon slumped to the pavement. He held on to just enough consciousness to realize that he had been struck by the back handle of a revolver, and now the barrel jabbed cold and deep into his temple. "Empty your pockets," the man growled, leaning over Dartanyon's chest. His cheap gold chain swung back and forth over the top of Dartanyon's nose. "And don't move, or I'll kill you."

"I don't have anything," Dartanyon moaned. "This bag of food is all I got."

The gunman patted down Dartanyon's pockets before ripping the sack out of his hands. Dartanyon took a breath of air, braced for it to be his last, and waited for the sound of the trigger to blow him away. Disoriented, he lay on the pavement, unable to see that the two thugs had slipped back into the shadows.

Arthur was waiting with a half-finished beer in his hands when Dartanyon finally staggered through the back door, hand spread across his face. "What took you so—," Arthur started in on him, only he didn't need to finish the question to know the answer. As blood splattered across the floor Arthur realized his boy had been jumped. He bolted out the door toward Shrimp Boat like a vigilante, yelling "Who just beat up my son? I'm gonna kill you!" No one owned up, and Arthur quickly ceded the search, winded after a few houses.

Arthur taped up the gash on his son's forehead and held a bag of ice on his lip. After Dartanyon fell asleep, Arthur knelt beside him and traced around the wounds with his finger. "Dar, nobody's gonna beat you up like that ever again," he quietly promised.

The next night, Arthur led Dartanyon into the backyard. "I'm gonna teach you how to fight so you can defend yourself," Arthur said. "No more walking like a target, like you don't have a good sense about you." Arthur had studied tae kwon do at the Cleveland Academy of Self-Defense in his early twenties. "My best friend and I were evenly matched, and it would take fifteen minutes or more for one of us to win," Arthur remembered. "So we said, 'Let's try this with our eyes closed. It'll be over faster.'" The twosome agreed on a set of rules, wrapped bandanas around their eyes, and branded it the "blind technique."

Arthur thought this would be a perfect training method for someone with low vision. He raised Dartanyon's fists to the ready position and pressed their wrists together. Arthur slowly slid his arms up and down, side to side, guiding Dartanyon's movement. "Keep contact and follow motion," Arthur explained. He wanted Dartanyon to anticipate his opponents' movement and hone his reflexes. "Feel how the person moves by how their hand is going

and then you go the opposite way," he instructed. Dartanyon's un-
usually long arms flailed wildly as he worked to land his punches.

Dartanyon wasn't keen on fighting at first. The assault had
shaken him deeply, and the bandages across his face reminded him
of all there was to fear. He stayed in the house every day for a week,
until Arthur returned home late at night and summoned him to
the backyard to spar. Arthur may not have known how to check
Dartanyon's homework or read him books before bed, but he could
teach him how to withstand the streets.

"Anyone who tells you they've never been beat up is a liar,"
Arthur told his swollen and scared son. "You can't learn to fight
until you've been beat up. Getting jumped is what gives you heart,
cuz you say 'That ain't gonna happen to me again.'"

With Arthur's guidance, Dartanyon's competitive spirit began to
emerge, and a fighter was born under the yellow moon. He learned
to feel his way through a duel, developing trustworthy instincts. He
settled into a sense of timing and soon outmaneuvered his old man
with ease. Arthur was elated by his son's quick progress. Little did
he know that his "blind technique" was a real thing, and because
of it, Dartanyon would one day see the world.

"After Dartanyon got a little confidence under his belt, his
whole demeanor changed," Arthur remembered. "He walked with
a swagger. I knew he would never be jumped like that again."

Two years passed before anyone tried.

Dartanyon, then fifteen years old, was walking home from
school in broad daylight when another teen came into his focus,
mumbling and gesturing like he wanted to fight.

"Run it," the thug ordered. Dartanyon knew what that meant:
empty your pockets, hand over your money, your phone, all that
you have. Dartanyon refused. The attacker pulled a six-inch knife
and plunged it toward Dartanyon. Dartanyon lurched backward,
causing the attacker to miss his abdomen but slash his forearm
instead. The attacker pulled back, preparing to take another stab;

as he did, Dartanyon landed a punishing right hook to the jaw, leveling the thug and sending the knife into the grass. Dartanyon straddled him and worked him over like a punching bag.

He left his victim writhing on the ground, only then noticing how deep his own flesh wound ran. The blood flowed steadily. He hurried home to wrap it in towels, applying hours of pressure until the bleeding ceased. He needed stitches, but he knew that even if he could find his father, Arthur would be too drunk or high to drive him to the hospital.

Things had turned from bad to worse when the new second-floor tenants moved in the previous year. They were crack dealers, and Arthur became their most faithful customer. When employed, Arthur went straight upstairs after work in search of his next hit. When he was between jobs—the polite way of saying he had been fired again—he would be out with his cronies as soon as the previous night's hangover wore off. Some weeks Dartanyon saw his father's dope boys more than his father. When Arthur was paid up, his runners watched out for Dartanyon, floating him a few bucks for food. When Arthur fell behind on his tab, Dartanyon fielded the angry calls from dealers or woke up to find that his video game console had been confiscated as collateral. The real trouble came in the car, though, where Arthur often drove under the influence as Dartanyon rode resigned beside him. "He'd be weaving back and forth, but I wasn't really afraid," Dartanyon remembered. "I couldn't imagine death being any worse than what I was living."

Dartanyon begged his father to stop drinking, even pouring salt in his beer. Arthur chastised him for meddling, raving a bunch of nonsense over and over as he always did when drunk or high. "Remember, my job is to make you into a better man than me," Arthur slurred. Dartanyon didn't think that sounded like a mighty aspiration, yet he clung to even this most vague attempt at parenting, choosing high roads when he saw them. When his father passed out in the chair, Dartanyon covered him with a blanket. When he came to, Dartanyon forced a few scraps of food into him before heading to school. Arthur was the only parent Dartanyon had left; he refused to lose his father too.

The only time Dartanyon could count on Arthur being sober was on Sunday mornings, when Uncle Famous picked them up in the Tried Stone Church bus. "Hello there, I'm Famous," Uncle Famous would introduce himself, pleased with his unique moniker.

"What are you famous for?" people would ask.

"Nothing yet, but God's got plans for me!" he would answer with a twinkle in his eye.

Regardless of what condition Arthur was in, he ironed his tailored two-piece black suit on Wednesday for church on Sunday, and made sure Dartanyon did the same. Drugs and alcohol may have stripped away Arthur's dignity, but they did not cloud his respect for the Lord.

"Just trust in God for everything, and He'll handle it," Arthur preached to his son as they boarded the ramshackle white bus.

"God hasn't been handling things for a long time, so we gotta figure something else out," Dartanyon shot back. Arthur scowled. Dartanyon snapped back to minding his manners like a good choirboy should. And Uncle Famous praised the Lord all the way down godforsaken Kinsman.

DARTANYON'S DAYS DID not get any easier, but he did grow stronger, in body and in mind. Once he immersed himself in sports, his teammates became his family, and Leroy, his brother.

"Come on, Beefcake!" Dartanyon barked as he stood over Leroy on the weight bench, my camera rolling. "You can do this, man!"

I returned to Cleveland in early March 2009 to begin shooting with Leroy and Dartanyon. I filmed Dartanyon holding his book up to his face and peering closely into his computer monitor. I got

Leroy angling through doorways and whipping around corners. After classes, I captured Dartanyon carrying Leroy up the fifteen stairs to Lincoln-West's weight room—a converted hallway lined with dinged-up lockers, out-of-date weights, exposed electrical wires, and a water-damaged ceiling that looked ready to cave at any moment. A small, petunia-pink portable radio blared Lil Wayne and Shop Boyz. This was their Swole Factory.

On the cinder-block wall in front of Leroy's bench hung a simple piece of white paper that read, "If you want something you never had, you must be willing to do something you've never done." For Leroy, that leap was trust. Could he have a friendship steeped in respect as opposed to charity? Could he know wholeness despite disfigurement?

Leroy wrapped his hands around the bench-press bar, which was loaded with 330 pounds, and looked up at Dartanyon. In a sense, Leroy had been powerlifting himself around since the accident, building massive upper body strength by scuttling around on his arms. He wore cut-off T-shirts even in the dead of winter because so few shirtsleeves fit around his fifteen-inch biceps. To leverage his massive shoulder girth across a nine-and-a-half-inch weight bench and balance the equivalent of a piano over his chest—while predominantly using his core strength for balance—seemed superhuman to me.

"Come on, man, you got this," Dartanyon urged. Leroy lowered the bar, pressed it up, and with that, marked his new personal best.

"Dude! I can't believe I did that!" Leroy roared, shaking in excitement as Dartanyon batted him with high fives. In his unguarded elation, Leroy even hugged me for the first time.

As they celebrated their way out of the weight room, what continued to strike me as just as extraordinary as Leroy's herculean strength was still the understated act that bookended the lift itself—the one that carried him up and down the gymnasium stairs.

"What do you think it was that drew you together as friends?" I asked Leroy and Dartanyon.

"The first time we met, I didn't know that Dartanyon was legally blind," Leroy said.

"And I didn't know Leroy was crippled," Dartanyon countered. "It was a blind date."

"But Leroy, why is Dartanyon the one you want carrying you?" I pressed. "Why are you so comfortable with him?"

"He's easier to get through doorways than my wheelchair," Leroy answered. "He doesn't get as many flat tires either."

Beneath the jokes and jabs, I suspected they were at least sub-consciously drawn together by their disabilities, as well as by race, by poverty, by transience. When Leroy joined the wrestling team, no one expected that Dartanyon would look out for the new kid, especially not one who was so obviously physically challenged, when he himself had his own physical challenges. Dartanyon entered school each day carrying just about every hardship a child can bear. And then he went out of his way to carry one more. Dartanyon's life had been a demonstration of strength for the sake of his own survival; now on display was his resolve to help someone else thrive.

"They both had handicaps that weren't their faults," Dartanyon's father would later tell me. "Dar didn't ask to be brought here with them weird eyes, with a daddy who only cared about getting high. Leroy didn't mean to fall up under the train and get his legs cut off. But they just went balls to the walls and did stuff didn't nobody think they were going to do."

Leroy and Dartanyon were inseparable, joined together at more than the hip. Throughout Lincoln's halls, wherever I found one of them, I almost always found the other—and they were frequently in song. Dartanyon would hum a few bars, Leroy would improvise a harmony, and before long they were grooving and singing like no one was watching—although such was rarely the case. Classmates inevitably gathered around them to dance and laugh along, drawn like magnets into Leroy and Dartanyon's playful charm. Faculty told me that their friendship had a ripple effect throughout the Lincoln-West student body, smoothing rough edges and tilling barren ground.

"You see a level of hopelessness here in kids who by the time they are fifteen or sixteen years old have already given up," Coach Hons explained. "They've seen people in their lives who put in time and energy, but because of how our economy is structured and how our society is structured, they are still in poverty. As much as there is opportunity in America, there is also a limit, and you see the psychological effects of that limit in our students."

The image of Dartanyon carrying Leroy suggested that perhaps there were alternatives—choices to combat hopelessness with compassion. These two boys eliminated the right for excuses with their bravery to play on. To those who were taught real men don't need help, Dartanyon and Leroy proved it was possible to be both tender and tough. Perhaps above all, they showed that giving lightens us.

"Leroy and Dartanyon give their peers a visual reminder that we're in this together," Coach Taylor said. "I'm on your back, you're on my back—whatever it takes, we can get to the finish line. Whatever it takes, we can succeed."

Following Leroy's record lift, I looked on as Dartanyon carried Leroy back down the gymnasium stairs. "Leroy's the man!" Dartanyon shouted, spinning Leroy in circles as he clung to Dartanyon's back.

"You have no neck for me to wrap my arms around!" Leroy said, laughing. Dartanyon bounded across the gym, completely unhindered by the bouncing ball of a buddy on his back.

"Wow, I forgot what it felt like to skip!" Leroy said, his eyes widening like moons as his spirit traveled back to this airy slice of lost childhood. Dartanyon shocked life into the numb and fraying corners of Leroy's soul. He pulled Leroy out of his shell and esteemed his accomplishments rather than pitying his disfigurement. And as a result, the bright smile from Leroy's youth returned, this time effortlessly. He didn't have to be Dartanyon's hero. He could simply be his friend. And therein, Leroy found his "somewhere better" that had always been promised to him.

As I watched them spring across the gym floor, I had a hunch that Leroy didn't need to know why Dartanyon carried him. All that mattered was that he did.

THROUGHOUT THE SPRING of 2009, I returned to Lincoln-West for two out of every four weeks—at times with my film crew, often without it. In the past, I'd coordinated shoots with minors through their parents, yet here there were no parents to give consent, and Pat Sutton thought everything I suggested sounded just fine. On most days Dartanyon lacked a working phone, and Leroy rarely answered his, so on more than one occasion, I planned to film powerlifting events or field trips, only to find that the boys had given me the wrong date or the school calendar was misprinted. As a result, I did a lot of showing up and sitting around with Leroy and Dartanyon. And surprisingly, the idle time together proved to be transformative in our relationship.

Leroy began greeting me with a "Hey"—a red-carpet welcome compared with our basement beginnings. I gathered he was simply tolerating my filming—likely for Dartanyon, who was enjoying his first media experience. Leroy liked seeing Dartanyon happy, and even more, he liked knowing he had a role in Dartanyon's happiness. Their friendship was slowly but surely deconstructing Leroy's self-imposed prison. Painful memories were being displaced by new ones of trust.

I continued filming them together in their classes, wanting to capture the best of their routines. Without fail, they were the featured act in Coach Hons's street law class.

"Leroy, walk over there and sharpen this pencil for me," Dartanyon said.

Leroy rolled his eyes. "How do I say 'sharpen your own pencil' in braille?" he replied.

The class roared on cue, sparking Leroy and Dartanyon to launch into their own vivacious laugh track. As the room quieted, I noticed something curious about the doodles on Dartanyon's papers. On the top of each page, he scrawled the phrase "Destined for Greatness" in shaded scrolling letters. His audacious declaration sent a shiver up my spine. While I appreciated his optimism, his environment certainly lacked ideal growing conditions for real-world greatness. Were those three words a defiant or oblivious response to the damning limitations upon his life? Could he not tell how high the deck was stacked against him? Had no one told him that poor, black, and disabled register as three strikes and an automatic out in our society?

After class, I followed Dartanyon to his locker. Inside hung another piece of notebook paper, branded with the same phrase. "Why do you write 'Destined for Greatness' on your papers?" I asked him.

He shrugged. "My dad was bragging on me to one of his friends at work a few years ago, and the guy said, 'You wrestle, lift weights, and sing in the choir? You must be destined for greatness.' So I just started writing it. Not sure why."

I knew why. Hope is a commodity in hardened places, and Arthur's friend had served up a generous portion of it to Dartanyon. His words echoed a sentiment Dartanyon had not heard since his mother had passed—that maybe he was worth noticing.

Later that week, during last-period art class, Leroy and Dartanyon worked quietly at a table toward the front of the room. Dartanyon's girlfriend, Jessica, a pretty Puerto Rican girl with long chestnut hair and suspicious eyes, worked beside them. I sat at an empty table in the back of the room while my crew filmed the boys sketching. Both were gifted artists. Dartanyon drew detailed, shaded landscapes, often embedding the phrases "She's Watching" or "Destined for Greatness" within his etchings; Leroy gravitated toward demons and angels, monsters and dragons.

"I like that constant struggle of good versus evil and the gray area in between," he said. "Like with dragons, people today think of them as fire-breathing and dangerous. But if you look at their background, their history in ancient mythology, they tend to be creatures that look menacing but are simply misunderstood."

Leroy spoke little to me, but every sentiment he shared further cracked open the window to his heart. I collected each clue he dropped, lining them up to decipher his enigmatic code. His comments, his sketches, his physical appearance, all struck me as dares for someone to take notice. The ringed piercings through his lip and eyebrow cried, "Look up here, not down there. Look at my face, not at what is missing." His artwork represented his inner battle with justice and injustice. He signed his sketches "Loki the Legless," after the enigmatic god of mischief in ancient Norse mythology. Loki was the black sheep of his family who tricked his way into becoming a deity yet remained void of any true loyalties. Dynamic and flawed, Loki was depicted as being neither completely evil nor completely helpful. He ran afoul of not only societal expectations but also the laws of nature. Just when foes thought they had him pinned, Loki shape-shifted into another creature. Like Loki, Leroy prided himself in being mysterious, solitary, and unknowable.

Shortly before the end of art class that day, I noticed whispers intensifying between Dartanyon and Jessica. She leaned closer to him, insisting upon something, as Dartanyon shook his head in disagreement. She pressed further, moving him to agitation.

Finally, Dartanyon boiled over, revealing the crux of the issue. "For the last time, I am not sleeping with the ESPN lady!"

The class collectively gasped and whipped their heads around toward the back of the room. Fifteen sets of hairy eyeballs waited for me to respond, which I did, physiologically: my face lit up like a Christmas ornament.

"She's an ESPN producer and married to a doctor," Dartanyon continued, concerned only with his own defense. "I'm seventeen, blind, and homeless. *Really?*"

The bell rang, perhaps signaling the end of my career. An accusation of sexual relations with a teenage boy is a matter for grave concern. I watched in full-body panic as Jessica stormed out and Dartanyon angrily fended off high fives from male classmates. In my own high school days, I was too inconsequential within peer hierarchy to be the subject of sophomoric rumors. This introduction to teen drama was neither pleasant nor warranting of the teacher's condemning stare as I left the classroom. Dartanyon was propped up outside the door, staring at the ground as though waiting for a scolding. I fumbled for the words that would get us both out of this ordeal with as little collateral damage as possible.

"Listen, if you really are destined for greatness, I don't think it's going to be with her," I said. "Without trust, you're asking for a lot of drama."

Dartanyon nodded. I rushed out to my car, anxious to put space between us. He broke up with Jessica later that afternoon, abruptly ending two years of dating. Jessica cried and begged him to change his mind. But Dartanyon never looked back. It seemed that for the first time, he cared about what someone else thought of his personal choices, and that someone was me.

CHAPTER 7

IMPASSE

On days when we filmed at the school, I ran out to get substantial lunches for the boys in lieu of their meager cafeteria meals. If I drove them home from practice, we stopped for dinner on the way. Big Ma always cooked for Leroy, but knowing I could get one more good meal into Dartanyon that day helped me sleep easier.

The boys' fine-dining request typically landed us at a Subway sandwich shop: a seafood salad sub for Leroy, and the Italian combo for Dartanyon.

"Who wouldn't wanna eat *fresh*!" Leroy would shout, mimicking the Subway commercial tagline.

"Nothin' fresh about what you're ordering," Dartanyon would say. "Don't you know better than to eat seafood out of Lake Erie?"

"Don't you know you're black and not an Italian?" Leroy would chide.

"Have them burn the bun so it's a black Italian sandwich," Kameron Mogadam, our cameraman, said. We'd initially used a handful of different crews, but Kameron had become a regular fixture in our days. He was a compact, fast-moving, faster-talking Persian in his early forties. Kameron liked to say that his brain ran on a caffeine-fueled stream of thoughts that had direct access to his mouth. And because he approached each day with the mind of an optimist and the heart of an aging cynic, he could be completely lovely and wholly irreverent in the same moment. Mix in a dash of self-effacing humor, and Kameron quickly disarmed even the most heavily shielded individuals. Even Leroy.

"Your name is Kameron, and you're a camera man?" Leroy snickered upon their introduction.

"Don't mess with me, Leroy," Kameron said. "I'm slightly taller than you."

"Kameron the Kamera Man! Kameron the Kamera Man!" Leroy teased. "Man, that's the funniest thing I've ever heard!" In addition to being a gifted videographer, Kameron could engage in the juvenile sort of teen-boy humor that I could not—silly Internet videos, satirical scenes from *Family Guy*, and heated debates over PlayStation versus Xbox. The three of them sang songs I had never heard and quoted movies I had not seen. But after those exchanges were exhausted, Leroy and Dartanyon were completely blank slates. Any time I felt completely lost in teen humor, or on the verge of losing all control, I put my reporter cap back on and did what I do best—kill the mood with serious questions.

"Dartanyon, what do you miss about your mom?" I asked.

"I don't know. I guess I miss her cooking. Her pancakes were da bomb."

"Oh, I love pancakes too," I said, excited about this connection. "I make them with lemon zest and cornmeal. Did she make them from scratch?"

"Sure, like she scratched together a few nickels and got us all a box of Aunt Jemima for dinner," he said, amused by my naïveté once again. "Yeah, I guess she scratched them up real good." Leroy nodded in understanding.

"Do you like your name?" I tried again. "I've never heard the name Dartanyon before."

"Only white people have time to sit around deciding whether they like their name or not," he said, chuckling.

"At least you have your own name," Leroy said to Dartanyon. "I'm like the fourth or fifth Leroy in my family."

"Yah, but you're the only one without legs, so you stand out over all the others."

When the three of us were together, I could count on Dartanyon to assume the role of group emcee, setting the rules of engagement and dancing around my awkwardness with a vibe that was always happy, always easy. Alongside Dartanyon, Leroy relaxed in my presence. But when we dropped Dartanyon off, either with a friend or a cousin or sometimes on a corner, the dynamic took a sharp turn.

During our twenty-minute rides back to Big Ma's, Leroy would retreat into an emotional and conversational shell I lacked the tools to crack. Was he deep in thought? Was he having phantom pain? Did he not want to be bothered, or was he waiting for me to speak first? Leroy was incredibly skilled at *not* showing you what he thought. I hoped he would speak first, to direct the conversation and thereby remove my risk of hitting a nerve. I feared that if I introduced any topic of substance, Leroy might recoil, reversing the weeks of positive gains. I could pepper Dartanyon with endless questions because nothing seemed to rattle him, but beneath Leroy's surface, thin and brittle, he had a heart of porcelain.

I rehearsed the simplest of statements silently, checking my words for notes of respect, thoughtfulness, and accuracy before volleying them out loud to Leroy. But on one such evening drive, the clanging bells of a railroad crossing filled our silence first. We reached the track as the bar lowered. Leroy looked down.

"Sorry, bad route to take," I said.

"Oh, it's fine," Leroy replied. "I'm okay with it now." The dirge of the engine's horn encroached upon us.

"You know, at some point, I am going to have to ask you about your accident," I said. "It'll be part of the story."

The shunting train passed in front of us, ringing and rumbling. *Clickety-clack. Clickety-clack. Clickety-clack.*

Leroy picked at his thumbnail.

"I was walking to school . . . the train was coming . . . and I slipped on the gravel," Leroy said. "My backpack got caught on the train . . . and . . . I just . . . went under." He fiddled with the sleeves of his shirt.

"Some people I've talked to think maybe you were trying to jump the train," I said softly. "They said that kids did that for fun. I wouldn't think any less of you if you were."

Leroy looked up at me with his eyebrows raised. "I lost everything," he said. "There is nothing to gain from lying about how it happened."

Coal cars and oil tankers lumbered past us in a lonely cadence. As I weighed my next question, Leroy noticed me fingering the small silver cross hanging around my neck.

"I used to go to church and sing in the choir," he said. "I believed in God, like really believed in him."

He said that Big Ma sat beside him, clutching her worn Bible, covering those long hospital days with prayer. "Lord, we ask you for protection from enemies seen and unseen," she called out, rocking back and forth in her chair. "Heal this child, Holy Father."

On one rare night when she went home to sleep in her own bed, Big Ma placed her Bible on Leroy's lap. "You turn to this here book marker if you have a bad dream," she told him.

Lying alone with a Bible got Leroy wondering about God. "I kept asking Him 'Why? Why did this happen to me?'" Leroy recounted. "And God never answered. Can you imagine not answering your eleven-year-old child when he's crying alone in a hospital?"

Leroy thought about the neighborhood kids who tortured gerbils by dangling them by their tails over a cigarette lighter flame as they flailed with fright. "That's what I felt like to God," Leroy said. "I was nothing more than a gerbil that He wanted to abuse for His own amusement."

Leroy had looked down at Big Ma's Bible in his lap at the hospital that night. He turned to her bookmark and her underlines in Psalm 23.

For though I walk through the valley
of the shadow of death, I fear no evil.
Thy rod and thy staff, they comfort me.

Leroy decided then that he would rather crawl through the hollow alone than be accompanied by one who had taken his legs. God could have saved him but didn't, and that surpassed any other kind of evil Leroy could imagine. He shut the Bible and closed the door on God.

"How sadistic and cruel of a person do you have to be to sit there and believe there is a good God?" he asked me. His eyes stayed on me, insisting upon an answer from the woman who so boldly wore a cross around her neck. I stiffened, shuffling through my index of tidy Christian answers, the ones that are supposed to fill these explanatory vacuums. Should I tell him that God is inherently just and loving and that our limited human emotions cannot always be trusted? Should I tell him that God does not cause suffering, but rather allows us free will in a broken world, where bad things happen to good people? Should I tell him that God does not always fix things in the ways we want but extends the strength to endure? I thought I believed those teachings as surely as I believed in the sun coming up in the morning. But how could Leroy trust in the existence of a loving God when so much of his experience was rooted in neglect? As the train vibrated in my bones, I could not say I would have responded any differently than Leroy had God dropped out of the race in my moment of greatest need. My tongue prickled under the demand of Leroy's waiting stare. My once reliable ideas on faith could not neatly fold and launder Leroy's history. I remained quiet, as did he. There seemed no answer big enough for a grievance so severe. And sometimes just sitting still in that galling impasse leads to the deepest spiritual understanding of all.

Darkness had fallen as we pulled up to Big Ma's house. Five stairs led to the front porch; Leroy insisted he didn't need my help.

He slid from his wheelchair onto the second step of the stoop, then hoisted his thirty-pound, twenty-eight-inch-wide chair up over his head by its wheels and laid it down with a controlled thud on the porch. I let out my breath. I didn't know I had been holding it. This extraordinary measure was quite simply how Leroy got into and out of the house each day. He saw nothing newsworthy about it, and yet to me, it painted the discordant portrait of Leroy the Loki: heroic yet resigned, determined yet desperate, neglected yet resilient. I had to film this. I had to fix this. And as the door closed behind him, I lingered on the porch steps, wondering: If I found this young man a ramp, would God consider using it to come down and sort this mess out?

I NEEDED TO visit the site of Leroy's accident. And so on an early April morning under a carbon-gray sky that looked like it was holding a grudge, I went. I parked at the end of Elinor Street, whose modest homes dead-ended into the open railroad tracks twenty feet from the street. No fence had been erected to keep children at bay, no signage indicating that life could be irrevocably altered in this place. In the distance sat the General Metals Powder Company, where Leroy's brother gasped for help. To my left was an abandoned automotive garage. Straight ahead was the steel rail that divided Leroy's life like the spine of an open book. Most lives possess a before and an after. A truth revealed. A path chosen. Words we cannot reel back in. But the marker separating the two sides of Leroy's story lay uniquely tangible in front of me. I folded my hands in reverence, as though visiting the gravesite of a person still alive.

Yet how much life had this place taken from Leroy? I wondered. Who was he when he walked out the door to school that morning, and who did he become later that day upon learning he would never walk again? And is there a difference? We all live at the intersection of our essence and our experiences, but how do we tease out one from the other? As William Butler Yeats wrote, "O body swayed to music, O brightening glance, / How can we know the dancer from the dance?"

I sat beside the rusted rails, as though waiting for them to divulge their secrets. A handful of rocks and gravel sifted through my fingers—the same sharp cinders that had gouged Leroy's cheeks as he rolled through them. I hoped that by connecting myself to the contours and textures of this place, perhaps I could better connect myself to Leroy. I lay between the rails, as though offering myself up as a messenger. What was to be learned? Where was the redemption? My body tensed in wait, vulnerable and still. No comfort came. Instead this place was loud with nothing, with no one. I forced myself to stay longer, needing to outlast Leroy's ghosts, to free him from their haunting. I wrapped my hands around the tracks. They remained unapologetically cold. And when I finally resigned to leave, I paid homage, mourning all that Leroy lost that day—his legs, his faith, his worth.

An hour later, I met my camera crew and a uniformed officer on Laird Street. I had called the police station the week before to let them know of my plans to film the outside of Leroy's childhood home, and the officer had advised me not to enter the neighborhood unaccompanied. "Noon's about the time those people start waking up," he said. "They'll be wondering what you're up to." I cringed at his "those people" remark—two words with the power to construct an entire sociological hierarchy steeped in suspicion.

Our crew's van followed the patrol car down the street, plodding together with the amble of a holiday parade to allow us to film what we call "scenic shots" out the passenger window. Laird's "scenery" possessed a hazy morning-after feel, with empty beer cans and plastic cups lining the tops of rotting wooden porch railings. At several points we got out of the car to film markers of the lower class—balding tires strewn on lawns, boarded-up windows, and stray dogs, hollow-stomached and mangy, roaming for food. The old man with the crazy hair framed just right with the broken window in the background. From the leaning homes to the scrubby grass to the barefoot children roving the streets, everything on Laird gave the appearance of being uncared-for.

I felt like I was on a field trip through poverty, riding a zoo tram through cautionary exhibits. *And over on your left, through that chain-link fence, you can see the Perpetual Misfortune Display.* I was doing my job, capturing the visuals of Leroy's backstory, just as I had done for so many of my other subjects before. Yet Laird felt disturbingly different, because this time I had a squad car in front of me, and eyes in the back of my head.

If the officer was trying to protect me from drawing attention to myself, this clearly was not the way to go about it. Several residents scrambled into their homes as our van approached, "probably fearing that we were filming an episode of *Cops*," our officer joked. I imagined them stashing drugs under mattresses. I imagined them pulling pistols out of bureaus. I began to pulse with the type of us-versus-them fear that I thought I didn't possess. I caught myself thinking the worst of them, which in turn exposed the worst of me.

We ensured that black trash bags and overgrown bushes were framed in backgrounds. We got the rusted basketball rim bending forward with a ripped net. We got the beater Chevy Impala cruising toward us with six layers of Saran Wrap duct-taped over the broken passenger window. In one trip down the street, we successfully and efficiently checked all of the boxes on our poverty scavenger hunt, equipped to show how Leroy lived as an eleven-year-old boy. Finally, we neared the corner white duplex at the far end of Laird where Leroy's life had ended and begun anew. An older man, leathery and worn, sat on the front steps. I did not get close enough to talk to him, yet I felt that what we collected on the tapes would have spoken volumes to him, and to all of his neighbors: *I don't know you, but I've gathered all of the necessary evidence to demonstrate that your world is sad and shameful.*

But how far off was I? "We call this Laird Land because once people are born onto Laird, they're like citizens of it," the officer volunteered. "They never leave. They just move down the street, house to house, following the drugs." Had there been no accident, would Leroy have become the sullen figure now sitting on what was once his porch? Had the train maimed him or saved him? The policeman didn't let me wonder for long.

"Your guy must have been real lucky to get out of here," he said, folding his arms across his chest. "Real lucky."

BY MIDSPRING OF 2009, Navid and I were "paper pregnant," which is the phrase couples use when enmeshed in the adoptive process. We filled out a forest's worth of forms. We recruited friends to write letters of reference. We provided three years of financial records. We passed physical exams, criminal background checks, and life-saving courses. We created photo books marketing our life to prospective birth mothers. Frankly, this type of gestation suited my compulsive love of lists and tasks more judiciously than a physical pregnancy.

Navid had an expectant glow about him too. He said that listening to me gush about Leroy and Dartanyon had fueled his eagerness to grow our family. "You realize you light up when you talk about them, right?"

"Well I don't know about that," I said. "I just think they're really neat kids."

"You talk about them like a proud parent," he said. "It's invigorating to see how quickly they have affected you." Whether I noticed it or not, Navid detected a maternal instinct welling within me, and it expanded the boundary lines of his fatherhood dream. "I could see Lisa starting to love these boys like sons," he would write in one of his adoption application essays, "and though I initially wanted a biological child, I realized through her experiences that I could love any child powerfully. Color, race, and blood do not define a family." Navid and I were unified in this overarching decision to adopt, and agreed to adopt a child from Cleveland to honor both my birthplace and the impact that Leroy and Dartanyon had made on us. However, we remained deadlocked on one significant aspect of this choice: the age of our prospective child.

I voted to adopt a teenager, arguing that we would never be younger than we were at that moment, allowing us maximum energy to devote to a child with significant physical or emotional needs. "I would rather adopt a kid that no one else wants and give them a chance to know love," I said. "That's what this world needs."

This made Navid nervous. He wasn't interested in parenting as a means of social justice. He wanted to hold babies. He wanted to kiss squishy toes and say "Oogly-googly." He'd delivered fifty babies during his medical residency, each time visualizing the day when he would welcome his own. And until that happened, my husband remained the only man in the history of our church to volunteer for Sunday nursery duty.

"I just think parenthood is something we need to grow into," he said. "We don't know the first thing about raising teenagers, let alone teenagers with complicated issues and physical disabilities."

In the forefront of my mind was Leroy and Dartanyon, and what great kids they were. How hard could it be to love them and care for them? How much could kids like them achieve in a peaceful, supportive home like ours?

Then we met Erin Joudrey, the social worker assigned to conduct our home study. She was a jovial woman charged with assessing our marriage, adoption goals, communication styles, and family histories. Though she worked with children of all ages, her niche was coordinating foster placement for teenagers with attachment disorders and violent behavioral tendencies. Clearly, this was a sign.

"Navid and I have talked about adopting an older child like that," I said. "Tell us, what type of parents succeed in those cases?"

"Honestly, it's the nice Christian families who fail most often. They think that if they just show a child love, God will take care of the rest," she said. "But it's not that simple. The parents who succeed tend to be the ones who grew up in extreme dysfunction or abuse themselves." These parents could handle school expulsions and kids hurling vulgar insults at them, because they themselves endured similar chaos and lived to tell about it. In other words, Erin said, crazy tolerates crazy.

I looked around at our well-appointed home, with its custom-coordinated throw pillows on the window seat, my golden Emmy Awards gracing the mantel, and an Ivy League diploma hanging on the office wall. Before I could even consider the clothes hanging in rainbow order in our closet, Erin confirmed what I suspected, and what Navid hoped: "Sorry, guys, but you're not crazy enough."

CHAPTER 8

ELEPHANT IN THE HOOD

A story, most essentially, requires change. The agent of that change gives each story its contour. The characters grant the fingerprint. If there is a formula, I suppose it can be briefly summarized this way: introduce the character, sketch his backstory, present him at the moment of conflict, and carry us to the result. To the change. We explore the mighty outlines of a character's life before the conflict—the greatness that lifts him into the place where strangers care. We introduce the first hint of the problem, and then travel through the character's struggle with that problem, and how he is changed by it. If a story succeeds, we are changed from the sidelines, just a tiny bit.

Here, in this feature I was developing for ESPN, both Leroy and Dartanyon had a compelling backstory. But there was something more magical and also far more delicate to capture and convey: their bond. Dartanyon carrying Leroy gave their connection physical form, but it was the jokes they traded, the songs they sang, the looks they shared, and their infectious wit and irreverence that provided the purest and richest vein of their story. But how to frame those moments—this largely intangible and kindred knowing—as reflections of their bond and in the context of a sporting season in their lives? And simultaneously paint the challenges of their lives outside the shelter of their friendship?

Friendship, as a theme, is easy to state and difficult to show. There was no schedule of events for Leroy and Dartanyon's brotherhood, and few visual images of how their relationship served as a catalyst for the change so central to the story's structure. Presenting a friendship in proper measure and in real moments was an assignment unlike any other I had attempted.

So quietly, I continued following them through their arduous routines, waiting for convincing moments. I met Dartanyon at the bus stop for his ninety-minute ride to school, just as the sun poked up. I followed him and Leroy through more classes, more weight-lifting sessions. I tagged along on class field trips and attended team fund-raisers. Though they were animated among their peers, Leroy and Dartanyon's gregarious laughter was replaced by muffled, monotone voices once it was just the three of us, as though I were a parent chaperoning a date. Directing them to "Be funnier on this take," or "Say that again in a warmer tone," or asking how they felt about one another, only exacerbated the problem.

Most features can be shot in two to ten days, yet after the better part of two months in Cleveland, I still struggled to capture the magic. While my colleagues investigated college recruiting scandals and chased Bret Favre in and out of retirement, I sat in Big Ma's basement watching two boys watch *The Simpsons*. At times, the journalist in me was unsure what I was looking for, but I knew these were the places to look. And although it appeared painfully unproductive and fiscally irresponsible from a managerial perspective, Victor allowed me to keep going back—in part because he trusted me, and in part because for the time and money spent, I needed to come back with a story.

What I found along the way challenged my own life story and my own patterns of thinking. As a child on the white side of town, I grew up believing that with willpower, one could overcome any circumstance. This is America, where people succeed or fail based on individual effort. And yet as I sat on Leroy's front porch, and as I met Dartanyon's extended family, I was struck by how hardship engulfed multiple generations of families. Nearly everyone I met was some combination of uneducated, unemployed, poor, tired, and drug-addicted. Why wasn't the "determination + perseverance = success" formula working? Why hadn't Dartanyon registered for the SAT college entrance exam? Why did Leroy owe $2,000 for a cell phone he never owned? Why did Big Ma have to calculate the cost of gas to pick up Leroy from lifting practice? Where was Leroy's father? Why had none of Dartanyon's brothers completed high school? Why weren't they all just trying a little harder?

"You ask an awful lot of questions," Leroy said one afternoon.

"And you don't want those answers anyway," Dartanyon added. "They'll just depress you."

My questions were met with reticence, for the only white people who came around here asking questions were the police, Leroy said, and nothing good ever came of that. On several occasions when Kameron's white crew van pulled up to Big Ma's house, neighbors bolted indoors and shut the blinds. "They all think you're with the Drug Enforcement Agency," Big Ma said. "You've got everyone calling up and down the street warning each other."

The more time I spent in their world, the more I wanted to understand it, and the deeper I dug for the roots of these mysteries. And Dartanyon was right. There were no pleasant answers to my questions. Dartanyon did not register for the SAT because he did not have the $26 registration fee. Katrina started putting phone and utility bills in her children's names after her debt piled too high, thereby digging Leroy into a credit-score grave before he knew what credit was. Big Ma understood that one all too well. She had cosigned Katrina's car loan after Leroy's accident, and once her daughter defaulted, Big Ma was forced into bankruptcy. The blame piled up with the bills. "Nearly lost my house," she told me. Her estranged husband, Big Daddy, and all four of their children had wrestled with drug addiction; she buried her eldest son too soon. Leroy was three years old when his own father took off. And all of Dartanyon's brothers dropped out of school for minimum-wage jobs to help keep the lights on.

"That's just how the world is," Leroy said. This was his sole explanation for the difficulties around him.

"It doesn't have to be," I said. "What would you like to change about your life?"

Leroy gave me a cockeyed look for thinking that changing anything in East Cleveland was going to be as easy as changing a lightbulb.

"I guess if I could change something, I'd find a lighter legless dude to carry around," Dartanyon replied. They routinely reverted to jokes—the easy, comfortable way out of my abstract questions.

"I'd change the 'hit him or I'll hit you' ritual," Leroy said, suddenly serious. "I hated that." He explained that, beginning when he was eight years old, his mother tried to toughen him up by ordering him to fight friends and strangers alike. Katrina would yell, "Hit him, Redd! Whup him good!" Leroy choked back the tears. He hated every swing, but he knew that if he refused to fight, his mother would beat him even harder with that nasty switch from Big Ma's backyard. With "hit him or I'll hit you," you were going to get it one way or another. In her defense, Katrina was following the law of the streets, like all of the other mothers in the hood who didn't have fathers around to protect their boys. She needed her sons to command respect on their own, just like her brothers and her uncles had. But all Leroy learned from this ritual was to loathe confrontation, and that extended to questions like mine.

Hit him or I'll hit you. Because that's how the world is.

I thought of Coach Robinson's early words to me—"This world's got nothing for them." I wanted to be more than a turkey lady—I wanted to emanate curative love and unconventional solutions. But I fell short, in part because there was an elephant in every room I visited. That elephant was me.

At times it felt like a charade—this suburban Ivy Leaguer roaming around East Cleveland. Neighbors greeted one another in excited tones but rarely acknowledged me. Neither Leroy nor Dartanyon introduced me. And why would they? I was the reporter lady forcing lame smiles, meddling with my invasive questions, and scrunching my nose at the cigarette smoke curling between us. Though I told myself that I was not fearful of this side of town, I was at the very least skittish. I was uncomfortable with their lifestyles, their decisions, and, as our social worker Erin had put it, the craziness of it all. Why couldn't they just stay in school, get jobs, pay the bills, and say no to drugs? My white privilege taught me that these were simple, universal choices equally afforded to all Americans.

But as I pieced together the tenuous details of their personal stories, one fact grew clear: few had chosen poverty, any more than I chose my advantages. Families like the Suttons and Crocketts were born into sets of disadvantaged conditions that cascaded into subsequent negative outcomes. As children, they attended underfunded schools and returned home to overstressed single parents unequipped to nurture their emotional development. As teens, while their parents worked, many turned to the streets for a sense of belonging and a cure for boredom. They moved frequently and experienced regular episodes of hunger, homelessness, and unemployment—not to mention the drug exposure, teen pregnancy, and lower graduation rates that dog lower-income youth. And from there the cycle ensnares anew.

My growing sense was that Big Ma, Katrina, and Arthur were not bad people. They were limited people. There were decisions they had made for themselves, and others that life had forced upon them. And as I began to understand the sheer complexity of their existence, I began to see them as people to respect rather than as mysteries to solve. I ceased my probing. I abandoned my questions. I stopped scrutinizing their conversations and got in on the jokes. I quit pitying their deficiencies. I settled in beside them to absorb their sadness and their sweetness, to listen and learn. I hoped to convince them—or perhaps more so, myself—that our differences need not separate us. And as we sat, I sensed the sacred whisper: *These are my beloved.*

"IF YOU'RE GONNA hang around here, you're gonna have to learn the language," Leroy said one afternoon on his front porch steps. "Let's start you off with some beatbox. Try it like this: *Boots-and-cats-and-boots-and-cats-and-boots-and-cats.*" I envied his ability to reproduce hip-hop sounds and percussion instruments with his mouth. But though he methodically broke it down for me until we'd squeezed every last bit of cool out of the riff, I still bit my tongue and spit on myself, like a baby attempting solid food for the first time.

Dartanyon tried to console me. "Don't worry, you can't expect to get your black card in two months," he said. "You gotta work to be this fly." We moved on to video games, where the blind guy sat inches from the television and beat me mercilessly. They eased my distaste for tattoos by explaining how in lives of limited possessions and mementos, they secured their memories in ink. They taught me how to hot-wire a cable signal and boost my cell phone volume by putting it into a plastic cup. "Ghetto speakers," Leroy said. "They work."

And fortunately for my employment status, all our weeks of perceived idleness were working as well. Leroy and Dartanyon began to shine on tape, the unintended by-product of my assimilation into their surroundings. As my guard relaxed, their grace extended. I found that the key to producing a story on a friendship is to become a part of it, just as the key to understanding a community is to sit within it.

By late spring, Big Ma and I were calling out *Wheel of Fortune* letters together. She said I might as well call her Big Ma, like everyone else. She started greeting me with a hug and offering herself as an escort to the highway entrance whenever I left after dusk. "Next time you come, don't wear those blue pants round here though," Leroy's uncle said to me with a soft wink and a stern nod. "You gonna get yourself shot."

I was still the elephant in the neighborhood, but I was their elephant. And therein laid the pivotal, delicate change that every great narrative requires. I was capturing their stories, while they were refining mine.

BY HIS SENIOR year, Dartanyon understood just how physically strong he was. And after so many years of people looking at him like he was an anomaly for those funny eyes, he enjoyed standing out as a different sort of freak—a freak of nature. In late March 2009, he finished second in the Ohio state powerlifting championships and set an individual state record of 580 pounds in the deadlift. Leroy had his own success, capturing the Ohio state bench-press title in his weight class. So one month later, as we set out to John F. Kennedy High School on Cleveland's east side for the Senate Conference powerlifting championships, the meet felt largely like a formality. Lincoln-West was the hands-down favorite.

Everyone in the gym knew who "Muscles" was, and Dartanyon's competitive acquaintances circled around to shake his hand and beat on his biceps as soon as we arrived. A significant police presence lined the perimeter of the gymnasium. Dartanyon and Leroy wasted no time lightening the mood, turning the simplest moments into launchpads for entertainment. Dartanyon led stretching, and in between exercises, he moonwalked around the circle, checking on people and firing them up. "Leroy, touch your toes!" Dartanyon called. Leroy pounded around the floor beside him as if searching for them.

"Oh, they're at home," Leroy goofed. After stretching, the two danced around the gym, cracking jokes and singing hip-hop like they were hosting a variety show. Yet the moment their names were called, the switch flipped. Dartanyon carried Leroy to his bench, both mentally locked in to the task at hand. With Dartanyon holding his hips, Leroy pressed 305 pounds, then 315 pounds, and finally 330 pounds. Not only did he outlift everyone in his own weight class by more than 100 pounds, he outbenched the entire gym, beating even the top heavyweight by 25 pounds.

"How does he do that with no legs?" kids marveled.

"If you think that's amazing, wait till you see his squat," Dartanyon joked.

Dartanyon's bench press was always fifty pounds short of Leroy's, but he made up for it with his deadlift. His first mark of 545 pounds instantly broke his own previous conference record by 25 pounds. Ten minutes later, he increased to 550 pounds. Lift. Squeeze. Hold. Got it. While waiting for his third attempt, Dartanyon walked over to the bleachers to check his cell phone. It was gone. He searched his pants pockets. His wallet was missing too.

"NOOOOOOOO!" Dartanyon flew into a rage. "Whoever stole my stuff, I'm gonna kill you!" He looked like he just might snap a neck, and the entire gymnasium stopped to see if he'd find the right one. Kameron grabbed his camera to resume filming Dartanyon as he flew around the gym, raving maniacally. I motioned for Kameron to stop. "But this is an important moment," Kameron said. "He just got his stuff stolen. We're here to film what's happening. Documentary. Root word *document*."

"Filming this feels voyeuristic, like we're capitalizing on his misfortune," I whispered. "Shouldn't we help him look for his things instead?" Kameron disagreed, but he ceased recording. Dartanyon puffed and paced like an angry bull along the bleacher's edge. "Who's the coward who stole my stuff?"

I had seen Dartanyon disappointed. I had seen him manhandle a competitive opponent as though it was his next meal. But I had never seen him look capable of inflicting savage violence, which is how he looked that day. Even I felt afraid to approach him. I took off to the principal's office instead.

"Ma'am, one of Lincoln's athletes had his belongings stolen from the bleachers. He's blind. Can you lock all of the entrances so we can find the culprit?" I asked.

"Honey, in the time it took you to get here, they probably already sold his stuff off out on the street," she said, turning away.

"You have to at least try," I pleaded. "Let me write down his name and my number in case you find them." I handed her my card. She rolled her eyes.

By the time I returned to the gym, Dartanyon had stopped pacing. He stood awaiting his final lift with his hands on his head. "When you take something from someone who has nothing, that hurts deeply," Coach Taylor said. "I was so glad Dartanyon didn't go beyond what he did, because it would have taken half of Cleveland to hold that kid back."

Dartanyon had slated his third deadlift attempt at 575 pounds. Though he had already set a new record and secured the overall title for his weight class, he needed to contribute as many pounds as he could toward his team's total. Taylor led him back to the bar. Dartanyon gave it a yank, but it was tough for his body to succeed without his heart. He had already won, but he had also lost. He let the bar crash to the ground and went off to kick some more bleachers.

The Wolverines held on for their fourth consecutive conference title that afternoon. Leroy and Dartanyon accepted Lincoln's trophy. But even with a gold medal around his neck and a plaque in his hands, Dartanyon had been stripped of his right to celebrate. I surveyed the school administrators and surrounding police; none considered Dartanyon's plight worth an incident report or even an "I'm sorry, son." The fighter needed someone to fight for him that day, yet no one did.

"How about when we finish here, we start replacing what was stolen," I offered. Dartanyon nodded, still too angry and hurt to speak. I said good-bye to Leroy and let Coach Taylor know that I was holding Dartanyon off the bus.

"Are you sure you have enough money for everything?" Dartanyon asked.

"I have my credit card," I said. "We should be fine."

"They don't take credit cards at the phone place, just cash," he said.

Though that seemed odd to me, I focused on solving the problem rather than questioning it. I knew my bank card would only allow me to withdraw up to $200. I turned to Kameron, who was packing up his gear and trying not to eavesdrop. "Can I borrow some money?" I asked. "I'll pay you back tomorrow."

Kameron ran his hand through his hair and scratched the back of his neck. I knew what he was thinking. A credible producer does not stop filming her subject during a theft as he flies into a frenzy in the middle of a championship tournament. A credible producer does not chauffeur her subject around town and buy him a cell phone. A credible producer does not drag her crew across ethical lines. For though we may have felt badly for Dartanyon's predicament, journalistic code forbade us to do anything about it. We were trained to keep our emotional distance, to remain objective. And I understood the necessity of this when working with professional athletes. Yet when working with vulnerable kids, the principle of drawing a line in the sand seemed duplicitous. How could I ask Dartanyon to travel into emotional depths, only to glean his experiences and leave him there?

"We can't *not* help him," I said. "I mean, look at him." Dartanyon sat hunched over a bleacher, drooping like a kicked puppy. Sports journalists like to identify turning points—in a match, in a season, in a career. Which at-bat changed the momentum of a series? Which interception sparked a comeback? Before us now appeared the balance not of a game but of a life. Here was a chance to go beyond talking about a loss. Here was our chance to redeem one.

Kameron reached into his pocket and drew out his wallet. "Go save the turtles."

"Go do what?" I asked, confused.

"You know, like those documentaries about baby sea turtles that hatch on the beach, and they have to waddle like a hundred yards out to sea in order to survive." He went on to explain that while these defenseless baby turtles are inching their way toward the water, vultures and other birds swoop down to eat them. If the hatchlings manage to avoid the air attack, they then have to outwaddle crabs the size of soccer balls that chase them down and drag them to an underground death. Because these reptiles are born into a predatory obstacle course, only one percent makes it into adulthood. And this grated on Kameron.

"You start rooting for them—*Go, baby turtle, go!*—and then *Noooo!*" He threw his hands into the air in animated disbelief. "And then it hits you. Why doesn't the camera crew just pick them up and throw them in the ocean? Sea turtles wouldn't be endangered if cameramen helped them!"

Leroy and Dartanyon's crawl to adulthood was also pitted with callous traps. But the rules of documentary required us to subdue our emotional responses or risk coloring our reports beyond the factual and objective. We were supposed to let the turtles die.

For three months, with his salt-and-pepper Persian eyebrow raised, Kameron watched me bond with Leroy and Dartanyon and bend the rules in the very ways we were warned against: buying meals, giving rides, growing attached. Throughout our filming, Kameron had seen it all. And finally, on that day, he had seen enough. He clumped a wad of cash into my hand and commissioned me for a journey over that sacred ethical edge. "Go save the turtles," he said again.

Dartanyon and I raced to the Bureau of Motor Vehicles to obtain a new state ID card. We were turned away for lack of a birth certificate, which Dartanyon did not have. We bolted downtown to the Bureau of Vital Statistics, where I bought a replacement birth certificate. We arrived back at the BMV at 4:59 p.m., one minute before closing, as the guard turned the lock on the door.

"Sir, please let us in. This young man is visually impaired," I begged, banging on the door. "His wallet was stolen, and without a new ID, he can't get a new bus pass. Without a bus pass, he can't get to school. And I think we can all agree that kids should be in school." The guard, a towering older black man, shuffled back to open the door, probably figuring it'd be less effort to let us in than chase me around a circle of half-baked logic.

Our last stop was for a new cell phone. I expected to drive to an Apple or Verizon store. Instead, Dartanyon directed me to the crumbling brick storefront of what appeared to be an antiquated beauty supply store. Hair dryers, brushes, wigs, and shampoos were locked up in glass-enclosed counters. And yet the store was packed with a swarm of male customers, being served by a crew of Middle Eastern and African American men. The clerks were in perpetual motion, darting back and forth behind a black velvet curtain hanging in the back of the store. Everyone seemed to be speaking in a flurry of broken English and unfamiliar slang.

"Ma'am, your money, please!" a man shouted at me from behind the counter.

"Already?" I asked. "But you, uh, is there paperwork to sign? Did he pick out a plan?"

"There's no plan, or paperwork," Dartanyon mumbled to me. "He just needs the hundred and fifty dollars." I handed over the cash. The clerk put it in his pocket and shooed us on.

"Dartanyon, that place felt really strange," I said, still trying to get my bearings as we walked back to my car. "It didn't look like anywhere I've ever bought a phone before."

"It was a front," he said. "But they sell cheap jailbroken phones too."

"A what?"

"You know, a front, like they sell drugs there." He explained how customers order in code, using words like *cush* and *bubble rum* and *bogga sugar* in their requests. Runners would then go behind the curtain to weigh the orders. I suddenly felt violated, like an accomplice to anarchy.

"Dartanyon, that was completely irresponsible to take me in there without telling me what it was!" I said. "I would have taken you to a real phone store."

He jerked to a stop. "You were perfectly safe," he said. "I would never let anyone lay a hand on you." With that, he took hold of my shoulders and moved me to the interior of the sidewalk so that he could walk closer to the traffic. He was a curious amalgam of refined etiquette and shrewd street smarts.

I stopped to pick up a sandwich for Dartanyon and then drove him to his sister's house. "I still don't know how you got us into the BMV when it was already closed," he said as we pulled into the driveway.

"And I don't understand how you got a phone from a drug dealer selling twenty-year-old hair dryers," I countered.

"I guess we make a good team. We each got some different skills."

Dartanyon started to open the car door and then turned back to me, serious and searching. "You know, there's no one in my life who would have had the time or the money to do what you did for me today," he said, his voice catching. "I'm pretty sure God dropped you into me and Leroy's lives for reasons other than television."

That day, moving from producer to protector, I was the turning point. I made the decisive play. I crossed the journalistic line and found that the good stuff—the stuff that matters—was on the other side.

I thought most of my childhood was a big wasteland
that I needed to keep hidden. I didn't know I had a story until
I saw it on television. I guess it's only later, when we tell someone else,
that it even becomes a story at all.

—DARTANYON

CHAPTER 9

WHAT WOULD YOU DO FOR A FRIEND?

As our shooting wound down in mid-May of 2009, I began gathering final creative elements for the edit phase, such as exterior shots of the school and time-lapse footage of clouds moving above train tracks, to transition between place and time in the script. Collecting photos from Leroy and Dartanyon's childhoods was also a high priority. Still photographs allow reporters and producers the versatility to cover various themes we might want to introduce as our writing process unfolds. For instance, images of Dartanyon as a child would allow us to cover plot points related to his visual impairment, his mother's death, or his transience.

If a picture says a thousand words, the absence of a photo can say even more. To my knowledge, only one childhood photograph of Dartanyon exists. He looks to be about six years old, and his face is right up against the camera, as though he may have accidentally taken the shot himself. In fact, he wasn't even sure he was the boy in the picture when I showed it to him. He had no other childhood images with which to compare it.

Leroy's only recent photographs were taken by Ed Suba from the *Beacon Journal*, during a time he would have rather not preserved. He had never seen any of his school photos—he had either transferred into a new school after class pictures were taken or transferred out before yearbooks were distributed.

In the absence of personal photos of Leroy and Dartanyon, I
hired a local photographer to shoot their portraits, to capture the
grit of their journeys as well as artfully depict their friendship in
a way other than carrying. The boys were pleased, to a degree, by
being asked to pose. It was an overt, definitive way to pause the
demands of their daily lives for the sole purpose of giving them
attention in a way that few other things, including a video camera,
can. The lens says, *You are important in this moment. You're the subject. Nothing else is the focus. It's just you. Your face, your eyes, your
smile, your brawn, your brow, your image—you.*

On that same day, reporter Tom Rinaldi arrived in Cleveland to
conduct Leroy and Dartanyon's on-camera interviews. Throughout the last few weeks, I had worked hard to prepare the boys
by encouraging them to explore their thoughts about their pasts
and one another. Their ability to articulate their memories and
emotions would make or break viewers' ability to connect with
them. In my mind, as well as in Tom's, our months of shooting and
the possibility for resulting opportunities for the boys hung in the
balance of these interviews. And though I had not shared these
pressures with Leroy or Dartanyon, they sensed the shift in tone as
I led them into the darkened school gymnasium, where four
video cameras hovered around two chairs. Leroy waited behind
closed doors while Dartanyon took his place beneath the heat of
the halogen lights. Tom led him into the specifics of his home
life.

TOM: How would you describe your family situation?

DARTANYON: Not really one of the best. There have been
times that I'd have to, like, scavenge the house for food
because we have so little. I've moved about five or six times
within the past three years because we didn't have money.

TOM: What has been the most difficult part for you?

DARTANYON: The hardest thing growing up was hearing everybody else talk about "I am going to do this with my mom" and all this other stuff, and I was like the only child whose mother was . . . well, like Mother's Day is still one of the hardest holidays for me because my mom is in heaven right now and I don't have a mother to give a gift to or say Happy Mother's Day to.

Then, after three months of grappling with the story's central tenet—the one that lured me out of bed and onto a plane—Dartanyon's turn to reflect upon his relationship with Leroy had arrived.

TOM: Why do you carry Leroy?

DARTANYON: Just to get him from point A to point B.

TOM: What do you think you give to Leroy?

DARTANYON: I honestly don't know.

TOM: What connects the two of you? What can the two of you uniquely understand about one another?

DARTANYON: We just have this bond.

TOM: How did you end up being the one to carry him?

DARTANYON: I pretty much just chose to. I can't imagine not carrying him.

As I suspected, Dartanyon wasn't sure why he carried Leroy. It was never a choice for him. It was simply the right thing to do.

TOM: What does it mean to you to have him sit there on that mat while you wrestle?

DARTANYON: It means a lot. It's like having my brother there. Like basically having someone I know I can trust. I know he's going to be there.

Leroy's turn came next. Tom approached the topic of the accident cautiously. He knew he needed to hit a soft spot, and yet, like everyone else, he did not want it to come at the expense of Leroy's smile. He began broadly, letting Leroy choose the direction.

TOM: What happened that morning?

LEROY: My brother and I were walking to school, and we're on either side of the track. It just comes by, comes by . . . and there was rocks and gravel and I kinda just slipped, kinda just went under. I was twirling and spinning and then I was just laying there and I just stared up at the sun . . .

Leroy's voice trailed off as the memories thickened in his throat.

TOM: How angry were you after the accident?

LEROY: Well, my anger cannot be expressed. I still have a lot of it inside of me. As the years go, it like decays, to where I am not even caring anymore.

TOM: What has been the toughest part for you?

LEROY: Making friends. Every time I moved to a new house, I tried not to make friends because I knew we would move again and I would have to leave them.

TOM: Why is Dartanyon the one you let in?

LEROY: I don't know.

TOM: Try.

LEROY: I don't even know how to explain it.

TOM: We asked Dartanyon what he sees when he looks over during a match, and he sees you sitting on the edge of the mat. What do you think he said? And I know you guys could joke all day, but this isn't a joke. What do you think he said?

LEROY: I don't know.

TOM: You can joke about how he sees a blob or a blur. But Dartanyon used another word. He said, "I see a brother."

Leroy covered his mouth with his hand and lowered his head, searching. His eyes grew moist. He looked up.

LEROY: You know how you get that feelin' when somebody says something that gives you a chill up your spine? That's what just happened right there.

TOM: Why, Leroy?

LEROY: Because that's how I see him. He's my brother. But I didn't know he felt the same.

TOM: What is that worth?

LEROY: To know that there is somebody who will actually put me on his back when I fall down. Not a lot of friends would do that, but I know he will. To know that you will like pick me up and throw me on your back is astounding.

TOM: What's the message in that?

LEROY: Basically there are good people out there.

The exchange would never make air, yet these healing words would resonate forevermore in the fractured heart of this once lonely boy. Leroy understood that the carrying was simply a symbol for the caring, that he had an ally whose love ran deeper than blood. Dartanyon's rides were restoring Leroy's faith in humanity, and although these sentiments had been long apparent to me, they weren't known to Leroy until he, himself, spoke them into existence.

On the drive home that evening, that truth set Leroy and Dartanyon free. They bubbled over, giddy and gratified, recalling the day: *Did Tom ask you that question too? What did you say? Dude, that shot of you against the lockers was awesome!* They realized that their pasts need not be shrouded in shame. They believed that perhaps their thoughts—their lives—were worth recounting. They looked at one other and saw a friendship unsurpassed. And that made me the happiest person in the car.

ON THAT EARLY June night, 40 percent of Lincoln-West seniors gathered on the auditorium stage for graduation, their gowns flowing and their tassels poised to swing, each ready to mark the end of their high school journey.

Leroy always believed he would graduate, but his true goal was even grander: to *walk* across the stage to get his diploma. No one onstage that night understood that goal more than Dartanyon. That's why, when Leroy's name was called, Dartanyon stood too, right beside him. He helped Leroy stand—upon new prosthetic legs he had been fitted for just weeks earlier—then moved alongside him as Leroy crossed the stage, step for step, eye to eye. When Leroy stopped, put out his hand, and grasped his diploma, the audience rose and delivered a standing ovation.

What would you do for a friend, one you carried on your back all year long? You'd put him down and walk beside him, which was exactly what Dartanyon did.

After the photos were taken, the music stopped, and the tears dried, the two sat in the theater, side by side. I asked them to describe what the evening meant to them. This time, they had the words.

"As long as I can remember," Dartanyon said, "I've been carrying Leroy from point A to B to C. Graduation was the first time I finally got to walk beside him." He paused. "It was a privilege. It was an honor."

Leroy's eyes moistened, and he looked up.

"It meant so much to me," he said, "to know I have a friend who was there to catch me if I stumbled."

There was no stumble. There was no pun or punch line, no joke or jab. Just two friends, sharing one moment, smiling together in silence.

THE NEXT MORNING, it was my turn to cross a threshold. Navid and I had received word that a prospective birth mother was interested in meeting with us. Her name was Jayda, and she was living in a home for pregnant women on the eastern outskirts of Cleveland. As I sat in my childhood bedroom preparing to meet her, I drew strength from Leroy's determined steps. I tried on a carousel of outfits, oscillating between a professional appearance and a more matronly one. I settled on a pleated summer skirt, chucked the string of pearls, and knelt beside my bed to thank God for planting this dream in my heart, in this room, and now bringing it to fruition. As I set out, palms clammy, I rehearsed answers to questions I thought Jayda might ask me—about our family dynamics, educational philosophies, and frameworks for discipline. I remained unprepared for her initial concern.

"I thought you'd be taller," she said to me upon opening the door. Jayda stood at five feet ten inches, nearly a foot taller than me. Her comment made me feel like I ought to have been selling Girl Scout cookies.

I handed her a small bouquet of gerbera daisies instead. "I always thought I would be taller too." This had been my wish in so many of the crossroad moments of my life—childhood camp, my ESPN interview, my first day at Lincoln-West, waiting in the car at the train tracks with Leroy. I often wished I stood a little taller.

Jayda's skin was the color of melted caramel, and her stomach was swollen with child. She was twenty-five years old and five months pregnant. Brave but scared, Jayda was torn between the profound love she felt for the baby she carried and the knowledge that her circumstances would conspire against the stability and opportunity this child deserved. Jayda explained that she lost her job in early 2009, then lost her apartment, and finally lost custody of her five-year-old daughter. She was embroiled in a court battle for the girl, and if she kept this unborn child, placement into foster care was inevitable.

I explained my lifelong draw to adoption, and how caring for this child was not my backup plan. This was what I was born to do. Navid and I could provide the best education, a loving extended family, travel, and the chance to develop any interest this child might have. Jayda said she had been a fast runner in high school and traveled with a show choir, so she expected this child to be able to carry both a football and a tune pretty well.

We both had first-date jitters, unsure as to who was supposed to be winning over whom. At the end of our hour together, Jayda slid an envelope across the table to me, signaling that she had made her decision. "This is my ultrasound picture," she said. "You are having a boy." I pulled out the sonogram of my fetal son. I could see his peanut nose and every bone in his spine. His heart glowed like a firefly, and tiny ethereal bubbles floated around him as he rested in blessed ignorance of all of the forces vying for his life.

"Please take care of my son," Jayda implored as she signed our adoption plan. The desperation in her voice echoed the voice of Juanita, Dartanyon's mother, which had swept through my head and my heart during Dartanyon's consolation match four months prior. It tugged, too, at the maternal instincts I felt toward Leroy, who was brought into this world by a woman similar to Jayda in certain ways.

As I drove away, my heart swelled with thoughts of all three boys, linked by the same calling. Back home, my father was less impressed with the beauty of this symmetry.

"Oh, jeez, she's black!"

That was his knee-jerk response to a photo I shared of Jayda and me posed together. He broke into a cold sweat looking at that picture, trying to figure out how to explain to his golfing buddies that he was about to become a grandfather to a black child. His reaction did not surprise me; hearing it aloud, so brazen and unapologetic, did.

Navid's and my choice defied the generational racism that had been handed down to my father by his parents, and to them by their parents, as well as by a culture that, during my father's formative years, enforced the belief that skin color should separate us. Segregation had prevented my father from learning the lesson that I'd gleaned on Big Ma's front porch: when you know someone's story, it becomes impossible to hate him.

My father could not reverse the beliefs that the culture of his era had instilled in him. And I could not dismiss the shame I felt toward him because of it. So there we stood, both hot in the cheeks. He disapproved of me, and I disapproved of him. And even though neither of us was speaking, we were still managing to have this conversation, all while staring at a photo of a black woman carrying a child who had the power to fix us both.

STORYTELLERS DISTILL MEANING. We boil down complexities. We extract importance. We erect guideposts. In television, the edit room is a storyteller's laboratory. It is where facts and art must reach equilibrium, as we cull the best elements to present to our viewers. With more than sixty hours of footage collected on Leroy and Dartanyon over four months—five times what I would have normally shot for a story—choosing the right moments in the proper order grew into a maddening chess match. We had to condense four months of nuance into ten minutes of compelling television.

In past edits, I'd relied upon my own intuition when I arrived at a crossroads. I had learned to look for the split second of video that caused me to hold my breath or clench my fists—and if it did that for me, I trusted it would do the same for a viewer. But for the first time in my career, I questioned my instincts. Did I like a shot sequence because it was truly fascinating, or because my bias toward Leroy and Dartanyon skewed my judgment? How could I detach myself? *Should* I detach myself?

I tried to focus on the key themes. Determination over despair. The rejection of pity. Humor as a weapon against challenge. Tom and I strove to weave these intricacies delicately throughout the piece, ensuring that each thread led back to the friendship, cast in sport and layered in the context of teammates. With my editor, Josh Drake, piloting our efforts, we worked twelve-hour sessions throughout the summer, after which I headed home to pore over music and rehash wordings, often until I fell asleep at my dining room table. By early August, our script had undergone twenty-two rewrites as we toiled to reconstruct something as mystical as the chemistry between two people. And this incessant dissection only spun me further into blurred confusion. Had I merely convinced myself that this was a compelling story, or was the supporting evidence truly on these tapes?

During one late-night session, Victor mentioned that ESPN was debuting oversize plasma monitors behind anchors for their on-camera lead-ins. To fill those screens, our features now needed titles. Leroy and Dartanyon's story would be the first on our network with a name more telling than "Sunday Feature."

"What do we call it?" I asked Tom as we looked at the crumpled stack of scripts on my desk, feeling a little like giving up. Paused on the monitor before us was a still photo of Leroy on top of Dartanyon's back, looking back at us with the same twinkle that had compelled me to get out of bed and onto a plane five months before.

"I think there's only one thing we can call it," Tom said. "'Carry On.'" We smiled at one another, renewed in our efforts to untangle the task before us, with Leroy and Dartanyon as our muses.

"Carry on," I repeated. "If they can do it, so can we."

For their part, Leroy and Dartanyon provided comedic relief, calling throughout the summer. "You need to come back," Dartanyon would say. "I'm riding on Leroy's back now. You gotta film it." They never asked how the edit was unfolding, or even when their segment might air. They weren't concerned with how they might be portrayed. They trusted me implicitly, which further drove my desire to fill every frame of television with the greatness they deserved.

On weekends, as I folded tiny blue pajamas and lined the crib with plush teddy bears in preparation for my son, the bulk of my thoughts remained with Leroy and Dartanyon. I grieved the tender touches they had likely missed out on as children. I missed their laughter. Then I worried about their harsher days ahead. Graduation was done. Our cameras had gone. Neither had submitted a college application. I wanted Leroy to dream bigger than Big Ma's fusty basement; I wanted Dartanyon to find his elusive home, to be rewarded for bypassing his father's footsteps. How could I plan for my unborn child in such thorough detail and neglect Leroy and Dartanyon's futures? Where did God's responsibility end and mine begin? What was the backup plan should *Carry On* air to mediocre reviews? As I looked at the empty bedrooms in our cozy home, the answer seemed apparent: Leroy and Dartanyon should live with us.

"Honey, that would be incredibly challenging," Navid said. "We are maxed out as it is."

"But they don't have anywhere to go," I argued. "They wouldn't need much."

"Lisa, we don't even have a ramp."

I knew "ramp" was metaphorical for "we can't do this." Navid, now in a sports medicine fellowship, worked up to eighty hours a week. I traveled frequently. We had a newborn on the way. But I stomped out to the garage to look for some scrap wood and nails any way. Regardless of what our social worker thought, I reckoned I might just be crazy enough.

Carry On AIRED in early August 2009, and the piece began with a simple question: "What would you do for a friend?"

Thirteen minutes later, it ended with this fact: "While both boys wished to attend college, neither had the means to do so."

That plea, issued against the backdrop of Leroy and Dartanyon's resilience, sparked an incredible response from viewers across the country.

FROM NEW YORK: Thank you to Leroy and Dartanyon for showing us that our lowest moments don't have to hold us back. They can make us better.

FROM FLORIDA: As Leroy explained, it is not about pity. It is, however, about the true meaning of the human spirit.

FROM CALIFORNIA: Nothing like crying in a cube farm. That was the highlight of my week.

FROM INDIANA: Not only does this bring tears to my eyes, but Leroy and Dartanyon restore belief in mankind!

FROM MASSACHUSETTS: There are no physical boundaries in life that are more powerful than a positive attitude to succeed. Thank you, Leroy and Dartanyon, for showing us that today.

These messages arrived in tidal waves to my in-box. I could

hardly finish one before another crossed. An hour may have passed before I blinked. Finally I dropped down on the kitchen floor, weeping, relying on the cold hardwood to shock me back from what was surely a dream. I had left the edit at four o'clock in the morning—just six hours before air time—convinced I had lost the pulse of the piece. And yet it worked. The piece took a template—overcoming challenges to achieve success—and amplified it in nearly every way. Here were two people, with physical challenges of different kinds, and another set of challenges that were less apparent. Here was success in terms not of victory but of persistence and selflessness. Here was a portrait of love shared by two young men of color—not always the central focus of such portraits. Here were two young men who so obviously needed help, but rather than wallow in wait, they helped themselves and each other, genuinely and selflessly.

As a result, viewers wondered: *Could I be that strong?*

FROM GEORGIA: Thank you Leroy and Dartanyon for never giving up. Because of you, I will never give up.

FROM CALIFORNIA: Tell Leroy, the next time he finds himself struggling with the question of "Why my legs?" to think about all the people who were wondering, "Where's my heart?" until he helped us find it.

FROM FLORIDA: I am missing a leg too and want to wrestle. Can I talk to the two wrestlers on ESPN? They are my heroes!

FROM CALIFORNIA: I have been an addict for nearly ten years. Today I am going to rehab. If Leroy and Dartanyon don't feel sorry for themselves, I am not going to either.

FROM LONDON: Every morning I take a train from Cambridge to London. Like most Mondays, it's tough to stay grateful. But as my eyes watered as Leroy walked onstage alongside Dartanyon, it made me realize how grateful I am for my own life today. Thank you.

FROM OHIO: I was not only touched by this amazing story of strength and friendship, I was humbled by the grace and humanity of these remarkable young men. Tragedy is not what happened to Leroy—tragedy would be not supporting his dreams. How can we help these boys?

With Navid away on a camping trip, I spent the day savoring these messages, treasuring them in my heart in the quiet of our house. The only ones not bowled over by Leroy and Dartanyon were Leroy and Dartanyon.

"The piece was good," Leroy said, as though trying to convince himself.

"Yah, that was . . . yah," Dartanyon said. "I didn't really know what to expect."

Over the next twenty-four hours, more than four million viewers tuned in to ESPN to watch *Carry On*, and another half million watched on ESPN.com. From Ipswich to Idaho, housewives to sports fans to NFL executives answered the question, "What would you do for a friend?" by emulating Leroy and Dartanyon's example: They offered to carry Leroy and Dartanyon in return.

FROM NEW JERSEY: Thank you for touching my heart. I have watched many stories over my lifetime and have wanted to do something to help but never did. Today I want that to be different. I don't have much, but I can do something.

FROM WASHINGTON: Unbelievable story on ESPN about Leroy and Dartanyon. My entire family is sitting here in tears. Does Leroy need a wheelchair van?

FROM TEXAS: I can't remember the last time I've been as affected by a story as I was today. Has anyone set up a fund for these two young men? I can't imagine two people more deserving of an opportunity to continue their education.

FROM PENNSYLVANIA: I for one do not want money to be the factor that keeps Leroy and Dartanyon from reaching any future goals. I don't have much, so I am heading out to buy a Powerball ticket. If I win, it's theirs.

FROM MARYLAND: If there is a scholarship fund or anything I can do to facilitate their college aspirations, I will contribute in a heartbeat.

FROM TEXAS: I would like to donate at least $1,000 to each of them for their education.

FROM ILLINOIS: With me being a college student myself, I don't have much money but would be willing to put $40 in to get the fund started.

FROM TENNESSEE: Amazing. Heartwarming. Goose bumps. Happy Tears. Sad Tears. I haven't much to give, but I sat on my bed this morning and said a prayer for both of them. For all of us.

I had prayed for one viewer with deep pockets and a heart of mercy to be drawn to Leroy and Dartanyon. Instead, I got a legion of allies—each one eager to right the wrongs of these boys' pasts. Every respondent that is, except one:

ESPN CANNOT BE ASSOCIATED WITH ANY FUND-RAISING CAMPAIGN ON BEHALF OF LEROY AND DARTANYON. YOU ARE NOT PERMITTED TO INVOLVE YOURSELF ANY FURTHER.

ESPN's mailboxes and phone lines had been receiving viewer inquiries throughout Sunday, and by Monday morning, the network saw the need to remind me that it could not incur the liability associated with collecting money for individuals. While I understood the corporate position, its lack of empathy hit me like a bowed arrow to the sternum. Wouldn't a phone call to brainstorm solutions have been more appropriate? Did they expect me to forward a torrent of e-mails to a blind kid with no computer? Leroy and Dartanyon had no bank accounts, no family members equipped to harness this outpouring of generosity. ESPN had to understand that to rebuff this support would have been exploiting two vulnerable, deserving boys. Miniature tornadoes of bewilderment, then anger, then betrayal spun through me, overtaking my sensibilities. I was pounding out my resignation when Victor appeared behind my cubicle.

"I saw the cease and desist order," he said, running his hand through his hair.

"Victor, I will quit before I turn my back on those boys. I'll quit right now," I said. That day, I would be brave. That day, I would stand tall. "This is their chance. It's the only one they're ever going to get."

Victor's eyes grew soft, and he nodded ever so slightly. "Take whatever time off you need, and don't worry about the legalities," he said. "Go change the world. Our secret."

CHAPTER 10

NEW LIVES

It has been said that our lives are shaped by only a handful of moments—some delicate, some severe. They are points of decision. Choices made. Consequences suffered. Love lost or gained. Our remaining hours are spent living out those pivotal moments and being refined by them. Who decides where our course will veer and in which direction it will head? The turn in Leroy and Dartanyon's story was decided not by them, nor by its narrator. Instead, a chorus of a thousand strangers made the decision.

Dear Lisa . . . What is the scope of Leroy and Dartanyon's needs? I'd like to gain a sense of scale. Five thousand? Ten thousand? Twenty-five thousand? One hundred thousand? I would like to make this real as soon as possible so that they may plan accordingly for their educations.

I did not tell Leroy or Dartanyon about the incredible kindness piled up in my in-box. I couldn't bear disappointing them if nothing materialized, and I needed a clearer picture of what was being offered—and what was needed. I had never itemized and priced Leroy and Dartanyon's needs. Both boys wanted to go to college. Dartanyon wanted to study law; Leroy aspired to design video games. Where were the best schools for each? Could they live independently? Did they need medical care? Did they qualify for disability benefits? Should I be raising money for the future, or to mitigate their daily needs now?

Too many questions to answer in too little time, I decided. And so began a frantic race against the clock to collect donations before viewer interest waned. My first call was to Michael O'Brien, a Cleveland attorney and family friend who specialized in estate planning. He donated his time and staff, and within three days a trust fund for the benefit of Leroy and Dartanyon was in place. Michael's firm gave me a credible Cleveland address to which people could mail donations. However, I imagined I'd lose a lot of interested people unless we had a website that could accept credit card payments. *Lord, this was Your doing*, I thought. *You're going to have to figure out how to build a website.*

It was then that I fielded a message from Akron: *Lisa, I was truly moved by your story about Dartanyon and Leroy. I live seventy miles south of Cleveland and want to help in any way I can. Paul Eckinger, Eckinger Marketing and Web Design.*

I phoned Paul immediately. An Ohio native himself, Paul not only remembered Leroy's accident but had fund-raised for Leroy's family in 2002. He knew the money had been squandered. "I'd like to help again," Paul said. "This time I'd like to see it handled the right way." Paul stayed up for most of the next four days, designing and programming a website from scratch. He even convinced the payment site to watch *Carry On* and waive their standard 6 percent commission on credit card transactions, ensuring that every dollar donated would go to help the boys. When Paul finished, I asked him how long those four days of work would have normally taken. "Four to eight weeks," he said.

I stayed up for much of that week too, personally responding to every e-mail until my eye sockets ached and my fingers curled. Navid pleaded with me to rest, but I dared not lose the public's momentum. Nor could I tear myself away from the gripping nature of these letters. A man contemplating suicide that day chose to live, explaining that if Leroy and Dartanyon could endure, he could too. A single mother of an autistic son had spent the last ten years blaming herself for his disability; now she wanted to celebrate her child and involve him in wrestling. A businessman wanted to grant Leroy and Dartanyon lavish wishes of their choice.

A private pilot volunteered to fly them on college visits. A high school wrestling team in Florida organized a Push-Up-A-Thon to raise funds. Hollywood wanted movie rights. Carpenters offered ramps for Leroy. Researchers proposed experimental treatments on Dartanyon's eyes. Television shows sought them as guests.

The Carry On website went live on Friday night—five days after the piece aired. In its first hour, $11,000 poured in. Most donations were in small amounts from inspired, everyday people—$5, $20, $50. The frenzy continued throughout the weekend and maintained a steady flow throughout the month of August. The grand total come September was $47,000.

On top of that, a handful of viewers offered to pay the balance of college tuition and living expenses for Leroy and Dartanyon—an unimaginable opportunity borne of remarkable charity. I vetted these donors by phone, determining whose intentions were pure and whose positions most stable. I narrowed it down to three shrewd, kind businessmen and asked if they might divide the expenses, wanting to fill Leroy and Dartanyon's lives with multiple accomplished role models. The three benefactors agreed, but not before one of them flipped the tables and interviewed me.

A vice president of a prominent global investment-banking firm, this gentleman peppered me with questions about my background, my education, my family, my workload. Having grown up disadvantaged, this man had made it his mission to use his wealth to educate kids from similar backgrounds. In doing so, he concluded that the single most determining factor in these students' success or failure was his or her support system. "More than knowing Leroy or Dartanyon, I need to know you," he said. "I need to know who is going to get them over the inevitable bumps ahead, and from what I can tell, you are all they have."

I knew Leroy and Dartanyon needed me here, now, to rally these resources and propel them forward. But I had assumed I would pack them up and wave proudly as they rode off into their new lives. It hadn't occurred to me that they might continue to need me in the months and years that would follow. I could not conceive of what might go awry, yet the grave tone of this man's questions communicated that he knew better. I wanted to ask what pitfalls to anticipate and what he expected from me. But I worried he might interpret such questions as wavering on my part. I feared my ignorance might cause him to reconsider his offer.

Sometimes commitment is a choice. Here, it was the only choice.

"I love them, and I am here for whatever they need," I replied. "You have my word."

LEROY AND DARTANYON remained oblivious to the activity within my house-turned-fund-raising-headquarters. Leroy seemed content hanging out at Big Ma's for the summer, and my mother helped Dartanyon get an internship at the Ohio Lottery, where she worked. Though nothing had changed in their daily happenings, they had achieved local rock star statuses that left them perplexed.

"Everywhere we go, people yell, 'There's the guys from ESPN!'" Leroy said.

"It's been real weird. People want to shake our hands and tell us we're awesome," Dartanyon added. "Not sure why." How could they be heroes, he wondered, when they were still sitting in the ghetto, living hand-to-mouth like everyone else? Leroy understood, though, and it felt like déjà vu.

"Who knew that getting run over by one train could get me famous twice," Leroy said. He couldn't conceive of how his circumstances were about to change this time.

I flew back to Cleveland over Labor Day weekend for the big reveal. I summoned Leroy and Dartanyon, Big Ma, Katrina, Arthur, Coach Hons, Coach Robinson, and Paul, our web angel, to Michael O'Brien's office. They were all assembled upon my arrival. No one, except Paul, appeared happy to see me.

"Why are we here?" Dartanyon asked. "Are we in trouble?"

"Trouble? Why would you think that?" I asked.

"Because the only time you gotta lawyer up is when you're in trouble," Leroy said. It had not occurred to me that an attorney's office would prompt anxiety in them. To me, attorneys were relatives, friends, and helpful resources. "Lawyers are your one call from prison," Dartanyon contended.

"Well, quite the opposite today," I said with a laugh. "I have good news for you. It turns out that more than a few Clevelanders want to shake your hand. It's the whole country. And they've donated money for you to go to college. You can go to college! Surprise!" The men gasped, and the women fanned themselves. I was reluctant to volunteer exactly how much money had been raised, and to my relief, no one asked. Dollars didn't matter to them. Hope for a future did.

I continued through the list of offerings with the glee of Santa slinging presents out of a sack. Designer workout clothing, NFL tickets, video game consoles, concert passes, speaking invitations, first-pitch honors at the Cleveland Indians game, and new wrestling shoes for the entire Lincoln-West team. With each announcement, Dartanyon alternated between pumping his fists, dropping his head into his hands, or looking to the sky in disbelief. On the contrary, Leroy sat expressionless. I assumed he was in shock. His mother spoke for him instead.

"What about LeBron?" Katrina asked. "When he gonna step up and help us?"

"LeBron's a very busy man, and we may not need him," I answered, and continued to my next piece of news. "Have you heard of the Paralympics?" No one had. "It is the Olympics for people with physical disabilities. There are many things that Dartanyon and Leroy could do competitively. And the United States Olympic Committee has invited you to Colorado to see their facilities and try out some new sports. You fly out next week.

"I want you to realize that while all of these opportunities are amazing, you are not rich," I continued. "You've been given something better. You have been given the gift of space and time in which to work hard so that you can create stable, productive lives for yourselves. We can talk through the specifics of how we are going to do that later, but for now, do you have any questions?"

Dartanyon meekly raised his hand.

"Yes," I said.

"Um, did you say we're flying to Colorado?" he asked, trying to suppress his excitement. "Because I've never been on an airplane."

"Me neither," Leroy said.

I smiled, indicating they were cleared for takeoff. And right there, in the middle of our ordinary lives, a whole great wonder took hold.

FROM MY LIMITED vantage point, alleviating Leroy and Dartanyon's poverty and accommodating their disabilities did not seem terribly complicated. On a basic level, Dartanyon needed food and clothing. Leroy needed a new wheelchair. Both boys would require medical checkups, college application fees, laptops, beds, and desks. I would make the to-do lists, write the checks, and take down the mighty walls of poverty brick by brick.

While Leroy thought through his college options, I focused my attention on Dartanyon. Our first stop was the Cleveland Sight Center, a nonprofit agency serving the visually impaired. I bought Dartanyon a checkbook ledger with large lines, a calendar with wide blocks, and adaptive software to enlarge his laptop's screen. I offered him the free magnifying glass that came with the purchases, but he ordered me to put it down as though I had pointed a gun at him. He hardly wanted to be seen in this place, let alone leaving with a shopping bag. Still, I was elated. Now he could see his responsibilities and organize them.

Our next stop was Cuyahoga Community College in downtown Cleveland. Dartanyon's sister, Dionna, lived a short bus ride from one of the school's satellite campuses, and she said Dartanyon could stay with her. We registered him for algebra, psychology, and English, and then headed to the bookstore to buy his textbooks. "Let's pick up some notebooks as well," I said. Dartanyon followed me around the store, but once in the paper supply aisle, he stood uncomfortably beside me, waiting for instructions.

"Go ahead and choose whatever you want," I said.

With great hesitation, he lifted a thin-ruled yellow spiral notebook from the shelf just beside him. "This should be good," he said.

"I think one with wide lines might be better for your vision," I suggested. "And you have three classes, so you'll need three notebooks."

"Oh," Dartanyon said. He remained fixed in one place. I wasn't sure why choosing basic items was so difficult. Then I realized the source of his uneasiness.

"You've never gone shopping for school supplies, have you?" I asked.

"No," he answered softly.

"How did you take notes in high school without notebooks?"

"I always just borrowed a sheet of paper and a pencil from whoever was sitting next to me."

I thought about my childhood, and how the end of summer launched a spirited quest for colorful binders and bouquets of freshly sharpened pencils.

"Well, then," I said, nodding slowly while forcing back tears, "allow me the distinct pleasure of showing you a few new products on the market, Mr. Crockett." I launched into my best showroom-model impression, opening notebooks with exaggerated arm movements and demonstrating their pocket dividers with flair. I waxed eloquent on the uselessness of the compass and protractor once high school geometry has passed and debated the pros and cons of three-subject versus one-subject notebooks.

"You see, with the three-in-one, you have everything you need in one place," I explained. "It eliminates having to find three different notebooks every day."

Finally Dartanyon's stance softened, in what had become a spiritual moment in aisle six of this community-college bookstore. "I understand your point, and for that reason, I think I'll get the single-subject ones," he countered. "If I get the three-subject note-book and lose it, then I'll have lost everything."

I laughed and told him to select his three colors and I would take him to lunch, just as my mother used to do in celebration of our school shopping excursions. Dartanyon chose his notebooks quickly and led the way to the cash register. It was the first time he had walked ahead of me since I'd met him, six months earlier. I suspected that having choices breeds that sort of confidence.

BACK AT MY father's house that afternoon, I received a call from an administrative assistant at the college. "I just thought you should know that Dartanyon put down your name as his emergency contact today," she said, her voice wavering.

"That is fine," I said. "Thank you for letting me know."

"No, that's not all I'm calling to tell you," she said. "Next to your name on the form is a space that says 'Relationship to Student.' Dartanyon wrote 'Guardian Angel.' I've just never seen anything like that. I don't know who you are, but I thought you should know."

A FEW DAYS later, Leroy and Dartanyon boarded their first flight for the Olympic Training Center in Colorado Springs. This idyllic Disney World for athletes spans thirty-five acres, with housing capacity for more than five hundred athletes. While the Michael Phelpses and Michelle Kwans of this world train at home with private coaches, the majority of less visible Olympians and Paralympians toil in relative anonymity at one of our country's four training compounds. Together, Leroy and Dartanyon floated around campus, taking deep gulps of crisp mountain air. They toured the swimming, gymnastics, and weight-lifting facilities. They were presented with Team USA tracksuits, Dartanyon declaring that he would never take his off for as long as he lived. Leroy learned that as an amputee, he could compete in Paralympic hand cycling, shooting, powerlifting, swimming, and wheelchair fencing. Dartanyon's visual impairment made him eligible for sports like goal ball, rowing, and track and field.

Seeing resident Paralympians training alongside able-bodied Olympians gave Dartanyon and Leroy a glimpse of the world through a new and refreshing window—an alternate universe in which disabled people were regarded for their abilities, not their limitations. Even the language oozed with empowerment. No one was "crippled" or "cross-eyed." Instead they were "differently abled" and "para athletes." Leroy was particularly pleased to learn that his bench press was competitive with national Paralympic powerlifting marks, and said he'd consider training for the team. But it was a new sport that piqued Dartanyon's interest: judo.

"Judo is a Japanese martial art, kind of like a cousin to wrestling," head coach Ed Liddie explained to Dartanyon and Leroy. Judo aficionados cringed when Liddie linked the two sports, which were born of vastly different cultures and utilize distinctive techniques. But Liddie knew that in the United States, laypeople see judo as little more than wrestling in pajamas. The primary objective of judo is to throw an opponent through the air, with control and force, flatly onto his back, both shoulders touching the mat. If the fight goes to the ground—entering what is called *ne waza*—one works to submit the opponent with a choke or an arm bar, or to pin his back to the mat for twenty seconds. If your opponent doesn't tap out, it's permissible to choke him unconscious or break his arms.

And though wrestling serves as a traditional favorite of Americans at the Olympic Games, judo is the second most popular sport in the world, behind only soccer.

"There are similarities, but judo is all takedowns and pins," Liddie explained. "No kicking, no punching. Striking is prohibited in judo."

Liddie's father Edward, an army veterinarian, learned judo while stationed in France during the 1950s. When the Liddies moved back to the hardscrabble streets of Harlem, New York, Edward opened a record shop to support the family. To support his judo habit, he laid mats across the back room of the shop and started an informal neighborhood judo club. Liddie went on to star at Cumberland College from 1978 to 1982. Two years later, he won Olympic bronze at the 1984 Los Angeles Games, making him the second African American judo medalist in US history. His smile told you he was a kind man. His stare told you he was studying his surroundings like a surveillance camera. And his sixth-degree black belt told you he could take you down a hundred different ways.

Liddie and USA Judo put on twenty or so demonstrations a year, for everyone from schoolkids to corporate sponsors to wounded warriors returning from combat. In these forty-five-minute sessions, participants learn a few basics, like how to grip the lapel of the robelike *gi* worn by judo players, and how to take a fall safely. Then they take to the mats to try it themselves. When Liddie teaches visitors a throw, he usually jumps over their backs and lands flatly on his to give them the thrill of thinking they actually threw an Olympic medalist, as their friends ooh and ahh.

Dartanyon stepped in for his turn. Liddie leaned in as he had hundreds of times before to facilitate the demo throw. But Dartanyon caught Liddie off guard.

"To my amazement, Dartanyon actually threw me. I didn't even have time to jump," Liddie said. Sensing that Dartanyon liked the sport, Liddie invited him back to watch the full squad of thirty practice that evening. But Dartanyon didn't want to watch practice. He wanted a turn on the mats—and that was where we learned that Dartanyon had been blessed with a coveted gift in the judo world: quick hips.

"Judo is a lot of hips, and it doesn't come naturally to many people," Liddie said. "People try to throw with their back and upper body because they can't get enough power in their hips to pivot and bend."

Liddie discovered that not only did Dartanyon's hips swing like hinges, but his mind sucked in instruction like a magnetic force field. "We showed him a throw. He absorbed it. We showed him another throw. He absorbed it." Though Liddie had dumbed down the drills for Dartanyon's safety, Dartanyon exhibited a feel for the basic movements. Liddie likened it to a young kid who picks up a baseball for the first time and throws a curveball into the strike zone. "He wanted to see another throw, then another one. I was like, jeez, who is this kid?"

But Liddie knew that judo is largely a pedigree sport in which children between the ages of six and ten years old are ushered in by their judo-loving parents. Only on rare occasions does anyone start in his late teens to emerge as a dominant force. Still, Liddie went home scratching his head that night. "Had I not been there to see it myself and someone later told me that this kid had potential, I would have said, 'That's great, but it's too late to start in the sport.'"

Paralympics officials had been impressed with what they saw of Dartanyon's athleticism on ESPN, but in question was whether he was blind enough to participate in blind judo. He needed to fall into one of three categories: B1, B2, or B3. Athletes with a B1 impairment suffer from complete or near-total blindness. B2 athletes possess a constricted visual field of less than ten degrees. B3 athletes present with a visual field of less than forty degrees. By comparison, one needs a clear field of vision of at least one hundred degrees to qualify for a driver's license.

Dartanyon was scheduled for an appointment at the United States Olympic Committee's (USOC) Director of Vision Services, which is charged with classifying Paralympians for competition. The optometrist put Dartanyon through an hour-long battery of tests. Her commands were rushed and curt. If Dartanyon said he could not make out a letter, she insisted he try harder. Dartanyon began to feel attacked and overwhelmed. And then he began guessing. His waffling caused the doctor to wonder if he was faking his condition—an idea utterly inconceivable to Dartanyon, yet a legitimate cause for concern, particularly in Eastern European countries, where Paralympians are paid handsomely. Finally, and with no warning, the optometrist announced her conclusion: "Dartanyon, you are a borderline B3, if that. You will never be cleared to participate." With that, she left the room, leaving the news to burn in Dartanyon's chest.

"My whole life I'm too blind to do much of anything. Then I find something that is designed for the visually impaired, and I can't do it?" Dartanyon said to me. He had let himself imagine, if for just one night, that perhaps his physical disability had not been a defect, that perhaps it was intended as his ticket down this golden path toward athletic glory. Instead, he headed back to the airport, and the experience faded behind him like a mountain mirage.

ULTIMATELY, LEROY DECIDED that he identified as an artist, not an athlete. His veins did not pulse with competitive juices like Dartanyon's did. He wanted to develop video games, and he wanted to do it in a region where his wheelchair would not get stuck in snow. Leroy quietly selected Collins College of Design in Phoenix, Arizona to pursue his studies. Together we filled out the application, and I coordinated details with the admissions counselor.

Throughout our visits and phone calls that fall, Dartanyon was full of thank-yous and hugs, broad smiles and slow exhales. But Leroy's apathetic posture never budged. Even when I called to congratulate him on his acceptance to Collins, he grunted, unimpressed.

"Leroy, if at any point you don't want this, you need to speak up," I said. "The last thing I want to do is inflict my desires on you."

"No, it's all good," he replied.

"But usually when it's 'all good,' people smile or say something," I said. "Each time I call you with good news, you are so quiet. I am not even sure you are on the line."

"No one's ever called me with good news before. I don't know what I'm supposed to say." Just as Leroy had not learned the language of lament, he lacked the prose of pleasure as well. "But I am happy inside," he finally said. "My dreams might come true."

CHAPTER 11

THE GENTLE WAY

Ed Liddie could not shake Dartanyon's demo out of his head. *The kid threw me*, he thought. Liddie knew that visual acuity testing involves a degree of subjectivity in interpreting the classification boundaries. Failing one eye exam did not technically disqualify Dartanyon. He could try again. Perhaps he had gotten lucky enough guessing letters that he'd failed himself. Still, attempting additional testing was fine for young kids and weekend warriors who wanted to compete as a hobby, but the stakes were higher for Liddie. If Dartanyon's vision was truly borderline, and he managed to pass a domestic eye exam, he could still be in jeopardy of failing one in international competition, where classification protocols are stricter. Liddie couldn't be on the hook for spending USOC development dollars on a kid who had a high likelihood of being ruled ineligible two or three years down the line, when he was being counted on for results. And of course, these issues hinged on the biggest question of all: Could an eighteen-year-old kid be taken, quite literally, off the streets and transformed into a formidable judo player?

Liddie didn't know the answer. Though he had coached thirteen Olympians since 1996, he had only absorbed the resident Paralympic responsibilities one year earlier, in 2008. The competitive landscape and the vision testing were still murky to him. All he knew for sure was that he'd inherited a roster with a gaping hole at −81kg, and Dartanyon could fill it pound for pound. Liddie decided to approach it like a chess match: make one move at a time, and see what ensues.

He told me to find Dartanyon a beginner judo class in Cleveland, just to see if he liked it enough to follow through.

THE JAPANESE CHARACTERS for *judo* represent two ideas. The *ju* embodies "yielding or giving way." The *do* means "the way." When translated into English, the name of this sport that allows one to literally choke the breath out of another is commonly referred to as "the gentle way." In a technical sense, the principle of "giving way" applies to how one responds to a stronger challenger. For example, if one is pushed, the instinct is to push back, leading to a strength-against-strength confrontation, with the stronger challenger emerging victorious. However, under judo principles, the win would not necessarily go to the more powerful athlete. The weaker judoka, when forcibly pushed, could give way—yielding to the energy by turning or dropping low. The challenger's momentum in turn would go through or over the judoka, leaving the challenger off balance and the weaker but more skillful judoka in optimal position for a takedown.

In the philosophical sense, "giving way" is also a life application, emphasizing maximum efficiency in the art of refining and perfecting daily life. "Take the energy the world is sending you—good or bad—and use it to your advantage," explained Shane Hudson, master instructor at MaxOut Sports, located on the southeast edge of Cleveland. "Don't fight back. Take the energy and adapt to it. Do you understand?"

Few understood better. "I've been adapting my whole life," Dartanyon answered.

I had cold-called Hudson the week before, giving him what was becoming my standard spiel about a blind boy, a train accident survivor, and their uniquely inspiring friendship. As long as I got an even marginal sports fan on the phone, those four letters I gave after my name—E-S-P-N—opened nearly every door I approached.

In this case, I needed a judo coach, and Hudson was the first one to pick up the phone.

Like Coach Liddie, Hudson grew up on military bases. His father served in the air force, and every base had a mandated judo club. As a teen Hudson briefly encountered a blind Vietnam veteran on base in North Carolina who coached and made an indelible imprint on him. Hudson was fascinated by how this man maneuvered by feel, and he often found himself doing his own drill work with his eyes closed to mimic the sensation.

Hudson fit Dartanyon's needs with the perfect trifecta of qualifications: a third-degree black belt, a bachelor's degree in business management, and theological training in biblical studies. He had skills, smarts, and sensitivity. He saw his dojo not just as a business but as a ministry. For two decades he had been donating training fees for underprivileged children and working side jobs to raise money for their uniforms and tournament expenses. He believed in the power of judo to combat the rough edges of life with a more wholesome way. And he radiated the Zen-like gentleness he espoused. A trim white man in his early fifties, Hudson had soft graying hair and kind, welcoming eyes. After watching *Carry On*, he wasted no time phoning me back to say that Dartanyon was welcome any time, free of charge.

Hudson may have been moved by Dartanyon's plight, but he was nonplussed by his athletic abilities. "When he first came out, he was getting thrown all over the beginner class like a rag doll," Hudson remembered. "I wasn't sure why the USOC was interested in him. There was nothing that made me say 'This guy is going to go far.'" Hudson pulled Dartanyon off the mats and put him through a series of skill tests instead: Sprint work to check his fast-twitch muscle groups. Vertical leap and broad jump to look at his explosive abilities. Clean and jerks to assess his strength. Core stability, endurance, upper back—everything from soup to nuts. "Judo relies on coordinated, explosive motion, all within a self-contained sphere," Hudson said. "And as it turned out, Dartanyon had it all. He had the tools to be the real deal."

Hudson continued, drilling Dartanyon further than he would drill anyone else. "I was looking for the point at which Dartanyon's intensity would wane. It never did." Hudson knew he had a true fighter—the kind who has nothing to lose and everything to prove. But in order for his physical tools and his interminable will to work together, Dartanyon needed to accomplish two difficult, somewhat contradictory goals: unlearn wrestling while learning judo. Hudson likened wrestling to a commercial airliner—wide in the base, giving one a longer setup time and a broader stance from which to throw. Judo is the jet fighter—a tighter, dynamic stance from which to twitch and quickly turn with your opponent. "In wrestling, you can just heave-ho someone. Judo is about timing and finesse," Hudson said. "Dartanyon quickly realized that overpowering people wasn't working. He had to learn the technique."

Hudson focused on Judo 101—hand placement on an opponent's *gi*, bowing to authority, how to take a fall. He pounded Dartanyon with rudimentary skills, over and over, until his muscles could remember them without his head having to try so hard. Hudson was encouraged, but he didn't have much to report when Ed Liddie called in early November, after just a handful of sessions, to check on his prospect. Hudson believed Dartanyon's greatest asset was the one quality he seemed to be missing—arrogance. "There is no belligerence or sass in him," he told Coach Liddie. "He's teachable."

DARTANYON HAD BEEN enrolled at Cuyahoga Community College for a month when the first crisis arose in October 2009.

"They're gonna drop me from school tomorrow because I can't get financial aid," he said.

"Who is going to drop you?" I asked. "Why can't you get financial aid? I thought we signed everything last month." He didn't know who had called him, and he hadn't asked for any further details. He seemed resigned that he would have to leave. I spent the next hour on hold with the school before sending Dartanyon to sign consent forms so the financial aid department could speak to me, and then languishing on hold once again. The simple answer: the school needed Arthur's 2009 tax returns to process Dartanyon's aid.

"Can you just call your dad and ask for his taxes?" I asked Dartanyon.

"His phone is off," Dartanyon said. "I won't find him by tomorrow." I called the school again to explain the dilemma and request an extension. We would have the taxes within a few days, I promised. The days turned into weeks, with Arthur saying he was just about to dig those up each time he saw his son. Finally, one weekend while Navid was on call at the hospital, I flew to Cleveland to find Arthur myself. I had promised the boys' trio of donors that I would handle these bumps in the road, and I could not in good conscience squander their money when this appeared to be an easy problem to fix. Besides, I told Navid, it was a good excuse to sneak in a visit with Jayda as well.

Arthur met with Dartanyon and me during his break at Applebee's, where he worked as a server. He had never heard of financial aid before. "I thought you said in that meeting that Dartanyon's college was paid for," Arthur said. I explained that it would be, but the benefactors were expecting us to take advantage of government grants to lower the costs, and these were dependent on parents' tax returns. "They are generous families, but I can't ask them to spend more money than they need to," I said.

"I didn't do my taxes last year," Arthur said.

"I can help you get those done pretty quickly," I said. "There might be a small penalty for being late, but it shouldn't be much."

Arthur looked down and picked at his thumbnail. "I haven't done my taxes in more than ten years," he confessed. Arthur had been evading child support payments for his kids, and since he made most of his money in undocumented tips, he had double cause to steer clear of the IRS.

"How much do you owe?" I asked.

"Lost track. Probably twenty or thirty thousand dollars. Let's just say that if I do my taxes now, I could go to jail," he answered solemnly. I looked at Arthur, and then at Dartanyon. I didn't know who to fight for in this situation.

"Arthur, I'm not here to tell you what to do. I'm just going to lay out the choices and the consequences. The decision is yours," I said. "If you work with an accountant, which we can cover, your son can be assured a college education and you may go to jail. If you decide not to pay taxes, I can't be as sure of Dartanyon's future."

Arthur pondered his next move for an uncomfortably long time. He no longer wanted Dartanyon to be a better man than himself. Instead, he wanted to be the man Dartanyon needed. He steeled himself, summoning every ounce of courage to face the challenge at hand. "I've put this boy through hell and back, and somehow, the love never left," he said. "You know you can only should've, could've, would've so many times. It's time I do the right thing for my son."

THE CALL CAME on November 13, 2009—a week earlier than we expected. I paged Navid in his morning meeting: "Our son has arrived." I threw together our suitcases, and we sped to the airport, calling for open flights to Cleveland as we drove. "Come on, Mommy!" "Hurry up, Daddy!" we sang as we danced to the boarding gate. We had been counseled to guard our enthusiasm throughout the pregnancy in the event that Jayda chose to keep her son. But now he was here, and Jayda had bid us to come.

We had also resisted finalizing a name, not wanting to personalize the process before knowing the outcome. But once on the plane, we pulled out our pared-down list of boy names. At the top of both of our lists was Saxon, the Germanic name for "warrior." Somewhere over Pennsylvania, we settled on the middle name Azariah, a Hebrew moniker meaning "with the help of God." After the pervasive struggle I had witnessed in Cleveland, I wanted my son to grow into a man of conviction who would defend goodness and justice, and who would speak for the downtrodden, all the while relying on the long arms of heaven. We wanted to brand a special purpose on this child's life, one that reflected how Leroy and Dartanyon had shaken my perceptions of race and class, re-shaped Navid's notion of family, and led us to this baby—not just any child but *this* child, this boy for whom I'd felt destined since my own youth.

Those lofty ideals quickly melted into pools of butter once we laid eyes on our ruddy, wrinkly little boy. This future warrior looked straight out of the land of dolls. He had ears as tiny as my thumbprint and a head of silky black hair so full that it looked like a toupee. As he yawned, I caught a hint of Jayda's darling dimples buried deep in his disproportionately large cheeks.

"I'd like you to meet your son," Jayda said, her voice catching. She offered him up into my arms, resolved to be brave even as her quivering lip betrayed her. She had known her son for just twelve hours. Why must she say good-bye so soon? How dire must her circumstances have been? And how deep her love, that she would not subject this child to hardship undeserved? Nothing had pre-pared me for the crushing sadness involved in taking a child out of the hands of the woman who had given him life. Saxon began to writhe and wail. I didn't know who to comfort first, this fragile baby or his broken young mother. To gain a family, my son had to lose a family. Grief twisted my insides, and yet on the outside, Jayda needed to see me welcome her child with joy.

The hospital staff, sensitive to the complexities of adoption, allowed Navid and me to stay in the adjoining room to maxi-mize our time with Saxon and Jayda. We took turns feeding him, changing him, and trying to offset Jayda's sadness with conversation about Saxon's perfection. Navid was instantly enamored of this child, and of fatherhood, while I fixated on Jayda's solitude. She remained uncertain of the birth father, had hidden her pregnancy from her family, and had delivered without anyone by her side. Soon she would have to walk out of the hospital, alone. But Jayda sat in her bed, drawing strength from her son's trusting gaze. She stared at him like he was her soul mate, and the longer she absorbed his love, the more convinced she became that she would do the right thing for her child.

I had prepared for Saxon's arrival by reading books on organic nutrition and classical education philosophies. I intended to be the perfect parent straight out of the box. But watching Jayda, I began to see that parenthood doesn't demand perfection. It demands grace—for the complexities of the journey, for resolving to be the hero a child needs, and for the letting go. This revelation softened me toward Saxon's first visitor as he walked through the hospital door.

"Congratulations, honey," my father said. "I hope you don't mind that I'm here." I was genuinely glad he had come.

"I'd like you to meet your grandson," I said, placing my swaddled newborn into his arms. I knew this wasn't how he'd envisioned the birth of his first grandchild, but the kindness in his eyes told me that this was not an obligatory visit, that we were not simply setting our differences aside. Gone was his nervous twitch. He looked more willing to accept a different kind of plan, made up of different kinds of people. He was spurred onto higher ground by his love for me, and now for Saxon, this tiny warrior for justice, who in his first twenty-four hours of life was already starting to right the past. I brimmed with a kind of pride I had never previously felt toward my father, followed by sorrow for having formerly lacked the grace to accept that we are all imperfect works in progress, tangled in history and hope as we try and fail and try again. And though my father and I didn't know how to express such huge and humble ideas to one another, there we were, arm in arm, having a different type of conversation than the one we'd had in the kitchen, standing over Jayda's photo. This time we were speaking the same language.

CHAPTER 12

TRANSITIONS

Just like that, I found myself sashaying along both ends of the parenting spectrum. By night I was sleep-training an infant; by day I was settling two teenagers into college life. Because Collins College operated on a unique term schedule, Leroy enrolled for a mid-November start. I bought his plane ticket, had three rooms of furniture delivered to his Arizona apartment, and scheduled the utilities to be turned on. On the morning of his flight, Leroy insisted that he was not nervous. "I've been waiting for my life to begin for a long time," he said. "I'm ready."

I wanted to fly with Leroy and hold his hand through this rite of passage, just as my parents had for me. But I could neither leave new baby Saxon nor take him with me. Leroy assured me he was a big boy. I promised him I would worry anyway. Once he arrived in Phoenix, Alicia Mandel-Hickey, a former Paralympic director who had recently relocated to Arizona, picked Leroy up at the airport for me. Alicia said Leroy rolled through the door of this modest apartment with a smile as wide as the desert sky, for he thought that home might last more than a few months this time. He laid down diagonally across the queen-size bed, and then vertically, and then horizontally, treasuring every inch of the biggest mattress he'd ever had. And then he did backflips on it. He repeated this cycle for nearly an hour before calling me.

"This is really all mine?" Leroy asked.

"Yes," I answered. "How are you feeling now that you're there?"

He went quiet, like he always did on the heels of a question. "I think I finally figured out what I'm supposed to say when something good happens," he said.

"What's that?"

"Thank you."

USA JUDO ARRANGED to have Dartanyon retested in Cleveland three weeks after Saxon's birth. I was still in town, staying with my mother as I waited for Saxon's interstate adoption clearance from Connecticut. This time I coached Dartanyon to refrain from guesswork—if a letter required a far-flung reach on his part, he should answer that it was unclear. Too many correct guesses could once again disqualify him from competition. We laughed about rooting for him to fail this exam. "It's gotta be the first time God's heard someone praying to be more blind," Dartanyon said. He promised to call the minute he finished, but after what seemed like too long, I rang him instead.

"How did the exam go?" I asked excitedly.

"Oh, I couldn't go."

"What do you mean, you couldn't go? This wasn't optional."

"It was raining, and my sister's windshield wipers don't work, so she couldn't drive me," he said, as though this was a reasonable explanation.

"Dartanyon, why didn't you call me?" I cried. "I'm in Cleveland. I would have taken you!"

"It didn't start raining till just before we were supposed to leave. I wouldn't have made it, even if you had come."

Dartanyon did not seem the least bit rattled, watching his second chance wash away.

"It's still coming down over on my side of town," he said. "Looks like it's gonna be like this for a while too."

These are the moments in which those removed from poverty

presume that the poor are irresponsible, or stupid, or just don't care. Prior to this scene, I could not conceive that something as innocuous as windshield wipers wielded the power to sabotage the greatest opportunity of one's life. Even after Dartanyon told me, the only thing convincing me it could be true was that it was too ludicrous to *not* be true.

I cringed, imagining my next groveling call to Coach Liddie. As suspected, Liddie was not pleased with this implausible excuse, and clearly doubted the efforts he had made on Dartanyon's behalf. "If he can't handle small obstacles, how is he ever going to handle the big ones?" he asked.

I argued that transportation was a large obstacle for a visually impaired person in poverty, and that the fault was mine for not coordinating a reliable ride.

"Give him a second chance," I pleaded, "and I promise he will be at the appointment."

"Okay, but it's not a second chance," Liddie said. "This is his last chance."

DARTANYON MADE IT into Shane Hudson's dojo about twice a week between January and March 2010, whenever he could bum a ride or I could arrange one with another parent in the class. Hudson pounded Dartanyon with rudimentary grappling and footwork over and over, until it was drilled into his muscle memory. The transition from wrestling to judo continued to be awkward, and the learning curve steep. What kept Dartanyon going was his burning itch to throw people, and Hudson scratched it by teaching him an *ouchi gari*. To initiate this most basic throwing technique, Dartanyon would pull his opponent forward with his right hand, thereby angling his opponent slightly to the left. Then, with a controlled and explosive force, Dartanyon would spring forward, with hips turned left, using his own right leg to displace ("reap," in judo terms) his opponent's supporting left leg from the inside. As a result, his opponent would stagger off balance, and Dartanyon would finish him off with a final two-handed push to the mat.

"Okay, I got it," Dartanyon said after a few tries. "Show me another one." Hudson refused. One throw and one throw only. "Master the basics, one at a time," he insisted. "You must make the *ouchi gari* your own before you move on." And though Dartanyon executed the throw with wrestling remnants thrown in, Hudson saw reason to hope. However, it wasn't reason enough to justify the next bit of news from Ed Liddie.

"I got permission to bring Dartanyon out here to train full-time," Liddie said during a surprise call on a gray March day. Dartanyon had passed his second eye exam and was finally deemed "blind enough." "It's been in the works for a while, but I didn't want to get anyone's hopes up." He explained that each Olympic and Paralympic sport has a fixed budget for a limited number of live-in training spots. Coaches fill their slots with athletes most likely to medal in the Games. Liddie's two Paralympic residency spots were full, but he had petitioned the USOC to create an additional opening for Dartanyon.

"This is insanely flattering, but isn't it awfully soon?" I said. "I mean, he's only been learning judo for a few months. What chance does he have of actually succeeding out there?"

"Fair question. Candidly, we are weak at eighty-one kilos. We need to fill that hole. If Dartanyon is here on campus training twice a day instead of twice a week at home, I can pack several years of judo into one year. And if he works exceptionally hard, there is a *chance* that he makes the 2016 Games. It's a pretty long shot, though, so don't put that idea in his head yet."

"Then why put the development dollars into such a risk?"

He laughed. "I better hang up before you talk me out of this," he said. "Listen, though, if we're going to do this, I need to know something from you."

"Go ahead," I replied.

"Does Dartanyon have the work ethic and the discipline to train full-time? Does he have it in him to fully commit and do everything we ask of him?"

"Yes, yes, yes," I assured him. "He absolutely does."

I hung up the phone. Five-month-old Saxon was sitting at my feet, grinning like he had been hanging on to every word. "I'm not sure what I just said is true," I told him. Yes, Dartanyon practiced hard in high school, but Coach Robinson hardly ran a boot camp. Could Dartanyon handle such an intense regimen? Did he even like judo? Did it matter? Ed Liddie was offering Dartanyon a competitive outlet, education, three meals a day, travel, and housing alongside some of our nation's most motivated athletes. This opportunity promised a far greater upside than slogging through community college while I funneled him meager weekly allowances. This was Dartanyon's winning ticket out of poverty. I looked at Saxon's eager brown eyes and met his sloppy grin with one of my own. "I guess we're just gonna have to make it true."

Dartanyon was at school, between classes, when I gave him the news. "Coach Liddie is calling you up," I said. "You're moving to the Olympic Training Center."

Dartanyon crouched in a corner and wept. He said he didn't know there was such a thing as tears of hope, the kind that make you feel like life might begin anew.

CELEBRATION HAD GIVEN way to trepidation by the time Dartanyon met with Hudson six hours later. How could he possibly be ready for the Olympic Training Center? "Dartanyon, this is amazing!" Hudson exclaimed. "This is a chance of a lifetime!" But as Dartanyon dressed for practice, tying his white cotton belt around his waist, Hudson felt his own throat tighten. "Who trains alongside Olympians as a white belt?" he panicked. "White belts come with the *gi*. Anyone who pays for a *gi* is automatically at white belt level." Perhaps wanting to save face for them both, Hudson dialed up Dartanyon's training so he could leave for Colorado with some rank. To test for a green belt, the second of five rankings before black belt, Dartanyon needed to demonstrate understanding of the fifteen basic building blocks of holding, falling, and throwing setups, which Hudson began throwing at him in a judo crash course.

Two nights before his scheduled flight to Colorado, Dartanyon passed his green belt test. The relief was momentary. He and Hudson and everyone in the dojo looked at one another as if to say, *Well, who the heck goes to the Olympic Training Center as a green belt?* He was as wet behind the ears as he now was green in rank.

"I'm going to get eaten alive in that lion's den," Dartanyon said. The only throw in his toolbox was the *ouchi gari*. He had never been to a judo competition. Was he an idiot to believe he could pick up a new sport as he headed into his twenties and emerge as an elite athlete? "Keep learning, keep applying yourself, and you will do well, Dartanyon," Hudson said. "A man's gift makes room for him."

NAVID, SAXON, AND I were enjoying our first family vacation in Mexico in April 2010 when an unexpected storm cloud blew in: Leroy called in a huff.

"My bank card stopped working for no reason," he said angrily.

He had been in Phoenix for five months.

"Did you call the bank?" I asked.

"No, I just called you." Leroy gave me his banking password, and when I returned to the hotel that night, I logged on to his account. He was overdrawn by more than $300.

"Your bank card stopped working because you have no money in your account," I explained. "And not only that, you've accrued overdraft fees."

"What's an overdraft?" Leroy asked.

"It's what happens when you spend more money than you have," I explained. "The bank covers you, but you're charged penalties." It had never occurred to me to explain an overdraft fee, because it never occurred to me that someone would allow an account balance to dip low enough to worry about one. Leroy received a monthly stipend from school to pay his rent, and a monthly disability payment to cover his utilities and food. His budget was modest yet achievable. "Are you not keeping track of what you spend in your checkbook ledger?"

"No," Leroy answered. "I thought there was enough in the account, and I've been stressed about getting to school." He explained that he had been using taxis to get to and from classes each day instead of the city's dial-a-ride shuttle system for people with disabilities, which I had set up for him. He said the shuttle often ran late, causing him to miss his first-period class, or if another client in the shuttle's network had a medical issue, that person had first priority for pickup, meaning that Leroy would be forced to miss school altogether.

"So the shuttle has been spotty for weeks, and you're just telling me now?" I asked.

"I thought I was handling it by taking the taxi."

"I understand," I said, not wanting to make him feel guilty. It seemed like an honest mistake. I transferred money to resolve the mounting fees and to get Leroy to school for the rest of the week until we could figure out a more economical transportation plan.

Meanwhile, Dartanyon's initial weeks at the Olympic Training Center felt far from a dream come true. I paid a visit to Colorado Springs, where I found him uncharacteristically sullen. With no friends and no school to fill his free time, he spent hours holed up on the phone with the girlfriend he had left behind in Cleveland. He wanted to go home. "Go home to what?" I asked. "This is where your opportunities are." I begged him to stay, to give it a six-month trial. I took him out to lunch and shopping. Together we set up a bank account. We signed up for a phone plan in a credible cellular store that notably lacked wigs and hair dryers. I took him to a dentist for his first cleaning in, well, ever. The news killed my efforts to cheer him up: thirteen cavities and two cracked teeth.

"You've never mentioned any discomfort," I said. "Don't you have pain?"

"Sometimes." He shrugged. "You get used to it."

If Dartanyon's mouth throbbed by day, his body ached worse by night. Although judo meant "gentle way," Ed Liddie had his own interpretation.

"He's taken some hard falls. He's walking like he fell off a roof five times a night," Liddie told me as I watched training. "I cut his practices short to keep him from getting hurt too badly." Training was indeed unkind to the newly minted green belt. In high school, he'd become accustomed to being the big fish in the small pond. Here there were nothing but big fish, and Dartanyon was a guppy.

A few weeks after my visit, Liddie sent Dartanyon to his first tournament—the Liberty Bell Classic in Philadelphia. "I need a flight and a hotel," Dartanyon said in a frenzied call, two days before he was supposed to leave.

"Doesn't judo pay for that?" I asked.

"Apparently not," he said. "What do I do?" I hastily booked his travel, growing ever more grateful for the trust fund that carried us through these emergencies. His next call came from the Chicago airport, where his connecting flight had been canceled. He had six hours before his new flight, an empty stomach, and an emptier bank account. He hadn't planned ahead, and had already blown through his weekly allowance from the trust fund.

"We can't let him go to his first tournament hungry," I cried to Navid. My good husband frantically searched for a terminal map, calling every restaurant on the concourse, pleading to pay for a meal over the phone. No one obliged. "There is a blind boy in the airport who has no food," Navid said in his second frenzied call to McDonald's. "He's an athlete. He was on ESPN. Maybe you saw him, carrying his teammate with no legs?" Exasperated, someone finally handed Dartanyon a cheeseburger. Navid and I were relieved. But Dartanyon felt like a homeless beggar once again.

"It's okay," I reassured him. "This trip came up so fast that we didn't have time to prepare properly. We'll work out the kinks for next time."

Navid, Saxon, and I drove down to Philadelphia to watch Dartanyon fight. After taking a hard fall halfway through his first match, he grabbed his knee and limped back to center, where he lost quickly and badly. Liddie pulled him from the tournament. No need to risk further injury when he's just starting out, he told us.

I had flashbacks to the faltering theatrics of the first high school wrestling match I'd watched Dartanyon compete in. Certainly it could be a coincidence, but I felt like I was growing familiar with Dartanyon's body language. I knew how his answers to questions grew short when he was unsure in a situation, and how he would turn his head away when he was not being forthright. I could read the dips in his voice and the shifts in his stance, and my instincts told me there was more at play here than his knee. I wanted to tell Liddie that he should push Dartanyon to continue, that exaggerating injuries might be his default way of masking insecurity. But I held my tongue, figuring a seasoned Olympic coach didn't need advice from a woman who had studied judo for all of one morning.

LEROY, DARTANYON, AND I reunited later that spring at the Olympic Training Center, along with Coach Robinson and Coach Hons. We had been invited to speak about the role of sports in empowering the disabled. My pride soared as I looked at Leroy and Dartanyon dressed in their button-down shirts, shaking hands with Olympic officials. But as we rehearsed our talking points backstage, Leroy suddenly went off script.

"Kayla's got a bun in the oven," he announced. No one so much as blinked, awaiting clarification. Kayla was Leroy's friend from high school. He told us the two had begun dating while he was home over the Christmas break, but none of us had considered it anything serious, considering the distance between them.

"That's it," he said. "She told me this morning."

"She told you *what*?" I asked, grasping for the table, for anything that wouldn't move.

"She . . . is . . . you know . . . making something in there," he said, pointing to his stomach. He couldn't even say the word. *Pregnant.*

"Is it yours?" I shrieked. "It can't be yours!" I whipped out my calendar and counted the weeks since Kayla's spring break visit to Phoenix. "It's only been four weeks," I said, my hands shaking. "It wouldn't have been detected by a pregnancy test already. It's too soon to be yours."

"It's mine. And this is good news," Leroy said, growing equally agitated. "I'm finally going to have a legacy."

"A *what*? Leroy, a legacy is something you leave behind," I insisted. "You're eighteen years old. You have nothing. What could your legacy possibly be?"

He looked down and released a frustrated sigh.

Robinson leaned over to me. "That's just one of those things people say in the hood," he whispered. "No one really knows what it means."

I locked eyes with Leroy, pleading for him to tell me this was not true. How could he be sincerely happy about an unplanned, out-of-wedlock pregnancy between two people with no jobs, minimal education, and two thousand miles between them? He stared back, wondering why I saw this as problematic. After all, his own mother had birthed Tony at the age of fourteen; Kayla's mother had had her first child at the age of seventeen. Teenage pregnancy was not cause for alarm in their experience. It was standard operating procedure.

"We'll figure it out," he said. "Kayla's going to drop out of high school. I'll get a job."

How dare he play roulette with his future? I thought. He had to finish college. Employers were not lining up to give jobs to disabled people with high school degrees. My mind raced through the decades of implications for Leroy, Kayla, and this child. Dartanyon mumbled an obligatory "Congratulations, man." Robinson shook his head and kicked a table leg. I wept in a bathroom stall. And then we all took the stage to preach empowerment.

The next day I sat beside Leroy, just he and I. I set aside my questions, my accusations, and my disappointment, clearing the way for him to speak. He struggled, as always, to find the words, but he managed to confide that the most difficult part of his accident was not losing his legs but letting go of the idea that anyone would want to marry him and grow a family. And now he'd found a girl who was happy about having his child. He believed this would be his forever family, the one that comes complete with nightly dinners, Christmas mornings draped in mistletoe, and cloudless, lazy summer vacations at the beach. He would never regain his legs, but with this news of a child, Leroy had recovered a lost dream.

"But you don't understand what goes into pulling off that idyllic sort of life," I said. "Children don't come out holding your white picket fence. They're expensive and demanding. Your mom couldn't give you the kind of life you deserved *because* she had you so young." I extolled the virtues of adoption. I offered to raise the baby myself until he and Kayla graduated. Leroy countered that having a child would improve his focus; it would give him the sense of stability and family that had always eluded Kayla and him. I argued that adding a child to a teenage relationship limited in education, income, and transportation was a recipe for disaster. But once Leroy closes on a decision, there is no changing his mind. "I am going to be the father that I never had," he said. "And that is final."

How could I discourage him from accepting responsibility? How could I tell him that in a world where men are chastised for walking away, he should do the same? In good conscience, I could not. And though every fiber of my being screamed that Leroy's choice was a catastrophic error in judgment, I was left with only one remaining question: "How can I help?"

I RETURNED TO ESPN in May 2010 after six months at home with Saxon.

"How are Leroy and Dartanyon doing?" Victor asked. I couldn't bear to tell him Leroy's news.

"They are well," I lied. "Things are evolving."

"Great, such an amazing turn of fate," he said.

"You have no idea," I replied. Victor handed me my next assignment—a series of World Cup soccer features that had already been shot while I was on leave. "I just need you to write the scripts and edit them," he said. "I figured I'd keep you off the road your first few weeks back, to ease into working motherhood." As he walked away, I moved the stack of soccer tapes aside and began helping Leroy compose a letter to his donors, breaking the news of Kayla's pregnancy and affirming his commitment to school. They each responded supportively to Leroy, yet called me separately to express grave concern.

Leroy had offered up little information about Kayla's pregnancy over her first trimester, which allowed me to indulge in a bit of denial. I tried to pack Leroy's remaining days of childless freedom with positive experiences and pushed him to resume power-lifting through the Paralympics. One of his donors paid for a gym membership, and Leroy got his bench press back up to 350 pounds. He participated in two domestic qualifying meets to earn a spot at the Paralympic World Championships in Malaysia in August 2010. We applied for his passport, had him classified, and reserved his plane ticket. The excitement served as a happy distraction, at least for me, until I received his term grades toward the end of that summer:

C-minus, D, F.

"Leroy, how did this happen?" I asked. "Every time I ask how you are doing, you say you're fine. People who are fine don't fail classes."

He confessed that the stress of Kayla's pregnancy had been weighing on him. They fought over the phone late into the night, causing him to oversleep and fall behind. Furthermore, he had overdrawn his bank account again, which added to his anxiety. "I started paying Kayla's phone bill and ordering her pizza when she has cravings," he said. This came at the expense of July's rent, which was overdue. I once again set aside the edit I was prepping and started tackling Leroy's predicaments.

AT THE END of the summer, Leroy returned from Malaysia as the eleventh best powerlifter in the world in his weight class. Dartanyon returned from a short break in Cleveland with an overdrawn bank account and an unpaid phone bill, which I discovered only when the automated message informed me that his number was no longer in service.

"I had to buy my own food over the summer," he said. "I couldn't eat and pay the phone bill."

"Why didn't you ask me for help?"

"I don't know."

As had been the case with Leroy's money woes, Dartanyon's explanation was understandable. But I couldn't grasp how they'd failed to plan ahead for routine expenses. Why were they repeating the same mistakes? I paid the last two months of Dartanyon's phone bill, and with him on the line, I asked to have the late fees waived. I hoped that forcing him to engage in groveling conversations with the phone company would serve as a future deterrent.

Like many of the other athletes, Dartanyon planned to take classes while he trained. He enrolled in his first semester of school at Pikes Peak Community College in Colorado Springs that September, registering for English, computer science, and micro-economics. We agreed that a part-time course load was a good plan as Dartanyon assimilated to his new school and schedule, but a third of the way into the semester, he was already struggling in economics. "The professor is just really hard to follow," he said. I suggested he go in for extra help. Instead, he stopped attending class altogether. And though he told me he was doing well in English and computer science, I learned toward the end of the semester that he was on the brink of failing those classes too.

"I don't think you're taking school seriously," I said. He did not respond. "Why are you not doing the work? Are you missing things because of your vision?" Still he said nothing. Feeling dismissed, I wanted to bash the phone receiver against my desk. "If you don't answer me, I'm left to assume you're just lazy!" This was the first time I had raised my voice at Dartanyon.

"No, I am trying," he answered weakly.

"You're going to have to start trying a lot harder," I reprimanded. "I don't think you know how fortunate you are to have people paying your tuition."

I hired a tutor, Wendy Allor, to see if she could save the semester. She called me after her initial evaluation.

"The good news is that Dartanyon does not have any learning disabilities," Wendy reported. "The bad news is that he doesn't appear to have ever done a lot of learning either." The results were grim: Dartanyon tested at a fifth-grade math level and an eighth-grade reading level. "How is this possible?" I asked. "He graduated high school with a B average. He passed all of his standardized tests."

I went on a mission for answers. I began tracking down teachers in the Cleveland public school district, desperate for insight. What I learned was disheartening. From the onset, Cleveland's schools expected less of Dartanyon as a visually impaired student. While mainstream kids needed 90 percent or higher to earn an A, Dartanyon needed only 80 percent. A passing grade for others was 60 percent; for him, it was 50 percent—or in other words, all he needed to pass a test was decent guesses. On exams, he was permitted to use calculators and have questions read aloud to him by teachers who at times used suggestive inflections to guide him. I learned of one elementary teacher who stood over him during tests and whispered things like, "You probably don't want to choose that answer. You might want to reconsider the one above it."

The lagging school district felt pressure to elevate its poor graduation ratings, and that pressure trickled down to teachers, who in turn passed well-behaved kids like Dartanyon along. "Some of the instructional assistants felt badly for him, and probably helped more than they should have," Val Barkley, head of the visually impaired program, told me. "After all, a high school diploma is better than no high school diploma." Staring at Dartanyon's string of community college Fs, I disagreed. Wendy confirmed that Dartanyon couldn't outline a book chapter. He didn't know his way around a decimal point. And he had never heard of a topic sentence, let alone knew how to compose one.

As I stewed over Dartanyon's deficiencies, suspicion about Leroy's downward-spiraling grades rose within me. He continually pointed to his impending fatherhood as the cause of his decline—a plausible line of reasoning that did not initially raise any red flags to me. But now, in light of Dartanyon's difficulties, I wondered if Leroy had similar academic shortcomings.

I obtained Leroy's syllabi and asked to see his weekly assignments. A bare minimum were complete. The assignments he did submit were littered with grammar mistakes and run-on sentences, and in many cases devoid of punctuation. Certainly Leroy's external stressors were not helping, but Dartanyon's assessment had crystallized an alarming realization: neither Dartanyon nor Leroy had any business being in college.

I went into a full-body panic, feeling like I had deceived viewers and defrauded donors. I had blindly assumed that when someone graduates from high school, they are ready for college. I didn't know that 42 percent of Ohio students need remedial coursework in their freshman year of college. "The Ohio Graduation Test is not a test of college readiness," one teacher explained. "It tests very basic skills."

In Ohio, Leroy had passed through ten schools in twelve years, never once transferring at the start of a school year. His trail of transcripts was replete with Ds and Fs, but since he rarely finished a school year in the same place as he started it, he too was ushered along. I spun myself in circles trying to decide whether the school system or the teachers or the parents or society were to blame. But pondering why it happened was akin to Monday-morning quarterbacking: A lot of fingerpointing, but none of it changed the outcome. All that really mattered was that the jig was up, and the resulting mess had landed in my lap.

LEROY'S BABY GIRL was due the week of Christmas. With only a two-week break from school, he and Kayla hoped to coax the baby out as soon as possible to maximize Leroy's time with her. The night he landed in Cleveland, they guzzled castor oil together and ate spicy rice and beans. Kayla did squats while Leroy did push-ups beside her in solidarity. They were giddy kids, naively in love, and five days before Christmas, their daughter Alani Kaylee Sutton was born.

"I had this whole plan where I was going to look at her and say 'Hi, I am your daddy and I am going to take care of you for the rest of your life and protect you,'" Leroy said. "But instead, I was completely speechless. Something about those big Martian eyes got me, and I had no words for her beauty and perfection."

Leroy used his Christmas money on a tattoo, inking a replica of Alani's birth bracelet around his right wrist. When he told me, I chastised him for foolishly spending money on a tattoo that he could have used for diapers and food. "No, it was well spent," he insisted, drawing my attention to the scarred slices and pinpricks of his tortured teens now hidden beneath the fresh green ink. "I needed to cover the darkest part of my life with the happiest part of my life."

THAT SAME WEEK, I said good-bye to some of the best years of my life. I left ESPN. Navid had completed his fellowship and received his ideal job offer from the north shores of Boston—the area in which he attended college and to whose craggy coastlines he longed to return. There I planned to divide my time between caring for Saxon and freelance work. Navid would have settled for a practice in Connecticut had I pushed, but I had fulfilled so many aspirations already. It was his turn.

On my final Friday night at work, I sat alone at my desk boxing up old beta tapes, filled with big moments and brave people. My father had told me that if I found a way to get paid for what I love, I would never work a day in my life, and that was true of this job—a job I had dreamed up on that crumpled bit of paper. Every encounter, every edit, every word I put on the air, felt like a gift.

I wondered if Al Jaffe would be proud of the girl who'd fumbled miserably before him thirteen years before, for I was leaving knowing that the Vezina Trophy awards the NHL's top goalie each season. I learned the difference between NFL nickel and dime defenses. I learned that sports shouldn't be reduced to questions and answers, dates and statistics. Sports can serve as a backdrop of resilience and a field of redemption, giving us a vehicle to move from who we are to who we wish to become. Sports are treasure troves of the heart's greatest stories, some of which need to be told and some of which need to be held.

As the clock ticked toward midnight and my key card turned into a pumpkin, all that remained at my barren desk was a black-and-white photo of Leroy and Dartanyon, taped to my cubicle wall. I took their image in hand, comforted that this story had not ended just yet, and I walked out the door for the last time.

THE NEXT DAY, Navid packed the U-Haul for our move to Massachusetts. I felt queasy as I watched him carry out boxes. "This is an emotional transition for you," Navid said. "I'm sure your body is just figuring out how to process it all." I was terribly sad to leave our first home, a home that had warmed so many memories in a short time—our marriage, Saxon's homecoming, Navid's residency. I went for a final walk around the nearby lake, stopping at my favorite bench to pray. Once there, I threw up.

"You probably caught a stomach virus," Navid said.

"This doesn't feel like a stomach virus. This is a new sensation," I said. "I think I am pregnant."

After our first miscarriage in 2008, we learned that Navid has a genetic translocation. The top half of one of his second chromosomes has switched places with the bottom half of one of his sixth chromosomes. The mutation is not linked to a specific disease or deformity, but it leads to spontaneous abortion in 50 percent of pregnancies. After four losses between 2008 and 2010, our doctor put my chances of carrying a child to term below 10 percent. This was sobering news to Navid; while he had fallen head-over-heels in love with Saxon, he still occasionally wondered what it would be like to have a biological child. I saw the prognosis as further confirmation of my calling to adopt and was almost relieved to learn I would never have to expel a pint-size human being from my body.

Needless to say, we were both shocked when we conceived for a fifth time, and this one stuck the landing. My pregnancy was immediately different from my previous gestations in two critical ways: I got sick, and then I got exceedingly sicker. My morning queasiness did not discriminate against times of the day. I hurled morning, noon, and night. In the first three months, I lost seventeen pounds from my already slight frame. The clinical term for my condition is hyperemesis gravidarum; the reality would be seven months of intractable nausea and vomiting, hospital stays for de-hydration, and biweekly ultrasounds to monitor our baby's anticipated low birth weight. Navid went ahead to Boston to begin work. My mother flew to Connecticut to care for Saxon while I writhed in bed. Once I joined Navid, we recruited care for Saxon, and in between naps and hovering over toilets, I tailed Leroy and Dartanyon's movements as closely as my compromised state allowed.

In February 2011, while the room was spinning early one morning, Ed Liddie called. "Listen, Dartanyon is not working out here," he said. "He's been late to the team's morning lifting sessions for the last few weeks. This morning he didn't show up at all. The guys who run the weight room have had it with him." Liddie planned to tell Dartanyon he would have to pack his bags and return home. "But what he doesn't know is that I'm going to give him one more chance, so if he calls you, don't book his flight yet. I want to see if I can scare him into taking responsibility first."

Five minutes later, the phone rang again. A terror-stricken Dartanyon was on the other end. "I messed up bad, and I don't know what to do," he said, his voice quivering. "Ed is kicking me out."

I calmly asked him to tell me what happened. He said he had been so worried about sleeping through his alarm each morning that he would lie awake, too anxious to fall asleep. "Why didn't you tell anyone you were having this problem?" I asked.

"I don't know."

I suggested he first write an e-mail to his coach, explaining his sleep issues and reiterating his commitment, and then follow up with a face-to-face conversation. Dartanyon worked all morning on his letter before sending it to me to check grammar and spelling. In it, he asked to see a sleep specialist, and said he would do anything to stay. "Asking for help isn't something I'm used to doing, but I know I need it now," he wrote. "I have never been so scared of losing something in my whole life."

Dartanyon fretted through the weekend, like a defendant waiting for the jury to return with its verdict. We spoke several times, during which he cried and repeated that he had "lost everything." Letting him believe his future hung in the balance was among the harder things I have done. I tried to turn this moment into a learning opportunity, talking about the importance of adjusting to structure and how real men do ask for help. "I know I messed up. I know I need to change," Dartanyon said. I believed him.

On Monday, Liddie summoned Dartanyon to his office. "Son, there are a hundred kids who would give anything to take your place," he said.

"They can't have it," Dartanyon replied.

"I took a risk on you, and you're making me look like a fool."

"Coach, I'll never oversleep again," Dartanyon promised. "I'll do anything you ask."

"If you're late to one more weight-lifting session, you are done here," Liddie said. "Last chance."

For several months thereafter, until his body clock adjusted, I called Dartanyon every weekday morning at 5:30 a.m. to rustle him out of bed. I had assured Coach Liddie that Dartanyon had the discipline to make this move. I could not let something as avoidable as oversleeping be the cause of his demise. And though our morning calls were void of any pleasantries, they were some-how unifying in our unsavory missions, for as Dartanyon made his way, groggily, to the weight room, I staggered, nauseated, to the bathroom to begin another day of ceaseless vomiting.

AS IT TURNED out, practice was not the only thing Dartanyon had trouble showing up for; he had been dodging his tutor, Wendy, as well. Wendy had helped him enroll in two more classes for the 2011 spring semester—remedial English and logic—thinking that if she worked alongside him, he could still earn college credit while she got him up to grade level. Though Dartanyon did not expressly oppose this plan, he objected in more passive ways, such as repeated tardiness and arriving to tutoring sessions without his books or his computer. Wendy sent him shuffling back to his room to retrieve his items, thereby eating up much of their time together. I began texting Dartanyon reminders thirty minutes before each appoint-ment: *Remember your books, computer, notes, and a pen. 10 a.m.* By midspring he had shown up for fewer than half of their meetings, rarely notifying Wendy in advance. Dartanyon unapologetically tossed out lame excuses like having to do laundry, or a conflicting appointment with a physical therapist, or that he simply wasn't feeling well.

"Dartanyon, it is completely rude not to show up for appoint-ments without calling," I fumed. "Wendy was waiting for you, and we still have to pay her for her time." My reprimands bounced off him like rubber balls, garnering silence. His lack of courtesy con-founded me. The Dartanyon I knew was so much more considerate than this. What was he hiding? "You have to tell me what you are thinking. Help me understand."

"There's nothing to understand. I just forgot, and I didn't see your reminder until it was too late," he would say. This was a boy who seemingly remembered every lyric to every song he ever heard.

Ed reported he was absorbing judo at an alarming rate. No, Dartanyon had a lock-box memory.

"I don't believe you," I would say. "Try again."

"Maybe I'm not cut out for school," he said. And he was right. In his current state, he was not. I thought that if I provided him with the correct tools and constant reminders, he would embrace learning in a way that led to success. Instead, I made him loathe school and avoid me. By late spring he'd given up entirely, ignoring assignments and failing both classes. I had little energy with which to fight. I was surviving on orange Popsicles, and as I entered my third trimester, I arrived at each prenatal checkup with a suitcase in tow, for if our child had not gained an ounce, I would be induced to deliver.

"I am sorry to give you this news, especially knowing the physical challenges of your pregnancy," Wendy wrote, "but I am convinced that my tutoring Dartanyon is not the best use of time or money. He simply does not believe that he needs help, at least from me. I am uncertain as to what the best course of action should be for Dartanyon. I will continue to pray for him—and you. With great sadness, Wendy."

"I don't like feeling dumb. I hate school. I hate studying," Dartanyon said when I confronted him yet again. "I don't want this goal for myself."

"All right, you have my blessing to quit," I said. "Just send me a detailed proposal for how you plan to support yourself for the rest of your life, because employers are not lining up to give jobs to visually impaired, uneducated black men."

Meanwhile, Leroy and I were engaged in different sorts of discussions, about diapers and infant reflux—conversations I'd never imagined sharing with him. I had begged him and Kayla to remain apart for the first year of Alani's life so that Kayla could lean on her family's support in Cleveland while Leroy remained focused on school and built up savings. But they were determined to raise their daughter together, in Arizona. Kayla would work at night when Leroy returned from school, they said. They would save, get married, and buy a house. They were eager to build a life together. I feared they were building a house of cards. But like Dartanyon, Leroy wasn't terribly interested in hearing my thoughts. Kayla headed west, and I braced for the worst.

History is like gravity. It can pull you down.
We wanted to succeed, but we needed someone to show us how—
someone who believed our potential was
more important than our past.

—LEROY

CHAPTER 13

THE DARK AGES

Our daughter, Talia, arrived on a hazy August eve after a phenomenal epidural and three pushes. I laid in recovery the next morning staring down Leroy's financial aid papers. I had planned to finish them the day before but went into labor instead, a bit earlier than expected. I cradled Talia in my left arm as I tapped Leroy's information into the computer with my right hand.

"You've already mastered multitasking," the nurse said. "How many children do you have?" I looked down at the paperwork, pausing to consider. "Four," I said slowly, speaking it aloud for the first time. "She is my fourth, basically."

"You're a busy mama," she said. "How old are the other three?"

"Twenty-two, twenty-one, and two," I said. The nurse looked at me quizzically, clearly wondering about the age spread but careful not to offend by asking. "Let's just say that God got creative and gave me the family I always wanted but didn't know to ask for."

We had Saxon, the child I'd felt destined to mother since my own childhood, and who had already moved my father to reach across racial lines; Leroy and Dartanyon, the teenagers in need of mothering, who were sent in the direction of a white lady who thought she might be just nutty enough for the job; and now here was new baby Talia, fulfilling Navid's hopes of knowing a biological child. Early on in my pregnancy, I questioned why God was sending this child, for at the time, Navid and I were about to begin our second adoption. We wanted to give Saxon a sibling who could share his racial identity and adoptive origins. Yet God impressed upon me that this little girl was being sent in large part for Saxon—to fortify his sense of belonging and to be his comforter. And so we gave Talia the middle name Shalom—the Hebrew word for completion—to remind us of how God longs to gather up our broken pieces and make each heart whole.

TALIA'S HOMECOMING WAS far from the hallowed bliss of Saxon's arrival. For as miserable as her gestation was, she arrived intent upon making life outside the womb equally uncomfortable for both of us. Her first two weeks of life were a dizzying cycle of insatiable feedings, protracted screaming, projectile vomiting, and watery bowel movements. And yet because I was propped up in a sleep-deprived survival stance—quite literally standing, breast-feeding upright, because my stitches made it excruciatingly impossible to sit down, as though I had sat on a cactus—I hadn't the presence of mind to see that Talia's patterns were abnormal.

"Maybe she has a milk allergy," my mother-in-law finally said. "Try a bottle of soy milk and see what happens." Talia inhaled it and went to sleep without bodily protest. But before I could enjoy the quiet, I doubled over with my own wrenching cramps and ir-regular blood loss, which intensified over a period of days. Navid rushed me back to the hospital on our fifth anniversary, where we learned that I had retained portions of the placenta during labor, and as my uterus contracted to its original state, these remnants were breeding infection.

Expelling leftover fragments of placenta taught me what a bowl-ing pin must feel like to be battered by a sixteen-pound ball for ten frames, and once I returned home, Talia greeted me with a bout of colic—incessant, inexplicable, inconsolable crying that left me wondering how I might trade her in for the gurgling baby on the box of Pampers. She screamed from nine o'clock in the morning to nine o'clock at night, forgoing naps. I had never heard of an infant surviving without naps. Her pediatrician smiled feebly and said Talia would grow out of it within twelve weeks, that colic is simply neurological immaturity and nothing to be concerned about. The concern was for my sanity, and for Saxon's, because he took Talia's screaming as his cue to howl along with her. I was woefully un-prepared for the isolation that came with having two children under the age of two, and when Navid left for work each morning, tears flooded my eyes as I wondered how I would survive the next twelve hours. I did it minute-by-ghastly-minute, never faster, never easier. Once Talia finally screamed herself to sleep at night, I laid her down in front of the humming dryer and stumbled into my office to check in on Leroy and Dartanyon's days.

Dartanyon sat out the fall semester of school with plans to return in the spring. I hoped that time off might break his cycle of failure before it did irrevocable damage to his confidence. Mean-while, he showed growth in other areas. He began adapting to the rigors of Olympic life. He learned to be punctual, and to socialize with people of position and pedigree. Liddie was pleased enough with his progress on the mat to send him to the Paralympic World Championships in Turkey earlier in that year, where he finished a surprising ninth. If he could break into the top three at the Para-Pan American Games that November, he had a sliver of a chance to qualify for the 2012 London Paralympics. Liddie pounded Dar-tanyon that fall, pushing him to peak in time, and each time I called to find out how he was doing, Dartanyon's breathless answer was the same: "Recovering."

I had gone more than a month without speaking to Leroy following Talia's explosive entry into my world. My e-mails and voice mails to him went unreturned. He ignored my requests to read over his homework. His professors were not updating the class websites with his weekly grades, so in my exhaustion, I hoped for the best and went to bed, dreading morning and Talia's impending assault.

Finally, in early November 2011, Leroy responded to an e-mail with a desperate message: "I'm in a huge dilemma. My grades are low, and I have to write a letter to avoid being dropped from school. By the way, my chair broke and won't fold down so it doesn't fit in my friend's car, so I don't have a way to get to school. We're almost out of food too. I am in a bad situation." I immediately picked up the phone.

"How did this all happen, Leroy?" I asked.

"I don't know."

"You have to know, or else it will happen again."

"I don't know how it happened," he repeated, more forcefully. He seemed genuinely ignorant of the architecture of his demise. I asked a slew of questions, searching for the crux of the issues. From what I could gather, the thrill of playing house was wearing thin. Kayla was filled with resentment as Leroy left for school each morning and left her behind to care for Alani. Leroy returned home late, hours after the family dinner they once dreamed of had gone cold on the table. He was at the mercy of friends for rides, he insisted; she accused him of cheating on her. He said they fought long into the night, keeping him from his schoolwork. The two of them couldn't navigate their finances any better than they could their mounting frustrations. Only eight days into the month, their $2,100 monthly allotment was gone. Their phone bills were three months past due. The electricity was one day from shutoff. The cupboards were bare. Leroy had already blown through his school stipends two months ahead of schedule. They were thousands of dollars in the hole and pointing fingers at one another.

"How did you guys spend two thousand dollars in four days?" I asked.

"I don't know," he said. I scrolled through his ledger. They'd frequented pricy restaurants, traveled in taxis, downloaded movies, shopped online, and bought an Xbox gaming console and a three-hundred-dollar pair of headphones.

"My headphones broke, and I can't do work without listening to music," Leroy explained.

"But you're not doing work. You're failing!" I exclaimed. "And your bills haven't been paid for months. Why didn't you tell me before things got so bad? I left you a lot of messages asking how you were doing." More than a year into college, how did Leroy still not know how to pay a bill?

He remained quiet, as if he was a child again, waiting on a whupping from his mother. And truth be told, I felt he needed one.

"I didn't want to be a bother," he finally said sheepishly. I regrouped with a deep breath and reminded myself that he came from a world where there were no solutions, where there was no one to ask for help, and where his needs were met with huffs. At least he had reached out to me, even if he was grossly late.

"Leroy, you are not a bother," I said. "I'm always here for you."

He remained quiet. I wished I could hug him.

I took a step back, as though surveying a messy room and trying to figure out what to pick up first. "How about we start digging our way out of this?" My inclination was to let Collins expel Leroy. I had grown convinced that he was not ready to handle the demands of college and fatherhood. But his landscape had become far more complicated than Dartanyon's. I could not simply send him back to Big Ma's basement, or even move him in with me, while also nurturing his academic skills. He had turned into a three-person deal, with Alani and Kayla now relying on his monthly stipends for their daily needs. In a sense, college was no longer his choice—it was his job. "School is your means of supporting your new family," I said. "Do you understand that?"

He mumbled that he did.

To keep him enrolled, Collins required a focused appeal, identifying a cause of the failings and presenting concrete steps for change. While I ordered a grocery delivery for Leroy, he embarked on his appeal letter, in which he brazenly blamed his professors for being uninteresting and squashing his motivation. "Leroy, you can't blame people for your problems and expect them to have compassion for you," I explained, wondering why this was not obvious. I outlined a new letter emphasizing the pressures of new parenthood and taking responsibility for his failings. He begrudgingly wrote a second letter following my bullet points, but this sort of bowing to authority clearly irked him. I drafted a supplemental appeal to the dean, expanding on Leroy's financial collapse. I committed to managing his money more closely to alleviate this pressure, monitoring his bank account daily and paying off his debts to clean the slate. The next day, Collins agreed to reinstate Leroy, with the provision that I maintain a tight rein, thereby cementing my involvement. I was relieved. Leroy sighed at the news—a declaration of feeling perpetually misunderstood.

I went on a high-powered offensive, in hopes of avoiding future pitfalls. I arranged for Leroy's monthly stipends to be deposited into my bank account for holding, and while I was at it, I made Dartanyon transfer his disability payments to me as well. I set up online payment systems to monitor their bills. I constructed budget-planning worksheets that they had to fill out by the first of each month before I would begin transferring their weekly allowances to them. They were not pleased, but neither could offer evidence of competency in their defense. "No matter what you achieve, if you don't learn to handle money, you will remain poor for the rest of your life," I said.

Still, no preventive measure curbed their impulsive spending. The idea of restraint and forethought was completely foreign. They were living out the financial model engrained in them by poverty. "Everyone in the ghetto gets their check on the first of the month, lives large that weekend, and then goes back to being poor for the rest of the month," Dartanyon explained to me.

"But doesn't this get exhausting?" I asked. "Do you like seeing zeros in your bank account?"

"It bothers me, but not enough to stop doing it, I guess." He and Leroy believed they deserved what they wanted, when they wanted it, as a reward for living without it for so many years. They had been taught to live for the moment, for the next one was never guaranteed.

"If you have no intention of helping yourself, then I'm wasting my time," I said, exasperated. "I quit!" It was a bold attempt at shocking him into compliance, and I startled myself as I said it. Dartanyon was not fooled.

"You can't quit," he said with a laugh. "That thirty-day return policy has long passed."

WHEN YOU ARE in the middle of a story, it isn't a story at all. It's confusion. It's darkness. It's a lingering ache in the gut. It's stabs to the chest. It's a feeling of being swept up in a reckless current with no boat, no life jacket, and no indication of whether you are headed for calmer waters or a deeper abyss. It is only afterward, when we tell someone else these experiences, that it becomes anything like a story at all.

We were too far in to start over in a more prepared way, and we were too far from the end goal of self-sufficiency to glimpse light. We were groping our way through dense fog, living beyond our expertise. Dartanyon was masquerading as an elite athlete in a sport he had heard of just one year before. Leroy was trying to be a father, with no template to follow. I dozed off each night with a book on toddler development in my left hand and a book on the complexities of teenage boys in my right. My seemingly foolproof plan of getting these boys off to college had made fools out of all of us. Leroy and Dartanyon really had no business living on their own, but with so much money invested and so many supporters awaiting their returns, what choice did we have but to continue fumbling our way through the encroaching darkness?

I lay awake many nights wondering where I went wrong. Had I set these boys up for failure by misjudging their maturity levels? Had I depicted them as survivors and champions, when in fact they had the life skills of young children? Had I deceived everyone, including myself? I had promised the Suttons and the Crocketts that their boys would return educated. I had promised countless Americans that their donations would indeed end the hardships. I had assembled a platoon of super supporters who were heavily invested, both monetarily and emotionally, in Leroy and Dartanyon's success. But I wasn't a mentor or a coach or an educator or a financial counselor. I was a television producer, and I had attempted to "produce" two lives. I'd assembled the elements on Leroy and Dartanyon's behalf, written their script, and expected a cinematic ending. Maybe it was my tenacity rather than Leroy and Dartanyon's that had led us to our current state. Maybe it wasn't their fault. Maybe it was mine.

And once self-pity set in, I found it difficult to shed. Navid worked long hours to establish his new practice and typically fell asleep upon returning home. Talia ended her bout of colic by staging a two-month hunger strike just when she was supposed to transition to solid foods. Saxon had speech delays, favoring violent, destructive tantrums over words. Both children were walloped by a bevy of winter illnesses as we entered the New Year, keeping me awake all hours of the night.

The phone rang six times a day, and I panicked each time I picked it up. A typical afternoon included any combination of these disheartening news items:

Leroy skipped class. Dartanyon skipped tutoring. Leroy's phone was shut off. Alani was out of diapers. Kayla was out of groceries. Dartanyon spent the money for his *gis* on video games. Leroy's femur broke through his skin. Dartanyon's ankle broke in half. Leroy failed his level design class. Dartanyon failed room inspection. Dartanyon's laptop crashed the night before his paper was due. Leroy's heart fractured beneath the weight of Kayla's scorn. Dartanyon forgot about his quiz. Leroy neglected the light bill. Alani was in the emergency room with a fever. Dartanyon's passport had water damage. Leroy's apartment had bed bugs. Dartanyon needed an emergency visa to Brazil for a tournament. The wheel popped off of Leroy's chair. Dartanyon popped a hamstring. Leroy's seat cushion was leaking gel all over his pants. Dartanyon left for a trip and forgot his pants altogether.

It was a storm in a teacup. There was always one fire still smoking while the next one kicked up. Worse, Leroy and Dartanyon were stubborn in their self-sabotaging ways, and pointing out their missteps led to a bevy of pathetic excuses. Where were the invincible warriors I'd met three years earlier? Were their superpowers deactivated when they moved apart? Had I been too easy on them? Had I expected too much?

All I knew for sure was that Leroy and Dartanyon were carving permanent stress lines into my forehead, which led me to be irritable with Saxon and Talia's needs. I resented Navid for his work obligations and inattentiveness. I called his office crying one afternoon, screaming at him while Saxon and Talia screamed behind me. "You have to come home!" I yelled. "I can't make it through these days by myself anymore!"

"You have to figure it out," Navid said. His voice was firm and low, signaling that his assistant was within earshot. "I cannot help you right now." I hung up on him in disgust, even though I knew he could not walk out on a full schedule of patients who also needed him. My demand was a desperate test. I wanted him to prove that he cared about me with the same fervor with which I was caring for everyone else. I wanted him to stop this carousel of chaos and rescue me.

That night, I escaped on a late-night walk under the stars and through the snow. The snow squalled that evening. It mirrored what I was experiencing within: gusting in all directions, at the mercy

of stiff winds, never landing, never resting. I once heard a meteor-
ologist explain that squalls differ from blizzards because the blowing
snow makes accumulation hard to measure until the weather system
passes. As I trudged on, I thought of how this is the case in life too—
how a storm's progress is difficult to gauge when you are caught in
the thick of it.

I arrived home to Navid's homemade cross on the back lawn.
Each January, he removes the branches of our Christmas tree and
saws off the top third of the remaining log. He fastens the two pieces
together to make a cross, and then he puts it unceremoniously back
in the tree stand. Navid does this as a visible reminder of how the
miracle of God entering this world does not end once the gifts are
opened and the carols go quiet. He does this to remind us that
God stayed, through more than two thousand dark winters since.
He does this to remind us that the power of the Christmas miracle
is available to us all year long. Yet standing before the wooden
cross, I did not feel strength. Instead, I throbbed with loneliness,
languishing in a spiritual chasm. I felt stripped of the qualities I
needed to mother successfully: the joy, the peace, the endurance—
the very virtues promised by my faith. I had never seen this de-
moralized version of myself before. I didn't like her. I thought of
my favorite Anne Lamott book, which says all prayers can be boiled
down to two types: Help Me, Help Me, Help Me and Thank You,
Thank You, Thank You. I lay in the snow beside the cross and
leaned on the first petition.

"Help me . . . ," I called feebly into the dark. "Anyone? Help?"

SAXON'S SPEECH THERAPIST encouraged me to speak to my son
in short, direct phrases when I wanted him to execute a task. "He
is not yet able to receive complex instructions or abstract concepts,"
she told me. "Break it down into chunks of language that he can
handle. Simplify the world for him." Shoes on. Brush teeth. Eat

apple. Hug mama. Saxon began to respond, his eyes brightening as his discovery of communication lent order to his world.

I hunkered down for the long, insular New England winter, operating a virtual command center with the mission of navigating my two little ones plus Leroy and Dartanyon through their days. I was wholly depleted of energy, yet I put one foot in front of the other and plodded ahead.

"Why didn't you turn in your animation assignment yesterday?" I asked Leroy.

"I didn't know it was due," he replied.

"How could you not know it was due? It's listed on the class portal. I'm looking right at it," I said, agitated.

"Oh, I never check that thing."

"Why would you not check the one place where your assignments are listed? It's the literal road map for your success."

"I don't know," he said. "The portal is stupid. A lot of time it's down for maintenance anyway."

Saxon waddled in. "Play cars?" he asked.

"Play cars," I answered. As I sat on the floor beside him, guiding him to pick up "red car" and "give Talia block," I wondered if applying a version of Saxon's modifications might benefit Leroy and Dartanyon. I could help break things down for them. So I began sending them daily to-do lists that typically read like this:

1. Complete English paper. Send to me for editing.
2. Study for quiz on chapter four.
3. Pay phone bill.
4. Ask professor for partial credit on late analysis assignment.
5. Complete budget worksheet and return to me.

But giving them five things to do in a day was like asking them to drink from a fire hose. They couldn't organize their time to handle multiple tasks. I lowered the bar—if they could complete just one task a day, while I picked up the slack on some of the others, I counted it a good day. "You're doing too much for them," my mother-in-law said late one night as I was writing to Leroy's professor, with Talia cooing on my shoulder. "They'll never learn if you do everything for them."

"But if they complete one task, they've at least learned to do that one thing," I countered. "And if I don't take on some of the other things, then this house of cards falls, and they lose the opportunity to learn that one thing well. But if they can learn to do that one thing, it will hopefully lead to them mastering two things in a day, and then three."

"Or they'll learn to take advantage of you," she asserted. "How many chances are you going to give them?"

"I don't know. I'm finding it's not easy to overcome the mind-sets of poverty." Leroy and Dartayon didn't have the same opportunities I had as a kid to make mistakes and learn from them with my parents' safety net beneath me. "One chance isn't enough. They may need a hundred chances to make up for lost time."

"Makes sense," she said, nodding. "Keep doing what you're doing. Give me the baby."

In many ways, growing up in abject poverty disabled Leroy and Dartanyon more than their physical challenges. Both boys were living out the consequences of being raised with no accountability, no responsibility, and few expectations. In my lucid moments, I saw these years as a training ground to acquire missing life skills and reverse the destructive habits they had absorbed throughout their youths. The only problem was, they didn't share my vision. Dartanyon was my procrastinator, always agreeable yet rarely productive. "Yeah, I was just about to do that," he said when reminded of a task, which really meant, "Not only was I *not* about to do that, but it had not even crossed my mind to do it, and even though you're telling me now, I probably still won't do it." Asking Leroy to so much as deliver the rent check to the leasing office was like asking him to roll a boulder across the Arizona desert on an August afternoon. My direction was met with disgruntled sighs, as though he was doing me the favor. "This is for *you*," I implored. "I am trying to help *you* achieve the goals that *you* set for yourself." Another sigh. Life's responsibilities seemed like a series of interruptions to both boys.

I walked regularly through the frozen nights to numb my frustrations. I knew that so much of my life had been comfortable compared with what is tragically possible in this life. I had thus far avoided the land mines of illness and suffering and loss. As a result, my fortitude for hard times was low. I feared prolonged discomfort and relationships I could not fix. I feared the unknown. I feared failing. And as I walked, I reckoned I needed the dark as much as I needed the light. How could I ever find the courage to walk through the shadows without practice?

Over time, the rhythmic crunch of the snow beneath my boots began restoring order to my heart. I reminded myself that Leroy and Dartanyon had not asked for my daily invasion into their lives. They were under no obligation to be my friend, or even to appreciate my efforts. I set my bruised feelings aside, and I focused instead on centering truths: The train. The crack house. The call. *Take care of my son.* I thought of how God gathered up the prayers of a destitute coach, a shaken paramedic, a strung-out father, a had-it-up-to-here grandmother—prayers of ammunition, from all who were willing to join forces to combat Leroy and Dartanyon's earthly plight. I traced these markers over and over again as I walked, for while my present feelings were capricious, these enduring touchstones served as a road map for me. They reminded me of how I got here. They reminded me that God wanted me here. They reminded me, in a whisper, to continue, for though the course is hard, the cause is not necessarily lost.

And each night I passed by Navid's Christmas tree cross. Easter was approaching, and Navid would soon hang a crown of thorns around our cross. He would remind me that though we celebrate with Easter lilies and resounding trumpets, the Resurrection took place in a dark cave. God and darkness had been friends for a long time. I was not alone here. I need not fear. I was part of a grand and beautiful plan, to soothe the human ache with a steady, inconvenient love. How dare I see it as anything less? And as spring began to peek up around the tree stand of the Christmas cross, I was finally able to sit beside it and offer up that second type of prayer.

Thank you.

THE GRADUAL RETURN of gratitude was rooted in the sense of love that my faith had infused in me during my teen years. I willfully called that love to mind now, and those memories served as spiritual keepsakes that anchored me. They restored me. And they made me wonder if my intensive micromanagement of Leroy and Dartanyon had muddied their assurance of my affection for them. Had I communicated their faults more often than their value?

I began calling Leroy and Dartanyon in moments free of crises, to simply say hello. I asked about their friends and movies they had seen. On weekends, I found them playing online video games against one another, over headsets. At first my lighthearted inquiries were met with reticence from Dartanyon in particular, who was waiting for the other shoe to drop. But I resisted the urge to correct during those calls. We needed to laugh again, like we did early in our relationship. We needed to heal. In sum, I told them that I loved them more than I told them what to do.

I also forged closer relationships with the boys' local support. Alicia, in Phoenix, drove Leroy to appointments and invited him over for Sunday dinners. Afterward, she called me with encouragement and insights into his state of mind. And when Dartanyon spent his schoolbook money on a PlayStation 4 and dodged his new tutor, Ed Liddie and I allied to drop a bombshell on him.

"If I hear you miss a single tutoring session or a single class, you don't travel," Liddie told Dartanyon. "Judo don't last forever, and it ain't gonna make you rich. Listen to Lisa, and get your education."

Dartanyon fell in line, for he had fallen genuinely in love with judo. His exposure to international competition and the path to Paralympic qualification lit a spark within him. In blind judo, players earn their spots in the Games by amassing points at three qualifying events: World Games, World Championships, and the Pan American Games. Athletes who finish in the top twelve in their weight class qualify that spot for their country. Each nation then holds its own Paralympic trials to determine which of its athletes will represent that weight class. Dartanyon had missed the World Games, mending his broken ankle. He'd finished ninth at the World Championships in Turkey that year. He needed to medal at the Pan American Games in Guadalajara, Mexico, in November 2011 to have a chance at securing the −81kg spot for the United States.

Instead, Dartanyon dropped three straight matches, against the Dominican Republic, Cuba, and Argentina. He bowed out of his final match with a suspected concussion and retreated into a corner with a sandwich and a juice box, looking scared and over-matched. "Everyone at that tournament had decades of experience," Liddie said. "We hadn't crammed enough in for Dartanyon to be competitive at that level yet." Dartanyon called me from the airport, tears streaming. Though we knew his chances of qualifying were slim, the defeats stung. "I don't feel like I should even be doing judo," he said. "I lost bad. Like real bad. Like I wouldn't be surprised if Ed just tells me to go back home, that I'm done." I listened, saddened by his loss while at the same time feeling fortunate to be the shoulder on which he leaned.

As a result of Dartanyon's poor showing, the United States could not send anyone to the Games in his −81kg division. But the US did qualify in the −90kg spot, where Denver-based Ryan Jones seemed to be a lock to win the bid to London at the April 2012 team trials. Liddie suspected Ryan was beatable, though, and had by no means given up on Dartanyon. In January 2012, Liddie sent Dartanyon to Finland for the Pajulahti Games. This was a smaller tournament than a World Cup, yet it was still represented by a handful of advanced European players. Dartanyon took gold. With the medal came a renewed sense of confidence and a hint of Dartanyon's vintage swagger. Moreover, the win in Finland gave him the international points he needed to challenge Ryan for his number-one seed—if, and only if, he could first win the US Nationals in Ryan's higher weight class. Liddie worked Dartanyon over that spring, force-feeding him as much judo as his body could withstand. "He's starting to get a rhythm for the sport," Liddie told me three days before the tournament. "His throws are looking better."

Feeding off that optimism, I called Victor. My pregnancy had kept me from taking on any projects since leaving ESPN, but Victor and I kept in touch periodically. I begged him to send a film crew to the US Nationals, hoping that if Dartanyon won, ESPN would follow him to London.

"So let me get this straight," Victor said. "Dartanyon has to win four straight matches against guys twenty pounds heavier than him, and if he does that, he then earns the right to fight the number-one seed in a best two out of three. And if he wins those, then he goes to London?"

"Correct."

"Is it common to win six judo matches in a day?"

"No. It's very difficult."

"And so after getting smoked in his own weight class in Mexico, you think he's going to pull this off in an even heavier weight class—why?"

"Because he sounds stronger when I talk to him, and he doesn't see obstacles like we do," I said. "Dartanyon wrote 'Destined for

Greatness' on his papers as a homeless kid. I don't feel like his story ends here." I had that hunch, just as I did when Dartanyon and Leroy lured me to Cleveland from the newspaper page in 2009.

"Have a nice trip to Texas," Victor conceded once again. I scrambled to book the crew—only this time I would not be able to join them. Navid was at a conference in Atlanta. My mother was visiting for her birthday, and I couldn't leave her with the two clamoring babies while I flew to Texas to be with Dartanyon.

On the morning of his matches, Dartanyon's voice sounded flat. "Everyone else has family here," he said. "I wish you could have come, even though I understand why you couldn't."

"I'm so sorry. I promise I'll never miss another one."

Minutes before Dartanyon's first match, Liddie was still squeezing judo lessons into him out in the open concourse. "Nope, pull this way. Circle your guy this way and then throw," Liddie instructed. "Create momentum and then turn him. And you can't have a straight back. If you do, he can counter you." Liddie's mantra was "one match at a time," and he promised to text me after each round. The first message: *Dartanyon won first match fast. Looked good.*

I received Liddie's messages while in the pediatrician's office. Saxon had been constipated for nearly a week, and there was growing fear of an obstructed bowel. As I described his symptoms and recent dietary intake to the doctor, *bing!* A new text message popped up. *He's through second match. Made a mistake but recovered.* I held my writhing son down for X-rays and exams while my own stomach knotted up, waiting for results from the doctor and from Dallas. *Bing! Won his third match in six seconds. He's focused. Just gotta keep doing what he's doing.*

The gastroenterologist sent us home. If Saxon didn't have a bowel movement by the next morning, surgery was imminent. My eyes welled, clutching my young son on my lap as he moaned, praying for him, and praying for Dartanyon.

And then: *Fourth match over. Dar is the US Champ.*

"So now he's in the challenge round. This is the part that really matters. He can do this," Liddie said, calling during the break. "He's just gotta stick to the plan."

I rocked Saxon, taking deep breaths, hoping for a big poop and for two underdog wins. After the stumbling blocks of Dartanyon's windshield wiper fiasco, his broken ankle, and his defeat and tears in Mexico, I couldn't believe he was in this position. In fact, his unlikely ascent to the finals caught even the tournament announcer by surprise: "Please turn your attention to mat six, for the ninety-kilo fight-off between Ryan Jones and . . . and . . . *Davey Crockett?*"

"Did he just call me Davey Crockett?" Dartanyon asked, incredulous. "He just called me Davey Crockett!"

Liddie slapped him on the backside. "Don't worry about it. Go out there and make 'em call you by your name."

Liddie and Dartanyon had studied Ryan intently that spring. He was skilled in groundwork, but less athletic than Dartanyon with his throws. Ryan would be trying to slow down the tempo to contain Dartanyon's quickness, waiting for the fight to hit the ground. "Don't go down there," Liddie told Dartanyon. "Move him and drag him. Create momentum, create momentum, and then *freeze!* and throw." Twenty-five seconds into the match, that is exactly what Dartanyon did, catching Ryan with an *ouchi gari*. Liddie's adrenaline rushed.

"Dartanyon's strong. You gotta be careful or he'll hurt you," Liddie said to a bystander. "I work out with him."

In their next bout, Dartanyon again accelerated the pace beyond Ryan's comfort, and again it worked. Dartanyon quickly finished him with an *uchi mata*. In total, Dartanyon needed just four minutes and thirty-five seconds on the mat to win six matches—every one of them by *ippon*—the highest score a fighter can achieve. Dartanyon would represent the United States at the 2012 London Paralympic Games.

His lips began to quiver as he came off the mat, trying to comprehend what he had just accomplished. Liddie greeted him with a hug, and then handed him the phone. "Lisa, I'm going to London," Dartanyon cried. "I'm going to London."

"You're going to London!" I squealed. "I can't believe you won!"

"I won. I won everything. I'm goin'," he said. "I don't even know what to do right now." There was nothing to do but revel in the moment. Weary and parched from wandering through the previous two years, this was the oasis we desperately needed. This was evidence that something we were doing was working, that effort could lead to results.

"I love you, Dartanyon," I said. "I'm so proud of you."

"I love you too."

Saxon had a successful poop that night, but once back home, our champion failed remedial English for the third time. I had to smile. There seemed no way around the "two steps forward, one step back" nature of our progress. But with London as our beacon, we dared to hope our steps might carry us toward brighter days ahead.

IT WAS LATE May 2012, and he called at four o'clock in the morning. He was crying.

"Leroy, I'm here," I said, getting my bearings. "What is it?"

"It's over." He seemed unable to say anything else.

"What's over?" I asked, and then waited.

"Kayla and me are breaking up," Leroy finally said.

I visited later that summer. The tension between Kayla and him was thick and uncomfortable. They were two kids, acting out a dramatic high school breakup, and yet between them was a young child who needed them to grow up. I tried to alleviate the stress by buying groceries and diapers. I helped Kayla pick up job applications. I went with Leroy to class and met with his professors, all of whom agreed Leroy had great potential as an artist but a questionable work ethic from which to grow his raw talent. I explained Leroy's background, hoping to persuade them to invest in him more fully.

I met Leroy's friends, all gamers—nerdy, unkempt, bodies that doubled as canvases for piercings and tattoos. I extended my hand to introduce myself to one of them. "I know who you are," he said. "Leroy talks about you all the time."

"He does? What does he say?"

"He says you're the mom he should have had from the beginning."

CHAPTER 14

LONDON

Dartanyon had no business being in London. Liddie said it was
akin to a walk-on making the starting five of the Miami Heat
when LeBron was their king. "And I don't mean like a college player
walking on," he said. "I mean like *some guy* just walking in off the
street." When Liddie realized he was about to send a green belt to
the Paralympic Games, he had a moment similar to Hudson's two
years prior. He quickly threw more skills at Dartanyon and tested
him for a brown belt—a milestone that once again felt insufficient.
"Who goes to the Games as a brown belt?" Liddie wondered. Then
he remembered that everything in Dartanyon's life had been a long
shot. Why not add this to the list?

Dartanyon looked positively dapper, dressed in his navy-blue
Ralph Lauren suit and beret for the opening ceremonies. Waving
his American flag, he walked in the Parade of Nations before
80,000 fans. But one spectator was notably missing: Arthur.
Though he had avoided prison time for the $25,000 in back
child support that he owed, the State Department barred him
from obtaining a passport. Arthur's level of debt designated him
a flight risk. I applied for an exception and personally vowed to
return Arthur to US soil. My appeal was denied. "I appreciate
how hard you tried," Dartanyon said. "But it still hurts that he
can't be here for me."

Dartanyon and I watched the opening day of judo competitions
together. London's ExCeL Center was filled to capacity, and legions
of raucous European nationals were cheering on their own athletes.

They would soon root against Dartanyon. "My heart is pounding, and I don't even have to fight," I said. "How are you feeling?"

"Not gonna lie. I'm a little bit scared."

But I had one secret weapon who could love louder than any European: Leroy. ESPN and I agreed that none of this felt right without him, and so the day before Dartanyon's scheduled matches, we flew Leroy over. I picked him up at the airport and hid him behind a plant outside the venue. I lured Dartanyon outside by telling him a fan wanted to meet him. Instead, Leroy rolled up from behind him.

"Hey, you bringing home gold?" Leroy called out. Dartanyon turned. *It couldn't be*, he thought. "I said, you bringing home gold!" Leroy repeated, his booming laughter giving him away. Dartanyon jumped into Leroy's embrace. Nearly two years had passed since they last saw one another.

"I thought you couldn't get out of school!" Dartanyon exclaimed, lunging for a second hug.

"Dude, nothing could ever keep me from being here," Leroy said. "You're my brother." With that, Dartanyon's posture relaxed, and his smile returned. Leroy wheeled down the Royal Victoria Dock with Dartanyon literally skipping beside him. They were off in their own world, singing songs and making up for lost time.

"Should we film this?" I asked Kameron.

"I think we should let them go," he said. "This moment is theirs."

DARTANYON STOOD IN the tunnel beside his first opponent, Olivier Cugnon de Sevricourt of France. Olivier was one of those technically proficient judo pedigrees, fighting since the age of six. He won bronze in the 2008 Paralympic Games and was coming off a silver medal in the last European Championships.

Dartanyon pounded his chest as US Paralympic head coach Scott Moore barked last-minute reminders into his ear. But Moore's words were drowned out by the two voices already sparring within Dartanyon. A whisper of doubt slithered around his mind like a viper, taunting him—*You have no business being on this world stage.* And that voice was right. He was a judo infant, the only brown belt in London. But then there was another voice, the steady voice of that young teenage boy who once sketched a daring kind of hope with his stubby yellow pencil, reminding him of the words that had gotten him this far—Destined for Greatness.

Dartanyon walked toward his mat, the voices battling inside his head, until he heard one that overpowered them both. "You can do this, Dar!" Leroy yelled, leaning over the padded wall. Dartanyon pointed as he passed, relieved to know his friend was once again alongside the mat, where he needed him most.

Olivier was known for his unconventional style of shoulder hunching, which made it difficult for opponents to get inside for a throw. The two appeared evenly matched for the first two minutes, trading attacks, relegating much of the action to the ground. Dartanyon worked quickly and walked confidently until halfway through regulation, when Olivier shot for a drop *seoi nage* and yanked Dartanyon's arm awkwardly. Dartanyon returned to center, clutching his left shoulder.

Sensing weakness, Olivier immediately attacked, and though he couldn't get Dartanyon on his back, he did get into his head. Each time the groundwork stagnated, it forced the official to call them back to center, eliciting a familiar theatrical response from Dartanyon: He rolled on the ground, holding his shoulder, then his knee, struggling to stand straight. "Come on, Dar, you gotta want this!" Moore yelled. The referee pulled Dartanyon upright; he slumped back over. She gave him a penalty for not attacking. Dartanyon huffed in disbelief, as though he had expected a hug instead.

After five minutes of regulation, the match was deadlocked and headed into the golden score—the sudden-death overtime of judo, where the first person to land a throw or score a point wins. But Dartanyon wasn't thinking about winning. He was thinking about how to explain himself if he lost. And so he punctuated every action with a melodramatic reaction—dragging his head along the mat, letting his leg give out, clutching his shoulder—as if to preemptively say, "See, I wasn't afraid. I was hurt." Certainly he entered the Games with nagging injuries—torn ligaments in his foot and ring finger, limited range of motion in his shoulder, screws in his ankle—but every judoka lives with bone shards and shredded joints. The voices were convincing Dartanyon that the pain cut deeper than it did.

"Get up, Dar!" Moore screamed, pounding his fists on the coach's table. "You gotta want this! Let's go!"

A section of French fans booed and brandished their flags. Leroy tugged on his lips. I pulled my knees to my chest and buried my head in my elbow. If he lost here, he went home.

Then, after twenty-eight minutes on the mat—twenty-three minutes more than he had ever spent in a match before—Dartanyon showed a flash of aggression, using his right leg to drop Olivier on his side for a *yuko*. He thereby earned an advantage point—and the win—in a most unconvincing fashion.

Dartanyon hobbled back to the athlete warm-up area, which was off-limits to me. I thought back to the day I met him and the first competition of his I ever watched—the high school wrestling match he was supposed to win easily. But the camera and the ESPN name put a pressure on him for which he wasn't prepared, and when he faltered, he explained it by limping and staggering and heaving over the trash. I thought of the Liberty Bell Classic, his first judo tournament, which he entered in full health and withdrew from two minutes later, blaming a strained knee. I had seen this drama before, and I could not let those lessons go to waste. I phoned Ed Liddie, who was with Dartanyon in the athlete holding area.

"Coach, I don't think Dartanyon's hurt. At least not as badly as he made it look," I said. "I think he is nervous."

"The trainers are assessing him now, so we'll see," Liddie said. I told him what I remembered from three years before and how the next day he'd bounced into the gym with Leroy on his back. "I think this may be what he does when he feels overmatched."

"I saw a similar thing with him in Mexico," Liddie said.

Dartanyon emerged from the training room. "Coach, my knee is really—"

"Come here, son," Liddie interjected. "You got a decision to make." Liddie refused Dartanyon praise for eking out his match. "You've gotta decide if you came here to win or if you are content to leave here with a nice pat-on-the-back-you-tried-hard-too-bad-about-the-leg kind of thing. Because you can either go home with sympathy, or you can go home with a medal. The choice is yours."

Dartanyon limped through the warm-up room to consider Liddie's words, surrounded by a sea of world champions and Paralympic coaches who were sizing up this new kid as he passed. Their stares bristled the back of Dartanyon's neck, reminding him that this was no place for rookies. But Dartanyon thought about his mother's funeral, about Kinsman, about the evictions. He had fought tougher rounds in this life, he thought. He walked back to Liddie—this time without the limp—and said, "I want some hardware, Coach."

Liddie leaned in. "That's what I want to hear," he said. "Let's go shock the world."

"LET'S-GO-INGRAM! LET'S-GO-INGRAM! LET'S-GO-INGRAM!"

It seemed the entire arena was chanting for Dartanyon's next opponent—hometown hero Samuel Ingram of Great Britain. Sam was the reigning European champion, and stood a full head taller than Dartanyon, reminding us that Dartanyon had not fully grown into this heavier weight class.

Sam went after Dartanyon like a street fighter. He quickly commandeered control of the match, securing the inside position on face-offs and maintaining a vise grip on Dartanyon's right sleeve to nullify his dominant throwing arm. But Dartanyon fought to shake free, convincing us all that he no longer wanted an excuse. He wanted to win. Gone was the limp, back was the warrior. Dartanyon staved off all of Sam's attacks for the first ninety seconds and got in a few of his own. But his inexperience showed against his veteran opponent, and Sam picked up on how Dartanyon preferred going to his left. With a *deashi braai*, Sam swept Dartanyon's right foot and planted the square of his back onto the mat. Victory Ingram, by *ippon*.

"Even though Dartanyon lost, we're happy because he fought better than he did in the match he won," Liddie said. "He didn't give up. He didn't give in. He just got caught."

Dartanyon still had a chance for bronze, if he could win his next two matches. "One match at a time still gets this done," Liddie told him.

JAPAN MAY HAVE birthed judo, but Brazil made a science out of it. Known as the most technically sound fighters in the martial arts world, Brazilians exhibit mastery of every technique and come armed with all the tricks. If Brazilian judokas were baseball pitchers, you could never be sure if they were going to come at you with a curveball, a change-up, a slider, or a knuckleball. And they could make a swinging fool out of you with any one of those.

Securing the inside grip, Dartanyon attacked Brazilian powerhouse Roberto Santos off the *hajime* (Japanese for "start"), immediately trying to throw him. Roberto didn't budge. "He was the strongest guy I had ever faced," Dartanyon later said. But Dartanyon remained comfortable and focused, finally believing he belonged there. He also knew it was win or go home. So he attacked off every face-off, keeping Roberto on the defensive and unable to set up his own moves.

Halfway into the match, Dartanyon worked Roberto on his side and earned a half-point *wazari*. The strategy shifted. He no longer needed to throw Roberto. He needed to eat time off the clock by keeping the action on the ground. Roll him around, mess around down there, act like you're trying to do something. But Roberto knew he didn't have time for the ground game. He shifted to aggressor, fighting out of Dartanyon's holds, fighting off the clock. Roberto kicked it into a new gear, one fiercer and faster than Dartanyon had the stamina to defend. With thirty seconds on the clock, Dartanyon wondered if he had enough to grind it out. But just as his will was starting to wane, a familiar voice echoed.

"Let's-Go-Crock-ett! Let's-Go-Crock-ett!"

Though Leroy was the only one chanting, everyone in the arena, including Dartanyon, could hear his booming voice. Dartanyon gathered himself, channeling the kindred spirit of his best friend. I joined Leroy, clapping rhythmically. "Let's-Go-Crockett! Let's-Go-Crockett!" Then, to our surprise, a legion of Japanese fans behind us joined in, waving their national flag and cheering "Let's-Go-Crockett!" Spanish fans were next, followed by a group of British children. And though it was probably only a few dozen people, it felt like a movement, as though Leroy had sparked the whole world to unite in cheering Dartanyon back to life.

Renewed, Dartanyon shot straight for a side pin, trapping Roberto between his arms. He squeezed him for ten seconds. Fifteen. Twenty. Twenty-five seconds. Pin. Dartanyon was headed to the bronze-medal match, and as he strode off the mat, he pointed, gratefully, to Leroy. I had flown Leroy over as a surprise. He turned out to be a savior. This time, Leroy carried Dartanyon.

IF BRAZILIANS ARE known for their sophisticated judo arsenals, Russians live and die by their fastballs. And Dartanyon was about to face Russia's equivalent of Nolan Ryan. Oleg Kretsul was a hulking Eastern European brawler who moved with the stealth of a cat. He began his career as a sighted athlete, breaking onto the scene at the 1996 Olympic Games in Atlanta. A year later, he married, and one week after his wedding, he suffered a serious car crash. His new bride was killed in the accident, and Oleg lost both of his eyes. The accident forced him to rebuild his life and his judo career— now as a Paralympian. Oleg reemerged as the silver medalist in the 2004 Paralympic Games in Athens and the gold medalist in the 2008 Paralympic Games in Beijing. He bore a resemblance to Shrek, with a square nose on a square head, planted atop square shoulders that could have doubled as bookshelves to hold his four world championship titles.

"Listen, you can handle him," Liddie told Dartanyon, while looking up at this mountain of a man and hiding his own sweaty palms behind his back. "It's just another round."

Oleg couldn't see Dartanyon, but his coach, Vitaly Gligor, could. He had watched Dartanyon compete in Finland earlier that year. "The American is strong, like a bodybuilder, but he doesn't have much technique," Gligor told Oleg. "He doesn't move like a judoka."

Dartanyon strutted out of the chute like a prizefighter, like he had grown ten judo years since his morning match against France. Both Dartanyon and Oleg attacked off the *hajime*, with Oleg gripping so aggressively that he reached over Dartanyon's shoulder and held him by the back of his *gi*. Oleg yanked him. Dartanyon yanked back. But it was no use, like trying to drag a tree stump out of the ground. *This guy is stupid strong*, Dartanyon thought about a minute into the match. And that's when his body overruled all other voices, his bones rattling with the early words and techniques Hudson had drilled into him: *Go toward the energy, don't resist it.* And then it happened. As Oleg jerked at Dartanyon's sleeves, Dartanyon changed gears and exploded toward Oleg. *Minimum effort, maximum efficiency.* With Oleg stumbling off balance, Dartanyon used his right leg to sweep both of Oleg's legs out from under him. Oleg crashed to the ground in a moment that both moved in slow motion yet passed in a blur. Dartanyon had defeated the decorated Russian with a most perfect and basic *ouchi gari*—the very first throw Hudson taught him as a white belt and insisted he make his own.

Dartanyon leaped around the mat in disbelief, pointing up to his mother, pointing to Leroy, pointing to me. The overhead screen flashed: "Winner, Crockett," sweeping us up in a staggering miracle that had quietly begun on a beat-up wrestling mat in an inner-city high school in Cleveland. Minutes later, in the media zone, Dartanyon and I stood before each other, thunderstruck. "I did it, Lisa," he cried, letting his head fall onto my shoulder.

"You did it. You did everything," I said as I wept. "I am so proud of you, Dartanyon." He'd begun the day as a judo infant and blossomed into an elite medalist before our eyes. He had encountered every style of fighting, from the Frenchman's stubborn persistence to England's street style to Brazil's technical proficiency to the Russian's brute strength. Dartanyon had risen above them all with a style of his own: indomitable spirit.

Leroy and I watched from the edge of the mat as Dartanyon took his place atop the podium, the bronze medal draped around his neck. Once forgotten by the world, Dartanyon finally stood on top of it.

THE NEXT DAY, Dartanyon, Leroy, and I rollicked around London, still trembling with joy. We decided that if you can't win gold, bronze is the next best thing—even better than silver. In judo, silver medalists end their day on a loss, at the hands of the gold medalist. Bronze medalists, however, end their final matches on a win. They earn the right to celebrate on the mat. "You win bronze. You are given silver," Dartanyon explained.

Dartanyon was not done surprising us in London, for there was one more honor to bestow. He learned that the US Olympic Committee provides American medal winners the opportunity to recognize the coaches who propelled them to the podium by presenting them with the Order of Ikkos medallion. This distinction, named for the first recorded Olympic coach in ancient Greece, acknowledges the countless hours of training and teamwork involved in achieving the athletes' success.

Dartanyon could have given this recognition to Coach Liddie, for taking on such a risky investment. He could have given it to Shane Hudson, for teaching him the throw that brought down the mighty Russian. But Dartanyon broke tradition. He didn't select a coach. He chose me. So on a sunny London morning, in the center of the Athletes' Village, with his teammates gathered around, Dartanyon carefully hung the silver medallion around my neck. And we understood that we had won, together.

"You know, I am leaving London with silver and you only got bronze," I teased as we posed for a photograph.

"Yah, but I earned bronze," he said. "You were given silver." I smiled, knowing that Dartanyon had given me more than a medallion that day. He'd given me the unexpected gift of love returned. "Although I think you earned it too," he added. "You worked just as hard these last three years."

We celebrated at a posh restaurant in Stratford. Dartanyon ordered salmon with an arugula salad, along with a prosciutto and sage flatbread—a million miles away from the syrup sandwiches and steam-ironed grilled cheese sandwiches of his childhood. We talked about the upcoming presidential election and a book he'd read while on the flight over to London. "How did you get all grown up, with your fancy food and politics, when I wasn't looking?" I asked.

He smiled playfully. "Occasionally I do something that you don't know about. And by the way, I want to go back to school next semester. I'm ready to take it seriously."

The years leading to London were mired in complexity, and our daily conversations were so often centered on problem solving. I hadn't had the time to step back and appreciate how those conflicts had refined Dartanyon. I stared in amazement at the young man who now sat across from me. Then I thought back to the unseasoned high school boy I'd met three years earlier, when I asked him which of his wins were particularly memorable to him. I wondered what his answer would be now.

"Dartanyon, how much of your bronze medal match do you remember?" I asked.

"Every second of it," he answered. "Like I could reenact it for you right here."

"Interesting, because the first day I met you, you said that you only remember the losses. Do you remember telling me that?"

"I do," he said. He looked up from his plate, thoughtfully considering the shift. "I guess the time for sadness is finally over."

CHAPTER 15

THE REAL EDUCATION

Leroy may have resuscitated Dartanyon's Paralympic debut, but he was having a difficult time saving himself. Once back in Phoenix, his fights with Kayla escalated. Though they were no longer romantically involved, they lacked the financial means to live apart, and as a result, their animosity grew with every passing day. Leroy's grades began to dip again. He self-medicated by excessively purchasing electronics and gadgets, compounding his stress. His conversational skills regressed; with his short, detached answers, he sounded like the boy I'd sat beside in the basement three years before. I had hoped that Dartanyon's performance in London would be the rallying cry Leroy needed to take his own steps toward betterment, and that our shared experiences in London would serve to deepen our connection. But instead, Leroy became unreachable for weeks at a time, refusing to answer my calls and texts.

When Leroy retreated into these black holes, it launched me into a vortex of emotions—first concern for his well-being, then anger at his obstinacy, then faked indifference, which led to reverse-psychological attempts to beat him at his own apathetic game by not reaching out to him for several days. I was certain he would wonder why I stopped caring. He didn't. So I circled back to concern, grave this time, fearing he was suicidal.

Only after I left messages threatening to call the police to check his whereabouts did Leroy respond. "No, I was fine," he said. He offered no apology, no acknowledgment of his peculiar behavior.

He played off his detachment as tiredness, and excused his lack of communication by saying he was asleep when I called, or his phone was off, or he meant to call me back and forgot. The miles between us left me exceedingly helpless. I couldn't grab him by the shoulders, look him in the eye, and say, "I know you're not okay."

Kayla reported that Leroy stayed at school until midnight most nights. She was irate that he was not spending time with Alani; Leroy countered that he had no choice; if he brought his work home, Kayla would sabotage him with another argument. The school said that either way, Leroy was not studying. "He plays cards all day," his adviser told me. "We can hear him laughing clear from the student lounge during times when he should be in class." His professors were not utilizing the portal to track grades and attendance that term, so I chased them down myself. I discovered that Leroy was rarely attending class or engaging in the work. He carried Fs in all three of his courses.

I began setting alarms to call Leroy before every class and make sure he was going. Sometimes he answered, usually he didn't. Always, I hung up feeling like I was standing in quicksand. I e-mailed his teachers for extensions and submitted my own ideas for extra-credit opportunities. Fortunately, they were supportive. Yet Leroy continued to drop every ball we handed to him. The harder I pushed him, the deeper he burrowed into his black hole.

"He seems to have given up," I said to Navid. "I don't know if I just let him get kicked out and learn his lesson the hard way, or if I keep fighting until he decides to fight for himself." If Leroy failed, the opportunity for that elusive lightbulb to click on in his head would be gone. But by continuing to intervene, I was enabling his shenanigans.

"My inclination is that you should keep the train on the tracks, so to speak," Navid said. But by November 2012, Collins College blew the whistle. They no longer believed Leroy was serious about his education and sent notice of expulsion. He had the right to a second and final appeal, but only if his plea was different from the original petition that we had made on financial grounds two years before. Leroy asked me to help write his letter. I said I could not; his behavior was as egregiously inexplicable to me as it was to the school administrators.

"You spend sixteen hours a day on campus, yet you're not turning in any work," I said. "If you can't tell me what's going on, you have no grounds to appeal." Was he depressed? Was he lazy? Was he on drugs? My mind ventured to the shadowy corners of his past.

"I don't know. When I can put the words together, I'll tell you," he said.

Three days later, he called. "There are parts of my days that I don't remember," Leroy said. "Like I'm conscious, and my friends tell me I was in class or in the lounge, yet I have no recollection of it." He equated it to a blackout, where sizable chunks of his time went unaccounted for in his memory. We went through events from the week and found them missing from his mental Rolodex. "And sometimes it's like I'm watching myself talk to people, but I'm not actually in my body."

This sounded like a problem beyond my pay grade. I couldn't fix this with a to-do list. I handed the phone to Navid, who questioned Leroy for twenty minutes before emerging with a diagnosis. "Leroy has post-traumatic stress disorder," he said. "It's a textbook case." I was familiar with PTSD, but thought it was a condition one suffered immediately following a trauma, not eleven years later. Navid postulated that because Leroy had not been treated properly at the time of trauma, he had been left with compromised coping mechanisms for subsequent stress.

Navid compiled academic literature on pediatric trauma to refresh his training and to educate me. As we pored over it together, I felt like I was reading the owner's manual that should have been sewn into Leroy's clothes so that anyone meeting him could interpret his behaviors: May shut down entirely in stressful situations, seeming unresponsive or detached. Problems expressing and managing emotions. Easily overwhelmed. Difficulty thinking clearly, reasoning, or problem solving. Unable to plan ahead, anticipate the future, and act accordingly.

Leroy's accounts of feeling detached from his body and watching his own experiences from somewhere else in the room had a name too: dissociation. He had likely learned as a child to dissociate as a defense mechanism, and now found himself automatically disconnecting when he felt unsafe or ill-equipped in demanding situations.

Leroy aligned with nearly every symptom of PTSD. His life had been a continuous reel of traumatic events: "hit him or I'll hit you," his accident, neglect, drug abuse, abrupt school transfers, gang exposure, bone reduction surgeries. Since early elementary school, Leroy had known just one trauma-free year—the year he relaxed in Big Ma's basement and rode on Dartanyon's back. Both places served as safe havens where Leroy's system could begin to recalibrate. But before any significant healing could take place, he was thrust into fatherhood, domestic disputes, and an academic environment for which he was woefully unprepared. With all of the disruptions to his emotional, mental, and chemical development, Leroy likely had the coping mechanisms of a ten-year-old.

Over the years I had known Leroy, I had grown to understand his trust issues and his academic deficiencies. I had also suspected that many of his issues were rooted in his accident and neglect, but I did not understand those roots could continue spreading like serpents beneath the surface, angling to throttle his future.

My heroic husband wrote a convincing appeal letter, describing how Leroy suffered from paralyzing anxiety attacks, and that his dissociation, misinterpreted as "spacing out" or ambivalence, was having adverse effects on his learning and classroom participation.

Navid recommended behavioral therapy, and Collins agreed to give Leroy a final chance.

Leroy had never heard of post-traumatic stress disorder. "It's kind of a relief," he said after Navid described the condition. "I was starting to think I had some kind of mystery psychosis and would end up in a padded room." Now that he understood the cause of his symptoms, I assumed he would embrace the help he needed. And initially he did. He went to four weeks of therapy sessions and genuinely liked them. But when his counselor got to the hard stuff—the part after she moved beyond telling him that he was a remarkable survivor and began probing his emotional wounds—Leroy stopped going.

"I feel better already, and besides, you're my counselor," he would tell me.

"This is about more than feeling better," Navid and I told him. "It's about learning the tools to cope with stress." Still, we could not convince him to return. I was going to have to step up into this role, somehow, someway. I was in this place, for this time, to fill this gap. And while a television producer is a far cry from a trained psychologist, my best was going to have to suffice. I had to settle into a new mind-set, though. I was not mentoring a college-age young adult; I was parenting a damaged adolescent who happened to be in college. My expectations needed to be different, and my approach needed to adapt. His progress would not adhere to time-lines or deadlines.

I continued reaching out to Leroy, but gone was the tension and the pushing on my part. Whatever he accomplished in a day would have to be enough, and if he accomplished nothing, I made sure he knew that he was still deserving of care. Behind the scenes, I continued working with his professors and advisers to get him through the last few months of school, for I couldn't bear seeing Leroy fail out six months from graduation. Leroy viewed himself as powerless, perceiving the world as a meaningless place in which planning and positive action were futile. I learned to guide him gently, without overtaxing his stress responders. With every detectable step of accomplishment, I showered him with praise. With every misstep, I affirmed my care. He needed a love free of strings and full of patience.

When I reached out to Dr. Norman Christopher, who had worked with Leroy at Akron Children's Hospital, he lamented how Leroy's family had slipped through the system's cracks. "Leroy experienced much of his life in toxic stress," he told me, "and when tough, adult things happen, his ability to rise up and overcome is based on his life experience and the faith he has in himself. Leroy learned to endure his challenges, but nothing and no one in his life showed Leroy that he could overcome them."

"Can a child who goes untreated for multiple complex traumas ever go on to thrive?" I asked.

"There are a lot of factors at play, but what we believe matters most is the nurturing, and particularly the relationship of the mother," Dr. Christopher said. "If Leroy's mother had been equipped to properly care for him, you and I probably wouldn't be having this conversation today."

Dr. Christopher told me that it was difficult to know if the outcomes could be reversed. But he emphasized that caregivers, at any point in one's life, have the greatest influence on a person's sense of self-worth and value. "I'm not aware of any data on it, but common sense suggests that you have a better chance of reversing the effects if you keep trying than if you give up."

IN MAY 2013 KAYLA was given a plane ticket to visit a friend in Hawaii. She took Alani with her and the two did not return to Arizona. "They didn't get on their flight back," Leroy said. "I'm not even sure they had one." He had cleaned their apartment and was dressed to fetch them at the airport when Kayla called, still in Hawaii. He was fighting back tears, stung by another loss and another failure. I wasn't sure how Leroy would recover from this blow, until later that month—on Mother's Day—when I received this letter.

Dear Lisa,

A few years ago, I never would have thought I would be writing to anyone for Mother's Day, but now I see that being a mother is more than having kids. It is sitting through the good, bad, and ugly with your child, which you have done with me. You are the steady rock with whom I can share my love, hate, pain, and sorrow. As you watched and helped me through transitions in my life, you proved to me that I could trust more than myself. Every moment I have cried, or that we have cried, those are the moments that drove me to love you. Those are the times that I labeled you mom. After years of disappointments, you have been the constant light in my life. You gave me faith in the human existence. Our bond is a bridge that links me to a home in your heart. Not much can make me believe in prayer . . . but you. So on this day, I pray . . . "Please let her continue to love and care for me like her own." I love you with every part of my soul.

Your son,
Leroy

And there we learned what Dr. Christopher suspected: A mother's love can revive a withered heart.

ON HIS TWENTY-THIRD birthday, as we continued working through his traumas, Leroy wished to relinquish his anger toward his father. He understood now how difficult it was to be an effective parent within the constraints of a teenage relationship. He was thinking differently about family and second chances. He wanted to find his father and hear his side of the story. So I set out to fulfill Leroy's birthday request.

Leroy only knew one thing about his father: his name was Big Leroy. When little Leroy was three years old, Katrina's brothers had beat Big Leroy with slabs of wood for allegedly raising his hand to her, and they told him never to show his face in the family again. But little Leroy didn't know this. All he knew was that his father was absent for his own birthdays, his accident recovery, and all the times when his mother went missing.

A quick background check on Big Leroy turned up a slew of arrests for domestic violence, attempted felonious assault, and kidnapping between 1996 and 2008. We found Big Leroy on the lower west side of Cleveland, in a grimy apartment above a corner grocery store. He lived with his girlfriend and her two young children who slept on the floor. A pit bull snarled in a corner cage, and twice during our hour-long visit, a scrawny man in a white ribbed tank top and enormous pants bounced through the door to ask Big Leroy if he wanted to smoke a blunt. No one in the apartment acknowledged my presence. I sat on the sticky floor in a corner, listening as father and son made small talk about movies and video games. We learned that Leroy is the oldest of nine children, meaning he had eight half siblings of whom he was largely unaware. Big Leroy asked his son if he had gone to high school and where he was staying now. I remembered the valor of Leroy walking across the stage to get his diploma and stepped out of the apartment to gather myself.

As we drove away, I asked Leroy how he thought the visit went. "As I expected," he answered. I asked if he'd grown up in similar conditions. "No," he said. "That was better than some of the places me and my mom stayed."

I could no longer contain my tears. "I'm sorry it took so long for me to find you."

"It's okay. I'm safe now," he said.

I approached my next thought with extreme caution.

"Leroy, I know you have long struggled with the question of why you lost your legs, and I don't dare try to answer that," I said. "But do you think that had it not been for the accident, you might still be living in a place like that, with a potentially more difficult life?" I had wondered as much since my early visit to Laird Land, yet I feared Leroy would interpret my question as one from a privileged outsider trying to put a tidy bow on his pain.

"I was actually thinking the same thing," Leroy said. "It's unlikely anyone would have tried to help me if I had legs." This was the closest answer to "Why?" that Leroy had ever found. And while we will never know why such a tragedy happened, Leroy's acceptance of this severe mercy moved him to a place of peace, and then purpose: "I think I would much rather change this world than walk on it," he said. "Now I have that chance."

Leroy uncovered few details about where he came from that day, but he found something more important. He caught a glimpse of who he wanted to become.

LATER THAT SUMMER, as we were planning for Leroy's college graduation in Phoenix, he said he wanted his father to attend. I, on the other hand, did not want Big Leroy to be present. I didn't think he deserved it. Though Leroy had made peace with his father, I resented him for the things I saw during our visit. How dare this man bring nine children into the world and hardly know where any of them were? I thought. How dare he spend his days getting high while children slept on the floor? How. Dare. He.

But I bit my tongue. Leroy was the first member of his family with a high school diploma, and soon would be the first member with a college degree. I understood why he hoped his family would step up and be proud of him. So I set out to get plane tickets for his dad, his mom, his sister, and Big Ma. I scheduled Coach Hons to take Big Leroy to the airport and give him spending money before he boarded. I explained that drugs and weapons could not be taken onto planes. I also asked him if his state ID was valid. But on the morning of their flights, Big Leroy called me from the phone of a friend to say his state ID was expired.

"Does that matter?" he asked.

"Of course it matters! I asked you weeks ago if it was valid."

"I guess I didn't know what that meant," he replied. He had four hours until his flight's departure. I said there was nothing more I could do. But Big Leroy was not ready to give up. He went directly to the Bureau of Motor Vehicles, where, due to his previous record of falsifying IDs, they would not renew his ID without a birth certificate, which he did not have. At that point, he said to me, "I'll call you back. I know a guy." An hour later, Big Leroy had miraculously secured a birth certificate and an ID, and when I asked how he pulled that off, he said, "Don't worry about it. I ain't letting my son down this time."

Leroy's family missed their connecting flight in Detroit because they were all at the food court when a gate change was announced—but I didn't know this because none of them had a cell phone from which to call me. I stewed at the Phoenix airport for four more hours, hoping they had found their way onto the next plane, while at the same time hoping they hadn't. I regretted my offer to coordinate their trip. By the time they arrived, I was ready to send them back.

Katrina, Keyiera, and Big Ma bunked with Leroy, while Big Leroy stayed at the hotel with me. During our first awkward breakfast together, he said, "So are you like a travel agent or something?"

I smiled. "Sometimes it feels that way. I am just here to do whatever Leroy needs me to do. He will always be your son first, but he is also like a son to me."

"Well, I can tell you're a real nice lady, and I don't know who you are, but I'm glad Leroy has you."

"Tell me something about yourself," I said. He clenched his jaw mid-chew.

"You don't want to know about me," he said.

"Sure I do. There's no judgment," I said. He raised an eyebrow, and I immediately understood that I had in fact been judging him from the moment I met him. Showing more grace than I had, he let that go.

"When I was five years old, my mom left my brother and I in an abandoned building," he said in a low, slow voice. "We went to the grocery store every day to steal our food. We hid pretty well, so no one ever found us, but now I wish they would have. We never went to school. I'd see my mom on the streets from time to time, but she never came back. I started selling drugs when I was nine years old to get some money, but I guess I was angry, because I started getting in fights too. I spent time in prison. Some of the things I did, some I took the hit. At least I learned to read and write a little in there. But overall, I guess I made some real bad decisions in my life."

Shame on me.

I held Big Leroy's stare and said, "You listen to me. You didn't make bad choices as a child. You made the only choices you had. You were five years old." Big Leroy looked away. I said it again. "You didn't make bad choices. You made the only choices you had. The only path you were offered in life was survival."

As we talked more, the details only grew sadder. I was softening toward this man, this person I had labeled an addict, a loser, and a bother. I had forgotten the lesson I learned on Big Ma's porch—that men like Big Leroy were once sweet-faced children who were forced to fend for themselves. I had forgotten the lesson I learned four years earlier with his son—that when you give someone a safe space in which to tell his or her story, when you *become* a safe person to whom a story can be told, that space births compassion. And with compassion, one's sense of self-worth can be reframed, and goodness can begin to grow.

Big Leroy said he was grateful for all of those who took care of his son, adding, "cause I never been able to do nothing for him."

"I don't think that's true," I told him. "This weekend you did one of the most important things a father could do for a son. You showed up. He needed you, you came, and you came proud." A tear streamed down Big Leroy's cheek. And then another. "This time you had a choice, and this time you chose to do what good fathers do."

Big Leroy said it was the first time he'd cried since his mama left him for dead in that old house. He said he had never told anyone about his life before, because he didn't think that could lead to anything good. But on that day, we found something good. We found connection. Big Leroy left thinking maybe he wasn't the failure this world painted him to be, and I sat a while longer, stunned by grace and its power to offer hope to a touched and tormented soul.

LEROY GRADUATED ON a sunswept day at the Phoenix Art Museum. I wish I could say I surged with the same pride as I did watching his high school graduation, but all I felt was relief that we did not have to slog through another term. I wanted to bolt out of the auditorium before the dean noticed Leroy sitting in the back corner of the stage and decided to recalculate his grade-point average. But Leroy had achieved what his mind and his body could manage, and on that day, it was enough.

The greater accomplishment came not on the stage, but in a backyard, where Alicia's family hosted a small graduation party for Leroy. On hand were the three families who had paid his tuition—three of the wealthier, more generous Americans one could meet—and they were joined by Leroy's family, four of the poorer Americans one could encounter. I slipped into corners to watch them learn to make conversation, to ask questions, to listen to stories. Perhaps the most poignant words of the afternoon came from Leroy, as he blew out his candles and addressed the room.

"It makes me really proud that I have each of you in my life. It warms my heart that you gave openly and stuck your necks out there on my behalf," he said. "You sacrificed for me even though I'm not the best student. But I have become a better person because you believed in me and didn't give up on me when I made mistakes. If you hadn't showed up in my life, my life would have been completely different. I want to tell you from the bottom of my heart that I love you, and it means so much that you came today to see me through another transition."

We had banded together over those years to carry Leroy, just as Dartanyon once did. In doing so, we filled the gaping holes in Leroy's heart with three foundational truths: You are never forgotten. You are wholly loved. You are worthy of celebration. This was Leroy's real education—learning to let each person there into his life, receiving love from his newer friends, and making peace with his family. This was his Olympic-size victory, and it was golden.

Your money, your family, your security,
your will, your future. Poverty takes a percentage of everything,
indefinitely, until the cycle is broken.

—DARTANYON

CHAPTER 16

UNLIKELY FAMILY

One. Two. Three.

We couldn't find her at first.

Seven. Eight. Nine.

We started at opposite ends of the row and headed toward the middle, counting the plots, shortly after Mother's Day 2014. As I walked, I caught Dartanyon out of the corner of my eye, bent close over each stone, straining to read the engravings. He had spent most of his life searching for his mother in some way. Each day, scrolling through those few grainy memories from his childhood. In the crack house each night, wondering why she had left him alone in the world. On the wrestling mat, channeling all of the strength she left behind in hopes that she was watching from above. And later, in me, this unlikely woman God had dropped into the gap. Yet today was as close as this boy had come to his mother since she left him fifteen years earlier.

Eighteen. Nineteen. Twenty.

"She's over here!" he shouted.

Section 34, Row 2, Grave 21. Coordinates of deep loss. A thick covering of dried lawn clippings blanketed the flat rose-colored marker, causing us to miss it the first time down the row. Dartanyon quickly dropped down on all fours, sweeping the stone clean with his hands. And there she rested: Juanita Keely Crockett. 1956–1999. Beloved Mother, Grandmother, Sister.

"Why aren't they taking care of her?" he asked as he scraped dirt out of the letters of her name with his thumbnail. Through all of those lean, trying years, he had wished for his mother to be there to look after him. Today he returned, ready to look after her.

I was nervous to meet her, to stand before this woman who'd spoken to me so clearly five years before: *Take care of my son.* Periodically, when I stood at a crossroads with Dartanyon, weighing what to do and wondering if his challenges were simply too much for me, I would hear her plea again: *Take care of my son.* And then over time, her voice grew faint. Perhaps she did not need to urge me on anymore. Perhaps she knew I was all in.

I wanted to ask her how she chose her little boy's big name and if he was nervous on his first day of school. I wanted to tell her how he became a young man who bronzed the London stage and finally aced that pesky English class last semester. Could she see that he had grown into his strong name with all of the tender grace and humble heroics she dreamed into him when she held him brand-new? And could she explain why I had been chosen to witness it all?

But I held back. I hushed my heart. Questions and answers were not why her boy had come today. No, he didn't need to know any of that. He simply wanted to sit up under her, just as he did when he was six years old and she was braiding hair, her love a prism that defined his blurry world.

Watching Dartanyon, I gained a stronger sense of what that means—"to sit up under her." To bask in the acceptance, in the wholeness, of knowing where you belong. I felt as though I was returning from a mission—from her commission—with a finished product of sorts. *Juanita, here is your son. May you be proud of us both.*

After some time sitting in the quiet, plucking the blades of grass around the edge of the gravestone, I asked Dartanyon what moments in his life he most wished his mother could have seen, other than every single day. "Probably my high school graduation," he said. "I was the only one of her sons to finish. I hope that would have made her happy."

I thought back to that ceremony, when this boy walked across the stage twice: Once for himself. Once for his best friend. "You don't have to hope," I said, and smiled up into the blue sky. "I know you made her happy."

I said that I hoped my son would one day love me as much as he loves his mother. Dartanyon put his arm around my shoulder and said, "You don't have to hope. I already do."

Two mothers.

One boy.

Loved into a man.

Mission accomplished.

THERE IS A photo of my father sitting beside Dartanyon on the sofa, at my house. They are in front of the Christmas tree. Saxon is playing next to them, and my dad is smiling. He is sitting in the middle of a story that he began.

This photo reminds me that story pries open narrow minds and closes imagined chasms. Story is the grease and the glue. Story is the counterforce to intolerance. In this story my father began, our family narrative on race took a healing turn. My father found that when you learn another's story, you can understand that person rather than fear him. Today, he looks not so much *at* people but *into* them—into their hearts, into the cores of their experiences—and he sees beauty. He may not be able to articulate this shift, but I can see it in the adoring way he looks at Saxon as he holds him on his lap. My father cares freely now. He smiles readily. He gives willingly. Only he is not thinking about any of that in the photo. Instead, he is caught up in this Christmas wonder, smiling contentedly between Dartanyon and Saxon, in a family that would have been vastly different had he not changed the order of it.

When Leroy and Dartanyon spend time at my home, they declare themselves my kitchen DJs. They're still trying to teach me how to beatbox. Dartanyon cooks breakfast and sculpts play dough with Talia. Saxon whizzes through the house in Leroy's wheelchair. And Leroy lies on the floor, beside the crackling fire, staring up at the skylight. He says he is most at peace at my house, and I see that calm in his eyes—that is, until Dartanyon dives on top of him and wrestles him into a pretzel.

"It feels good to finally have a Hallmark family," Dartanyon once remarked. He explained that "five o'clock dinners, a warm house, good conversation, and nobody drunk or high" marks such families. Then he added, "And in our case, blind and legless dudes. Every family should have a couple of those."

In two years' time, I essentially became a mother to four children of different races, ages, and abilities. It is not the family my husband and I planned. In fact, it is far better, far richer, than any we could have imagined. It is a family that reframed my understanding of what it means to be blessed. There was once a time I believed that blessings were things we possessed: stable jobs, good health, promising opportunities. I believed these were heaven's rewards for living well. But I now understand that a blessing has less to do with what we have and everything to do with what we are able to give. I understand that blessings come from being part of a redemptive journey here on earth, in allowing God to work out the injustices through us. Blessings come when we walk alongside another to pick up the broken pieces and together restore the beauty.

I gave up asking Dartanyon why he started carrying Leroy. In the end, it didn't matter. It didn't matter where they started or where they were going. It didn't matter how heavy the load or how far the destination. All that mattered was who they compelled us to be. They moved me, and countless others, to be the ramps and the vision, the mothers and the fathers and the guides. They drew us out of safe spaces to become bridges across perceived barriers of race and class. They taught us about darkness and light and our ability to be the living difference between the two. They taught us that when we accept what we are called to do, we become who we are created to be. They taught us how to carry on.

EPILOGUE

Story allows us a window into another person's experience, free of risk, through which we can stand at that character's crossroads, watching them live out their choices. Story allows us to vicariously test our limits and measure our endurance. We examine the boundaries of our moral fabric, and story either shows us the strength we hope to find in our hearts or, at times, depicts the worst of our fears about what else may be inside our darkest selves. With story, we can love and yearn and chance without the penance of consequence. And then we turn it off. We close the book. Because it is someone else's story. We are under no obligation to continue in reflection once the story ends. But on a rare and mysterious occasion, a story does not end. It lodges itself inside us, and more broadly, into the bloodstream of a culture. The change that was necessary to move the story arc at times continues moving, through the hearts of those aching to be stirred.

In August 2013 ESPN aired *Carry On II*, a twenty-two-minute follow-up feature on my relationship with Leroy and Dartanyon. Initially, I asked Victor to forgo my inclusion, arguing that this was Leroy and Dartanyon's story, and that they had a proven chemistry with viewers that we risked diluting by adding me into the mix. Ultimately, I lost the battle. The exposure once again catapulted Leroy, Dartanyon—and, this time, me—onto a world stage. And once again, thousands of people reached out in teary-eyed gratitude.

This outpouring seemed different, though. Four years prior,

Carry On motivated people to care about Leroy and Dartanyon; this time, people were inspired to care about *one another*. They wrote to me personally to say that today was the day they would become foster parents. Today was the day they would show their families how much they cared. Today was the day they picked up a mentoring application at the juvenile facility that they had driven by every morning for the last twenty years. As people discovered connections between our journey and theirs, they found renewed encouragement to live with hope, with generosity, and with an ever deeper love.

Big Leroy went home from his son's graduation in 2013 wondering what potential laid in wait within him. He enrolled at Edwin's Leadership and Restaurant Institute, a French cooking program in Cleveland for former inmates. Big Leroy graduated and now works as a caterer in North Carolina. Motivated by Big Leroy's success, Katrina enrolled next. She graduated in 2016.

Laurie Moline, the Akron Miracle Network producer who interviewed Leroy shortly after his accident and left feeling like something was amiss, saw *Carry On II* in 2013. As she watched, her chest tightened. She wondered if Leroy's life would have been any different had she reported her suspicions twelve years prior. She wondered if she could have done more. And then she decided to make up for lost time. She began a mentoring program for teens and now shepherds dozens of kids from backgrounds similar to those of Leroy and Dartanyon toward self-sufficiency. Together, Laurie and I partnered to transition Leroy's brother, Tony, into a drug and alcohol rehabilitation program in 2015. I found Tony while researching this book. He reported still having nightmares about pulling his little brother off the train tracks. Tony was homeless, hopeless, and high before breakfast. He had hit rock bottom and started digging. Under Laurie's watch, Tony emerged sober and gainfully employed. He moved into Big Ma's house, where she faithfully and lovingly guards over him.

Arthur has held the same restaurant server job since *Carry On* aired in 2009. Once Dartanyon learned how to save his own money, he took a chunk of that savings and moved his father out of his drug-infested boardinghouse and into a suburban efficiency apartment. Arthur's entire living space measures three hundred square feet, yet he calls it his Taj Mahal. Here he works earnestly at his sobriety. Dartanyon said he's learned that the difference between winning and losing at this life is having just one person who believes in you, and he wants to be that person for his father. Dartanyon is pursuing a social work degree in hopes of guiding many more out of poverty one day. He won a second bronze medal at the Rio Paralympic Games in 2016 and continues to compete at an elite level.

In talking with Leroy for this book, I found that he remembered very little about the years following his accident. He retained the things he could live with and blocked out the rest. I turned to his doctors, teachers, coaches, and family members to fill in the voids. What I uncovered was at times uncomfortable, and I sensitized Leroy slowly, giving him the innocuous pages first to read for accuracy. When he proved he could stomach those, I shared the more astringent stories. We grew brave together, me as a writer and he as a survivor.

"I always thought I was over the train," he said one day over the phone, "but your book made me see that I'm not. I can see now that it affects everything I do—the friends I choose, the bad decisions I make and the good ones I avoid. Way too much was put on my plate, at way too early of an age."

I gripped the phone tightly, pressing his words against my skin. He started to cry.

"I didn't try in school or with my art or with handling money because I wanted everything on my terms. All these years have been like a big temper tantrum over what happened to me," he continued between breathless sobs. "After seeing it all on paper, it feels like this huge weight has been lifted off my chest."

Leroy's epiphany was the very one I had prayed for, from the first day I walked into Big Ma's basement, all the way through the last chapter of this book. The portrait of Leroy served as a mirror for the person of Leroy, reflecting healing truths.

Shortly thereafter, in 2016, Leroy was hired as a tester by a top gaming company. On his breaks, he travels back to Ohio, where Alani and Kayla now reside.

And as for my dad, he still reads the *Plain Dealer* sports section every morning beside my grandfather, looking for my next great story. On his coffee mug is the face of his favorite grandson.

ACKNOWLEDGMENTS

Shortly after Leroy and Dartanyon graduated from high school in 2009, LeBron James invited the three of us to his charity fundraiser in Akron, Ohio. When we arrived, LeBron's manager asked us how many people were in our entourage. The boys and I laughed in bemusement. "Could you imagine having an entourage?" we wondered. Today we laugh because we no longer wonder. We actually have one. It is made up of those who have come alongside us with timely support and steadfast encouragement. Some we knew for an hour, others for years. We consider all of you a special part of our Carry OnTourage.

To those who have watched ESPN's *Carry On* and contributed to Leroy and Dartanyon, we thank you for rising up at such a critical crossroads in their lives. You kick-started their futures and insisted they have the opportunity to develop their untapped potential. Though we do not know you all by name, we remember you daily and dearly in our hearts.

To our trio of super supporters: Ira and Beth Leventhal, Jonathan and Delia Matz, and Bob Lamey and Paige Heid. All of you saw two young men flash across your television screens on the same day in 2009 and were drawn to act. You understood something that initially I did not—that to lift one out of poverty, it takes more than love. It requires financial commitment. You offered both. You invested freely, and you cheered us on at every turn. Your generosity inspires me to do more and to be more in the lives of those in need.

Ira likes to call me the best general manager in sports. You began as my teammates. You became forever family.

Patrick and Alicia Hickey. Thank you for being Leroy's Arizona family through the thick and the thin. Alicia, you have been my sounding board, my soul sister, and my secret mole. You make me brave.

To Mike O'Brien, Renee Bohinc, and Katie Kotkowski at the O'Brien Law Firm—thank you for scrambling as you did to set up Leroy and Dartanyon's trust fund in record time. You understood the importance of momentum and put the needs of two boys ahead of your busy schedules. You continually use your powers for good.

Jay Lavender, you were the first to insist that I take on the challenge of writing this book. I told you I couldn't, that I had never written anything longer than twenty pages. "Perfect," you said. "Just do that ten times." The process turned out to be slightly more complex than that, but were it not for you, I would never have begun. Thank you for reading pages and relentlessly rooting for me.

To Dan Conaway and Chris George, my dynamic literary agent duo. Thank you for believing in my proposal, for taking it to market, and then for insisting that I believe in myself.

To Sarah Murphy and Karen Rinaldi at Harper Wave, thank you for saying yes to this book, for believing our lives held a message worth sharing, and for taking that message enthusiastically to the wider world.

To my attorneys, Mitch Smelkinson and Aron Baumel, thank you for giving your time and attention so lavishly. As many contracts as you review in a week, you treat each one uniquely and carefully.

To my neighbors, Mark and Sybil Coleman, thank you for allowing me to slip in and out of your dining room unannounced to write when the clamoring little ones in my house were less than supportive of this endeavor. You sustained me through many blurry afternoons with prayer and plates of sliced fruit.

Thank you to Akron Children's Hospital, the United States Olympic Committee, and the *Akron Beacon Journal* for fielding my many inquiries.

Thank you to ESPN for believing that "spunk" is an asset and for entrusting me with stories that transcend sports. You gave me some of the best years of my life, and I will forever be your greatest fan.

And lastly, to Navid—my husband and best friend. You have read every page of this book, and you know how to read me. Thank you for sharing the vision. You are My Guy.

ABOUT THE AUTHOR

A three-time winner of the Edward R. Murrow Award and a six-time Emmy Award–winning feature producer with ESPN for thirteen years, LISA FENN interviewed every big name in sports. Then, in 2009, she met two impoverished, disabled, resilient young boys, and it changed her life—and theirs—forever. Today she is a sought-after public presenter, speaking on leadership, poverty, and transracial adoption, in addition to her Christian faith and its relevance in both her media career and her daily life. Lisa received her BS in communications from Cornell University. Her work has been featured on ESPN, *Good Morning America*, and *World News Tonight*. She continues to produce sports stories and write about the redemptive power of love. Lisa resides in Boston with her husband and two young children.